*cut here*

# Windows' Wondrous Windows

Title bar

Maximize button

Minimize button

Close button

Menu bar

Toolbar

Up scroll arrow

Scroll box

Border

Scroll bar

Status bar

Down scroll arrow

Our neighbors have a daughter who thinks she's a chicken. They were going to put her in a home, but they're poor and need the eggs.

What do you call a nerd who graduates from college? Boss.

What do you call a group of surfers? A multidude.

For Help, press F1      NUM

## Windows 95 Mighty Mouse Moves

| To | You |
|---|---|
| Size a window | Drag the borders. |
| Move a window | Drag the title bar. |
| Minimize a window | Click on the Minimize button. |
| Maximize a window | Click on the Maximize button. |
| Restore a minimized window | Click on the window's Taskbar button. |
| Restore a maximized window | Click on the Restore button. |
| Close a document window | Click on the Close button. |

## Windows 95 Shortcut Keys: A Baker's Dozen

| Press | To |
|---|---|
| Alt+Enter | Switch a DOS application between full screen and a window. |
| Alt+Esc | Cycle through the open applications (shows each program's window). |
| Alt+F4 | Shut down an application. |
| Alt+Spacebar | Pull down an application's Control menu. |
| Alt+Tab | Cycle through the open applications (shows only the program name and icon). |
| Ctrl+C | Copy the current selection. |
| Ctrl+Esc | Fire up the Start menu. |
| Ctrl+F4 | Shut down the current document window. |
| Ctrl+Tab | Trudge through the tabs in a tabbed dialog box. |
| Ctrl+V | Paste the most recent cut or copied selection. |
| Ctrl+X | Cut the current selection. |
| Ctrl+Z | Undo your last gaffe. |
| F1 | Start the Help system. |

# An Explorer Expedition

Current folder or disk drive

Pull-down menu

Toolbar

Folders list

Contents list

# Explorer Mouse Machinations

| To | Do This... |
|---|---|
| Expand a folder | Click its plus sign (+) |
| Collapse a folder | Click its minus sign (–) |
| Copy a file or folder | Hold down Ctrl and drag it |
| Move a file or folder | Hold down Alt and drag it |
| Create a shortcut for a file or folder | Hold down Ctrl+Shift and drag it |
| Delete a file or folder | Drag it to the Recycle Bin |

# Explorer Keyboard Coups

| Press | To |
|---|---|
| + or -> | Expand the highlighted folder |
| – or <- | Collapse the highlighted folder |
| Ctrl+A | Select all files in the current folder |
| Delete | Delete the highlighted file or folder |
| F2 | Rename the highlighted file |
| F3 | Find a file or folder |
| F5 | Refresh the current drive or folder |
| Shift+Delete | Delete the highlighted file or folder (bypasses the Recycle Bin) |

# The Taskbar: A Launch Pad and Radar Screen in One

Click here to display the Start menu.

Current time (double-click to set the time)

Click these buttons to navigate your running programs.

Information area

The

# COMPLETE

# IDIOT'S

GUIDE TO

# Windows® 95

*by Paul McFedries*
*with Faithe Wempen*

A Division of Macmillan Computer Publishing
201 W. 103rd Street, Indianapolis, IN 46290

*To Sandy (my big sister), Chris (Beethoven wails!), Emily (the first female major league pitcher?), Stephen (Pearl Jam wails, too!), and my goddaughter Katy (the hockey and baseball star).*

## ©1995 Que Corporation

International Standard Book Number: 1-56761-495-7

Library of Congress Catalog Card Number: 94-71081

97  96  95    8  7  6  5  4  3

Interpretation of the printing code: the rightmost number of the first series of numbers is the year of the book's printing; the rightmost number of the second series of numbers is the number of the book's printing. For example, a printing code of 95-1 shows that the first printing of the book occurred in 1995.

*Printed in the United States of America*

**Publisher**
*Roland Elgey*

**Vice-President and Publisher**
*Marie Butler-Knight*

**Publishing Manager**
*Barry Pruett*

**Director of Editorial Services**
*Elizabeth Keaffaber*

**Managing Editor**
*Michael Cunningham*

**Senior Development Editor**
*Seta Frantz*

**Senior Production Editor**
*Michelle Shaw*

**Copy Editor**
*Audra Gable*

**Cartoonist**
*Judd Winick*

**Cover Designer**
*Scott Cook*

**Designer**
*Kim Scott*

**Indexer**
*Kathy Venable*

**Production Team**
*Claudia Bell, Chad Dressler, Joan Evan, Amy Gornik,
Barry Jorden, Bob LaRoche, Todd Wente*

*Special thanks to C. Herbert Feltner for ensuring
the technical accuracy of this book.*

# Acknowledgment

Thanks to Microsoft for their assistance and cooperation. A special thanks to Tim Breidigan, Scott Raedeke, Michael Losh and Tracy Van Hoof.

Dear Readers,

Congratulations. Upon picking up this book, you're taking the first important step in redefining your relationship with that cold, dark monitor glaring at you from your desk. You've endured the age-old stand off: technology versus you. And, while it's true that you could just keep plugging away at your grandfather's old typewriter, the time has come to face the bitter truth—computers have become a vital part of our personal and professional lives. But that doesn't mean you like it.

We understand that you care more about the end result than about the means for getting there. You're a smart person who just doesn't have time to sit down and learn all the intricacies of the latest operating system or spreadsheet program. After all, you don't need to know how a car works in order to drive one. The same should be true about computers.

Our *Complete Idiot's Guide* series was designed with you in mind—the beginning computer user who is new to operating systems and a bit intimidated by the vast amounts of information to comprehend. Our books do more than meet you halfway. They pick you up at the point where you're just about ready to call it quits, and give you the boost you need to keep going. And as a bonus, we make you laugh about it.

Whether you're a struggling entrepreneur working to get your business off the ground or a student writing a research paper, you'll find the computer topics you need, presented in a witty, humorous language you can understand. You've got my word on it.

Sincerely,

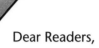

Roland Elgey
President of Que

# Contents at a Glance

# Contents

**xiii**

# Introduction

These days, there's no shortage of ways we Windows users are made to feel like complete idiots. Armies of alleged "Windows experts" and "Windows consultants"—their pockets appropriately protected—charge exorbitant fees for prattling on in some techno-language that bears only the faintest resemblance to English. Magazines spout Windows "tips" and "tricks" that give a whole new meaning to the word "esoteric." The shelves in bookstore computer sections groan under the weight of more bloated and incomprehensible Windows volumes than you can shake a stick at. (If you plan to check this out for yourself, be careful: I think public stick shaking is illegal in some states.) And, of course, the worst offender is Windows itself, with its genius for turning routine tasks into heart-stopping adventures.

Well, a pox on all their houses! We are definitely *not* complete idiots. (*Partial* idiots? Well, okay, maybe sometimes; but *complete* idiots? No, never.) In fact, we're smart enough to know a thing or two ourselves:

➤ We're smart enough to know that, despite the claims of those geek-speaking gurus, Windows isn't brain surgery or even rocket science. So it shouldn't take a Ph.D. to figure out how to use it.

➤ We're smart enough to know that the only truly useful tips are those that either make Windows easier to use or make it easier for us to get our work done.

➤ We're smart enough to know that life's too short to read five kazillion pages of arcane and mostly useless information about a computer program. We have lives to lead, after all.

➤ And we're smart enough to know that there *has* to be an easier way to work with Windows.

# A Book for Smart Windows Idiots

If you're no fool, but Windows makes you feel like one, welcome to *The Complete Idiot's Guide to Windows 95*! This is a book for those of us who aren't (and don't even want to be) computer wizards. This is a book for those of us who have a job to do (a job that includes working with Windows 95) and just want to get it done as quickly and painlessly as possible. This isn't one of those absurdly serious, put-a-crease-in-your-brow-and-we'll-begin books. On the contrary, we'll even try to have a little fun at Windows 95's expense as we go along. (I do, however, feel compelled to apologize for some of the jokes in advance.)

You'll also be happy to know that this book doesn't assume you have any previous experience with Windows 95. I'll begin each topic at the beginning and build your knowledge from there. However, if you have used a previous version of Windows, I'll be pointing out the differences in Windows 95 so you can get productive posthaste.

With *The Complete Idiot's Guide to Windows 95*, you'll get just the facts you need—not everything there is to know. This means I'll be avoiding long-winded discussions of boring, technical details. Instead, I'll present all the information in short, easy-to-digest chunks that you can quickly skim through to find just the information you want.

# What to Expect

With Windows, *anything* can happen (and often does). So my best advice as you cross over into Windows 95 territory is to expect (you guessed it) the unexpected. However, the last thing you need is to be thrown a few curve balls by the book that's supposed to be your trusted guide in this newfound land. So, to get you better prepared for the journey to come, let's bone up on some of the flora and fauna you'll be seeing along the way.

First, the itinerary. The *Complete Idiot's Guide to Windows 95* is organized into seven reasonably sensible sections. To help you find what you need fast, here's a summary of what you'll find in each section:

**Part 1: An Introduction to Windows 95**

The three chapters that open the book are designed to help you get your Windows travels off on the right foot. Chapter 1 lists the top 10 things you need to know about Windows 95; Chapter 2 gives you some general Windows 95 tidbits and answers a few common questions; Chapter 3 tells you about the all-important chore of installing the program.

**Part 2: Workaday Windows 95**

Ninety percent of learning Windows 95 involves learning a few simple techniques that can be applied to almost any Windows 95 program. These universal skills are the ones you'll be using day in and day out, and they're the subject of Part 2. You'll learn how to start Windows 95, how to use the mouse and keyboard, how to crank up programs and commands, and how to get through fundamental tasks such as opening and closing files, and printing.

### Part 3: Navigating Your Computer with Windows 95

*My Computer* and *Explorer* are the Windows 95 tools that give you an easy, graphical way to work with your computer's files, folders, and floppy disks. The three chapters in this section explain the basic features of both My Computer and Explorer.

### Part 4: Okay, Enough Gawking. It's Time to Get Some Work Done!

This section of the book covers a hodgepodge of topics that'll help you get the most out of your Windows 95 investment. The first few chapters concentrate on the various freebie programs that are part of the Windows 95 package. I'll discuss WordPad (a word processor), Paint (a drawing and painting program), and lots more. Then I'll show you how to share info between applications, use Windows 95's multimedia programs, work with fonts, and use Windows 95's networking features.

### Part 5: A Few Windows 95 Odds and Ends

The chapters in Part 5 prove that, yes, you *can* have Windows 95 your way. The program comes with a fistful of customization options that enable you to give Windows 95 a complete makeover. In particular, I'll show you how to change the colors and background pattern of the Windows screen, set up a screen saver, customize the mouse and keyboard, and add new hardware and software to your system.

And for you modem-hounds in the crowd, I'll take you through the basic communications doodads in Windows 95. I'll begin by showing you how to set up your modem. From there, I'll tell you how to use your modem to dial your phone, call bulletin boards, and connect with online services. Then I'll take you on a tour of the Microsoft Exchange program's e-mail and fax capabilities. (And at the back of the book, check out the section on Microsoft Network, the latest member of the online world.)

But before that, I've thrown in two chapters that tackle Windows' most common problems and give you easy, non-technical solutions.

To make the instructions easier to read, *The Complete Idiot's Guide to Windows 95* uses the following conventions:

➤ Text that you're supposed to type, items you select, and text that you'll see on your screen appear in **bold**.

➤ As you'll see, Windows 95 uses quite a few keyboard shortcuts. These shortcuts almost invariably require you to hold down one key and press another. For example, one shortcut you may use a lot requires you to hold down the **Ctrl** key, press the

Esc key, and then release Ctrl. To avoid writing out a mouthful like that over and over, we needed an easier way to express these *key combinations* (a sort of "shortcut shorthand," if you will). So key combinations appear with a plus sign (+) in the middle, as in **Ctrl+Esc**.

➤ The names of dialog box controls appear in a special font like this: Select the Create from File option button and then click on the Display As Icon check box.

Also, look for the following features that point out important information:

**By the Way...** These boxes contain notes, tips, warnings, and asides about Windows 95 that are interesting and useful (at least theoretically!).

**Transitional State** I realize that many of you aren't new to Windows, just to Windows 95. So, to make the transition a little smoother and a little more manageable, these icons point out major differences between Windows 3.1 and Windows 95.

**Technical Twaddle**

These "geek boxes" contain technical information you can use to impress your friends (and then forget five minutes later). But really, you may find these fascinating if you're a closet geekwannabe, or if you're interested in background information and technical details that will help you feel more like an "insider" in the computer world.

## Acknowledgments and Other Assorted Tips of the Hat

I'd like to thank the members of the Academy... Whoa, wrong speech! I'd like to thank Barry Pruett, Seta Frantz, Audra Gable, Michelle Shaw, and the other members of the Que family who contributed to this project (they're all listed at the front of the book).

Special thanks to my buddy Faithe Wempen who helped write the communications chapters.

# Part 1
# An Introduction to Windows 95

*Okay, you've got a computer, you've got Windows 95, you've got your favorite accessories (coffee, relaxing background music, and so on). Hey, you're ready to go! However, just to build the suspense, this section presents some "look before you leap" stuff. (But if you're a dedicated leaper, don't let me stop you; feel free to head right into Part 2.)*

# Chapter 1

# The Top Ten Things You Need to Know

I know, I know. You can't wait to get started. What is it? A looming deadline? Unfettered curiosity? Type-A personality? Well, not to worry. This chapter gets you up to speed quickly by presenting a "just-the-facts" description of the 10 most important Windows 95 tasks. Of course, each of these tidbits is discussed in more detail elsewhere in the book, so I'll also point out the relevant chapters that you can flip to if you want to know more. If you're one of those people who likes to read ahead to the good parts, this chapter's for you.

## 1. Starting Stuff from the Start Menu

The Start menu is the Windows 95 launchpad for not only the freebie accessories that come bundled with Windows 95, but also for the programs you install yourself. To use the Start menu, you need to display it first. You do that by clicking on the **Start** button found in the bottom-left corner of the Windows 95 screen (see the figure below). If your mouse is buried under a mound of paper, you can also press **Ctrl+Esc** (i.e., hold down the **Ctrl** key, press **Esc**, and then release **Ctrl**) to get the job done.

Start button

*Click on the Start button to display the Start menu.*

Once you've coaxed the menu into view, you then choose a menu item using one of these methods:

➤ If using your mouse, click on the item.

➤ If using your keyboard, find the underlined letter in the item's name (such as the "P" in Programs) and press that letter on your keyboard. If there's no underlined letter, use the up and down arrow keys to highlight the item and then press **Enter**.

If Windows 95 displays another menu (you may have to trudge through three or four to find what you want), repeat the above procedure until you find and start the program you're looking for.

To get the full scoop on all this, the section in Chapter 5 titled "The Start Menu: Your Windows 95 Launchpad," is the place you oughta be. Other relevant chapters include Chapter 8's "Opening a Document from the Start Menu" section (in which you learn how to load individual documents from the Start menu) and Chapter 23's "Customizing the Taskbar and Start Menu" section.

## 2. Using Pull-Down Menus

*Pull-down menus* are sneaky, hidden menus that list the commands available for each Windows application. To pull down a menu with the mouse, move the mouse pointer onto the menu bar area (the horizontal strip along the second line of an application's window), and then click on the name of the menu you want to pull down. To use the keyboard, hold down the **Alt** key and press the menu name's underlined letter.

Once the menu is displayed, you can select any of the available commands. With your mouse, simply click on the command you want to execute. With your keyboard, press the up and down arrow keys to highlight the command you want and then press **Enter**.

See Chapter 6 to learn more about pull-down menus.

## 3. Getting Help

If Windows 95 goes wonky on you, or if you simply find yourself in some unknown Windows neighborhood, you can crank up the Help system by using any of the following methods:

➤ Press **F1**.

➤ Click on a **?** button in a dialog box and then click on something in the dialog box.

➤ In most Windows applications, you can click on **Help** in the menu bar or press **Alt+H**. The Help menu that appears will have one or more commands for accessing different parts of the program's Help system.

For a heaping helping of Help info, jump to Chapter 5 and read the "Help! How to Get It" section.

## 4. Working with Wizards

In an effort to make all our lives easier, Windows 95 delegates certain routine-but-too-complex-to-memorize tasks to the care of various "Wizards." These Wizards take you by the hand and lead you through the appropriate steps for a task by asking you questions and providing places for you to enter your answers. You'll be dealing with Wizards regularly, so it's a good idea to get to know how they operate and how to get along with them.

It's quite simple, really. Each Wizard displays a series of dialog boxes in which you provide the info necessary to complete your chore. You move between these dialog boxes by selecting one of the following buttons:

**Next >** Select this button when you're done with the current Wizard dialog box and you want to move on to the next one.

**< Back** Select this button to retreat to the previous Wizard dialog box.

**Cancel** Select this button to bail out of the Wizard altogether without doing anything.

**Finish** Select this button to complete the task.

Check out Chapter 7 to learn more about Wizards in particular and dialog boxes in general.

## 5. Opening a Document

When you start an application, the program usually displays a new file automatically. If you'd prefer to work with an existing file, you need to open it. Follow these steps to open an existing file in most Windows applications:

1. Pull down the application's **File** menu and select the **Open** command. This displays the Open dialog box.

2. If necessary, use the Look in drop-down list box to select a different disk drive.

3. Select the folder that contains the file.

4. Double-click on the file name.

For more information on the Open command, see the sections in Chapter 8 titled "Reunited: Opening an Existing Document" and "Opening a Document from the Sta

Menu." To learn more about list boxes, buttons, and other dialog box elements, head for Chapter 7 and check out the section called "Dialog Box Gadgets and Gizmos."

## 6. Saving a Document

One of the most gut-wrenching experiences in computerdom is when you work on a document for hours and then lose everything because of a system crash or power failure. A big-time bummer. You can minimize the damage, however, by saving your work frequently. To do this in most applications, pull down the **File** menu and select the **Save** command. If you're saving a new file, the Save As dialog box appears. Select the drive and folder to which you want to save the file, and then type a file name in the **File name** box. When you're ready, select **Save**.

See the section in Chapter 8 titled "Save Your Work, Save Your Life" for more details about saving a file. To learn more about dialog boxes, see Chapter 7.

## 7. Printing a Document

Once you've finished working with a document, you'll probably want to print a copy to show off to your friends and family (or perhaps just to line the bird cage). To do this, pull down the application's **File** menu and select the **Print** command. In the Print dialog box that appears, set the number of copies, the specific pages you want printed (if you have more than one), and various other settings (depending on the application). When you're ready to print, select the **OK** button (or the **Print** button in some applications).

For the big printing picture, take a look at Chapter 9.

## 8. Undoing a Mistake

Many Windows 95 applications include an Undo command that you can use to reverse your most recent action. This is great if you cut something when you should have copied it, if you've just consigned your entire day's work to some deletion la-la land, or if you've made some major gaffe that has your boss so steamed, your coworkers are clad in nothing but towels. (I know, I know, *you* don't make mistakes. But you probably know plenty of people who do, so you can pass this information on to them.) To use the Undo feature, pull down the application's **Edit** menu and select the **Undo** command.

I discuss the Undo command in more detail in Chapter 8, in the section called "To Err Is Human, to Undo Divine."

## 9. Switching Between Multiple Applications

Windows 95 supports *multitasking*, which is just a fancy way of saying that you can run multiple applications at the same time. The number of applications you can run at once depends on how much memory you have in your computer, but even a bare-bones Windows 95 system should be able to get two or three medium-size programs going.

Once you start a program, Windows 95 adds a button representing that program to the taskbar at the bottom of the screen. For example, the following figure shows the taskbar with three programs on the go: Explorer (that's the Exploring - My Computer button), Control Panel, and WordPad.

Each of these buttons represents
a currently running program.

*When you launch a program, Windows 95 places a button for it on the taskbar.*

To switch between the open programs, you can use any of the following methods:

➤ Click on the application's button in the taskbar.

➤ If you can see any part of the application, click on it.

➤ If you have two applications open, press **Alt+Tab** to switch between them. If you have more than two applications running, hold down **Alt** and press the **Tab** key repeatedly. Each time you press Tab, Windows 95 displays the title and icon of one of the active applications. When you see the one you want, release the Alt key.

Chapter 5 gives you more information on navigating running applications. In particular, see the sections "Taking Windows 95 to Task: The Taskbar," and "More Methods for Switching Between Programs."

## 10. Quitting Windows 95

When you've had just about enough of Windows 95 for one day, you can quit the program by displaying the Start menu and selecting the **Shut Down** command. In the Shut Down Windows dialog box that appears, select the **Yes** button. (If you want to restart your computer instead of shutting it down, choose the **Restart the computer** option and select **Yes**.)

See Chapter 4's "Shutting Down Your Computer" section for additional information on quitting Windows 95.

# Chapter 2

# Walking in a Windows Wonderland

## In This Chapter

➤ What Windows is and what you can use it for

➤ How Windows makes your life easier

➤ Why you can still keep your old DOS programs

➤ What's new with Windows 95

➤ A leisurely amble through the Windows landscape

As strange as it may sound, I was actually at a baseball game when I first realized Windows was a Big Thing. Where I live, we have one of those state-of-the-art baseball stadiums with all the modern-day amenities: artificial turf, a McDonald's, and the main attraction: a huge 110-foot TV screen (the biggest in the world, I hear) that tells everyone when they're having fun.

Of course, with tens of thousands of people as a captive audience, you'd better believe this monster TV is going to show commercials. So there I was, shelling peanuts and waiting to root root root for the home team in the next inning, when on comes a commercial for (wait for it) Windows. Whoa! Here I am sitting with 50,000 of the faithful, and we're all watching a Windows ad. The specifics of the ad have faded from memory (although I *do* remember some slinky blonde getting all hot and bothered in front of a PC), but I recall thinking that if Microsoft (the publisher of Windows) was willing to shell out megabucks to peddle this new software at a major league baseball game, something BIG was happening.

Actually, with Windows now selling over a million copies a month, "humongous" might be a better word. Windows is, truly, a phenomenon unlike any other in the world of personal computers. This chapter explores the Windows mystique and attempts to answer no fewer than five questions:

➤ What's with all this Windows hoopla?

➤ Is Windows really as easy to use as everyone says?

➤ I've got Windows; now what the heck do I do with it?

➤ Do I have to toss my DOS programs?

➤ What's new and improved in Windows 95?

# What's with All the Windows Hoopla?

Windows ads don't appear only on 110-foot TVs. You see them on normal-sized TVs, inside newspapers, and on billboards, sandwich boards, bulletin boards, and ironing boards. (Yeah, I made up that last one; but, hey, with Microsoft you never know.) You name it, Windows is there. Computer magazines (and even some real magazines) are stuffed full of articles with titles like "57 Cool New Ways to Make Windows Bark Like a Dog!" and "He's Hot and You're Not—How Windows Can Help!" Everywhere you go, people are talking about Windows (well, okay, *almost* everywhere). So why all the fuss?

Well, in a nutshell, Windows represents an entirely new way to get things done with a computer. The old way (that is, the DOS way) involved typing commands on your keyboard and waiting (or more likely, praying) for the computer to respond. There are two major drawbacks to this approach:

➤ Most of us are pathetic typists.

➤ Most of the things you have to type bear only the slightest resemblance to the English language. I mean, imagine having to type—or even *remember*—a command like this:

xcopy c:\*.* a: /d:04/15/95 /v

Gag me! Using DOS is like going to a fancy French restaurant where you have to write down your order. If you get anything wrong—like spelling crème as créme (or is it the other way around?)—you don't eat.

Windows changes all that because it works the way human beings work: visually. Your programs and all the commands or options you need to choose are represented visually on the screen (or they're a few mouse clicks or keystrokes away). Just think: no more convoluted commands and snaggled syntax to remember. In fact, Windows may be the first computer application that doesn't require you to remember anything!

### Well, When I Was a Kid...

Although the keyboard may not be the best way to operate a computer, things used to be worse. In the old days, intrepid users had to enter information through a series of toggle switches on the front of the machine. I think it took about three days just to enter your name.

# Is Windows Really As Easy to Use As Everyone Says?

Well, yes and no. I mean it's not like you're boiling water or anything (yes, bachelors, boiling water *is* easy). On the other hand, it's not exactly brain surgery, either.

When you get right down to it, Windows, like just about anything else, is as easy or as hard as you make it. This is a fully loaded piece of software that comes with a veritable cornucopia of bells and whistles. It's possible to sink into its mired depths and never be heard from again (except possibly as a story on "Unsolved Mysteries"). If that's what you want, you're reading the wrong book. My goal is to show you just how easy Windows is to both learn and use. The secret, as you'll soon see, is to learn just what *you* need to know—not what everyone else thinks you should know.

How does Windows make it easier to use a computer? Well, as I said before, images are the key. When you start up a Windows application, most of what you can do with the program is laid out visually in front of you. Carrying on the French restaurant example, using Windows would be like ordering from a menu that has nice pictures of each of the dishes. You point to the selection you want, and voilà, your meal is served up piping hot. Windows 95 even maps out your entire computer (floppy disks, hard drives, CD-ROMs, printers, and all) in a nice, neat visual display like the one shown on the following page. (The program you see is called Windows Explorer. I'll tell you all about it in Part 3, "Navigating Your Computer with Windows 95.")

**11**

*The box on the right gives you a visual representation of all the components of your computer.*

Of course, cute little pictures are only part of the story. Another feature that makes Windows easy to use is the *dialog box* concept. Although you'll learn about these in detail in Chapter 7, a brief introduction here won't hurt. As the name implies, a dialog box is simply a means by which you and Windows communicate. Now don't expect long philosophical discussions that last into the wee hours of the morning. Windows is good, but not *that* good. No, you'll see a dialog box any time Windows needs more information from you or needs you to confirm that what you asked it to do is what you actually want it to do. Here's an example of a confirmation dialog box.

*This Windows 95 dialog box asks you to confirm a file deletion.*

## It's a What?

Windows is an example of what computer nerds call a GUI—a *graphical user interface*—which is pronounced *goo-ey*. (No, I did *not* make that up.) Personally, I think *pictorial user interface* would have been better, but I suppose the pronunciation (*poo-ey*) would turn people off.

The third key to Windows' ease-of-use is consistency. Certain operations, such as opening and saving files, are implemented the same way in almost all Windows applications, and most Windows applications look more or less the same. These consistencies from program to program mean that you have that much less to learn with each new program you use. (This is a real benefit to those of us whose brain cells are the innocent victims of our misspent youth.) Check out Part 2, "Workaday Windows 95," to find out about many of these consistencies.

# Okay, I've Got Windows; Now What the Heck Do I Do with It?

I'm not here to be an evangelist for Windows, so I'm not going to tell you that Windows can do everything except wax the cat. And I'm certainly not going to tell you that the only limit to Windows is your imagination. This is bunk. Computers and the programs that run on them (including Windows 95) are big, dumb galoots that exist only to do your bidding. They are pack animals—mere beasts of burden born only to handle the grunt work that the rest of us don't want to bother with. If you're new to computers, please tape this statement on your forehead now: *you are infinitely smarter than your computer will ever be*. This, of course, does not mean you've just wasted several thousand dollars; it just means there's a limit to what one can reasonably expect from a machine.

However, donkeys live useful, productive lives, and so can Windows. For one thing, Windows will still allow you to do what people have been doing with personal computers for years: write letters, mess around with numbers, draw pictures, and play cool games. Windows, though, brings a number of advantages to the table:

➤ Once you're comfortable with the Windows way of doing things (which won't take you very long), you'll be able to do all those normal computer tasks more easily and quickly.

➤ Your finished product will be, generally speaking, more professional-looking.

➤ Windows lets you work on multiple projects at once (called multitasking). For example, while a letter or report is printing, you're free to muck about with a completely different program. (So you could, for example, reward yourself with a couple of rounds of FreeCell—one of the games that comes with Windows 95.)

**Check This Out...**

**Multitasking**
The capability to run several programs at the same time. This simply means that Windows (unlike some people you may know) can walk and chew gum at the same time.

Windows by itself is easily worth the price of admission (especially if it came bundled with your new computer), but there's actually a lot more fun stuff lurking in the Windows box. The Windows programmers—bless their nerdy hearts—have included, at no extra charge, a hatful of small programs (they're called *accessories*). With these programs you can do all of the following things:

➤ Write letters, memos, résumés, or even your latest Great American Novel.

➤ Draw and paint pictures, logos, cartoons, and whatever else your inner child feels like doing.

➤ Make quick calculations (so you'll know if that check is going to bounce *before* you write it).

➤ Make backup copies of your important files (just in case disaster strikes).

➤ Play cool games (all work and no play...).

See Part 4, "Okay, Enough Gawking. It's Time to Get Some Work Done!" for information on these and other Windows tricks.

## Do I Have to Toss My DOS Programs?

In a word, no. The creators of Windows looked at the tens of millions of people using DOS programs and figured they'd better keep these people happy. So they made sure that DOS applications would work reasonably well under Windows. They'll run a bit slower, and some of the more misbehaved programs might give Windows a little gas, but they will run.

## What's New and Improved in Windows 95?

In the time from its inception in 1993 to its release in 1995, Windows 95 reached new heights of marketing hype (or new lows, depending on your tolerance for hyperbole and puffery). But for every "Gee, whiz" type who insisted that Windows 95 was the greatest thing since the Veg-O-Matic, there was a skeptic who insisted equally vehemently that the program was nothing but the "same old, same old" dressed in a shiny new suit.

Who's right? Well, as usual, the answer lies somewhere in the middle. Windows 95 certainly isn't the Second Coming, but it's definitely not just a warmed-over version of Windows 3.1. It boasts a boatload of improvements, big and small, that are sure to make the few hours you spend each day hunkered down in front of your monitor a little less drudging. I'll be giving you the details on many of these improvements as we go along, but just to whet your appetite, here's a list of the major ones to watch out for:

**Keep it simple, stupid.** The overall design of Windows 95 is simpler and cleaner than that of Windows 3.1. For example, Program Manager is history; to crank up a program or accessory, you simply click on the **Start** button, and then select what you want from the Start menu that appears.

**Belly up to the taskbar.** All the programs you have running appear in a special area at the bottom of the screen called the *taskbar*. Using the taskbar, you always know which programs are loaded, and you can switch to any of the programs with a simple click of the mouse.

**Examine your computer with Explorer.** Windows Explorer is easier to use and more ergonomically sound than its predecessor, File Manager. For example, Explorer treats your computer as a whole, letting you work easily with all your floppy drives, hard drives, CD-ROMs, printers, and whatever else you have glued to your machine. And you may as well remove the word "directory" from your Windows vocabulary. Directories are now called "folders" in Windows 95, and you better get used to them because they're *everywhere*.

**A Mecca for mouse mavens.** Although Windows 3.1 was designed with the mouse in mind, most people eventually found they preferred the keyboard for the majority of tasks. Windows 95 may change all that, because, while it too is made for the mouse, it's smart about it. Lots of tasks take only a single mouse click; things can be dragged hither and thither; and there are toolbars to beat the band. (A toolbar is a strip of buttons that gives you one-click access to common functions.)

**At last! The right mouse button becomes useful.** Speaking of the mouse, did you ever wonder what the heck the right button was supposed to be for? True, some programs made use of it, but not Windows itself. With Windows 95, however, the right mouse button is used to display *shortcut menus* that give you quick access to frequently used commands and features. This will often save you from having to hunt through endless pull-down menus to find what you want.

**Hallelujah: longer file names!** For my money, Windows 95's Most Valuable Feature award definitely goes to its support of longer file names. That's right, no more trying to shoehorn a meaningful name into a measly eight characters. Now you can go crazy because the limit has been bumped up to a positively verbose 255 characters! (One word of warning, though: only programs designed for Windows 95 will be able to understand these long-winded names.)

**Wizards: The Windows 95 pit crew.** With Windows 3.1, you were on your own when it came to performing tasks like setting up a new printer. With Windows 95, however, you're never alone because the program comes with a whole crew of so-called *Wizards*. These helpers take you through common Windows tasks (such as installing a printer) by asking the right questions and recording your answers.

**15**

**Helmets off: Windows becomes crash-proof (well, almost).** By far the most annoying thing about Windows 3.1 was its perverse tendency to go up in flames whenever an important deadline or meeting was looming large. Windows 95 was designed from the ground up to be more stable and not to give up the ghost as easily as Windows 3.1 did. (Again, however, you'll need to use programs created specifically for Windows 95 to get truly bullet-proof operations.)

**Less dirty DOS dancing.** Many of the things you used to have to do in DOS are now built right into Windows 95. For example, DriveSpace (the program that creates more room on your hard drive) is now a seamless part of Windows 95.

**Help for hardware headaches.** Windows 95 has built-in support for something called "Plug and Play" (PnP). This means that if you add PnP-compatible hardware to your system, Windows 95 will recognize it and configure the device for you automatically.

**Where's the beef? Check out the new accessories.** Many of the no-charge programs that come with Windows 95 have been beefed up from their Windows 3.1 versions. For example, WordPad (the word processor) has quite a few more features than Write, its anemic Windows 3.1 cousin. There's also a bunch of brand new accessories that are making their debuts in Windows 95. These rookies include Phone Dialer (which dials your phone for you), CD Player (which plays music CDs on your CD-ROM drive), and Microsoft Fax (which enables you to send and receive faxes right from your computer).

**Get online with the Microsoft Network.** If you have a modem, Windows 95 includes an easy link to the new Microsoft Network. This online service boasts electronic mail, programs, lots of info, and even links to the Internet.

**Windows and DOS: Now a happy couple.** Before Windows 95, DOS and Windows were, at best, acquaintances. They got along reasonably well most of the time, but their spats could be nasty ones. Now, however, DOS and Windows have shacked up and are living happily together under one Windows 95 roof. This, combined with the new Windows 95 versions of some important DOS programs (see the following page), should mean that most of us can say goodbye to the old DOS world.

# The Transition from Windows 3.1 to Windows 95

Lots of people will be heading into Windows 95 having already struggled with the intricacies of Windows 3.1. While Windows 95 isn't completely different from Windows 3.1, it's different enough that you'll have a bit of a learning curve ahead of you.

To help you get through, I'll be pointing out the significant differences between the two products throughout this book. To give you a bit of an idea what to expect, though, the following table summarizes what became of the Windows 3.1 programs (and some DOS 6 ones, too) in the move to Windows 95.

## Windows 3.1 Programs and Their Windows 95 Counterparts

| Windows 3.1/DOS 6 | Windows 95 |
| --- | --- |
| Program Manager | Start menu |
| File Manager | Windows Explorer |
| Calculator | Calculator (new version) |
| Calendar | Same |
| Cardfile | Same |
| Character Map | Character Map (new version) |
| Clipboard Viewer | Clipboard Viewer (new version) |
| Clock | On the taskbar |
| DEFRAG (DOS 6) | Disk Defragmenter |
| DriveSpace (DOS 6) | DriveSpace |
| Media Player | Media Player (new version) |
| MS-DOS Prompt | MS-DOS Prompt (new version) |
| Notepad | Notepad (new version) |
| Object Packager | Object Packager (new version) |
| Paintbrush | Paint |
| Print Manager | Control of individual printers |
| Recorder | Gone |
| ScanDisk (DOS 6) | ScanDisk |
| Solitaire | Same |
| Terminal | HyperTerminal |
| Undelete | The Recycle Bin |
| Write | WordPad |

# The Least You Need to Know

This chapter gave you a brief introduction to the world of Windows and showed you how it can make your computing life easier. From here, you have two choices. If Windows 95 isn't yet installed on your computer, move on to Chapter 3 where I'll take you through the installation process. If Windows is already installed, skip ahead to Chapter 4 to get a tour of the Windows 95 screen and learn some mouse and keyboard basics.

# From Floppy Disk to Hard Disk: Installing Windows 95

**In This Chapter**

➤ Preparing to install Windows 95

➤ The installation steps

➤ Some post-installation chores

➤ Everything you need to know, from go to whoa

My favorite thing about having a computer (except possibly switching the unruly beast off at night) is probably the moment a new software package arrives. It sits there gleaming in its shrink wrap, full of nothing but possibilities and great expectations, innocent as a baby in the womb. Awwww. But, alas, this blissful state soon ends. The wrapper gets torn off, the box gets mangled, the contents (the manuals, the disks, and the registration card that I always forget to fill out) get spilled and scattered. And then, just as a baby must be slapped to induce breathing, so, too, must our software be installed to bring it alive on our computers. (Okay, so that last metaphor was a bit of a stretch. Whaddya want, Hemingway?)

If you've just purchased Windows 95, this chapter leads you gently out of the age of innocence and shows you how to install the program on your computer.

# Is This Installation Rigmarole Necessary?

Before diving into the deep end of the Windows 95 installation process, you should dip a toe into the waters to see if you even have to bother. Why? Well, most new computers come with Windows 95 preinstalled by the manufacturer, so the legwork may have already been done. If you're not sure, turn on your computer and see if it loads Windows 95. If you see a screen that looks something like the one shown here, you're in luck: Windows 95 is ready to go. In this case, you can safely bail out of this chapter and head for Chapter 4.

*If you see this screen a minute or two after you fire up your computer, Windows 95 is installed on your computer.*

# Getting the Installation Show on the Road

When I was a kid, I used to get nervous when I received Christmas presents that said "Some assembly required" on the box. I *knew* what that meant. First of all, it meant I couldn't play with the toy right away—a major bummer. Second, it meant that someone (usually my father or a slightly inebriated uncle) would have to do the assembling. Several hours and several missing parts later, the poor thing would have been relegated to a corner somewhere, half-assembled and sad-looking.

Installing computer software fills me with the same apprehension. Most installation programs are written by people who assume that everybody will know what they mean when they say, "Change the BUFFERS setting in your CONFIG.SYS file to 50" or some such nonsense. What this world needs is a simple installation program that you don't have to have a Ph.D. to figure out.

Well, I'm happy to report that the Windows 95 installation program (it's called Setup) comes pretty close. Setup handles all the installation dirty work behind the scenes. All you have to do is answer a few simple questions and shuffle the installation disks in and out when Setup tells you to. (And even all that disk swapping can be avoided if you install Windows 95 from a CD-ROM.) Sound simple? It is, so let's get to it.

## Step 1: Get the Installation Disks Ready

If you're installing Windows 95 from the floppy disks, liberate them from their plastic wrapper and look for the one that says "Disk 1/Setup" on its label (it should be on top of the pile). Keep the others nearby.

If you're installing Windows 95 from the CD-ROM, pluck the Windows 95 compact disc from its jewel case.

## Step 2: Insert the Setup Disk

For the floppy disk installation, place Disk 1 in the appropriate drive (the one that matches the size of disk you have). To insert a floppy disk, hold it so the label is facing up and away from you. Then insert the disk into the drive as far as it will go. The 3½ inch disks will snap into place with a satisfying clunk.

If you're installing from a CD-ROM, insert the disc into your CD-ROM drive.

## Step 3: Start the Installation Program

How you start Setup depends on whether you're upgrading to Windows 95 from an earlier version of Windows or installing Windows for the first time.

**If you're upgrading from an earlier Windows version,** you need to install Windows 95 from Windows. Here are the steps to follow to get started:

1. Start Windows (if it isn't started already) by typing **WIN** at the DOS prompt and pressing **Enter**.

2. Pull down the **File** menu and select the **Run** command. Program Manager displays the Run dialog box.

3. In the **Command Line** text box, type the letter of the drive where you inserted the Setup disk or CD-ROM, followed by a colon (:), followed by \\**setup.exe**. For example, if the disk is in drive A, type **a:\\setup.exe**.

4. Select **OK**. The Windows 95 Setup screen appears.

**If you're installing Windows for the first time** (i.e., you're a newcomer to the world of Windows), you need to install Windows 95 from the DOS prompt.

Your first order of business is to make sure you're at the DOS prompt. You should see one of the following four things on your screen:

➤ **The DOS prompt.** The DOS prompt looks something like this:

C:\>

You may see a letter other than C, or you may see something like **C>** or **C:\DOS.** In any case, your computer is ready for the Windows 95 installation.

➤ **The MS-DOS Shell program.** If you see **MS-DOS Shell** at the top of your screen, hold down the **Alt** key, press the **F4** key, and then release Alt. This will return you to the DOS prompt.

➤ **Some kind of menu system.** Many computers are set up with a menu system that gives the user a list of programs to run. Look for an option called "Exit to DOS," "Quit," or something similar. You can also try pressing the **Esc** key.

➤ **Some other program.** If you're in another program, exit the program to get to the DOS prompt.

Now that you're at the DOS prompt, type the drive letter of the drive where you inserted the Setup disk or Windows CD, type a colon (:), and press **Enter.** For example, if the Setup disk is in drive A, type **A:** and press **Enter.** In this case, you'll see an **A:\>** prompt.

## You're in Trouble!

After you type A: (or whatever) and press Enter, DOS may report this ominous message:

**Not ready reading drive A**
**Abort, Retry, Fail?**

Yikes! Most likely, the problem is that there's no disk in drive A, which means the Windows disk must be in drive B, instead. In this case, press **F** (for "Fail"), type **B:,** and press **Enter.** This should give you the B prompt (**B:\>** or something similar).

Now type **setup** and press **Enter.** Setup chugs away for a few seconds and then lets you know it's going to "perform a routine check on your system." Sounds harmless enough, so press **Enter** to set things in motion, and then just follow the prompts on the screen. You'll eventually see the Windows 95 Setup screen.

## Step 4: Continuing the Installation

From the Windows 95 Setup screen, either click on the **Continue** button or press **Enter** to proceed with the installation. Setup takes a few minutes to rummage around in your system while it's "preparing the Setup Wizard." (Which conjures up images of some elderly gent hurriedly donning his robes, searching frantically for his wand, and saying "My hat! I can't go on without my hat!")

If you're installing from floppy disks, you'll eventually be asked to insert Disk 2. Remove Disk 1, plop Disk 2 into the same drive, and then click on **OK** or press **Enter**. (CD-ROM installers can smile to themselves, smug in the knowledge that this disk shuffling rigmarole is beneath them.)

Setup continues chugging along until, eventually, the Software License Agreement dialog box appears. Click on **Yes** or press **Enter** to continue (although you can read the legalese if you're feeling brave enough). Next, you'll see the Windows 95 Setup Wizard dialog box, shown in the figure below.

*The Windows 95 Setup Wizard will guide you through the installation process.*

This is your first contact with one of those Wizards I told you about in Chapter 2. This dialog box sports the following three buttons:

**< Back**     Select this button to return to the previous step in the Setup process. (You can't select this button yet because this is the first Setup Wizard dialog box.)

**Next >**        Select this button when you've completed the current step and want to move on to the next one. In most cases, you can choose this button just by pressing Enter.

**Cancel**        Select this button to bail out of the Setup process altogether.

The first Setup Wizard screen just gives you an outline of the steps to come. Once you've read it, select **Next >** to move on.

# Step 5: Finishing the Installation

The rest of the installation procedure involves nothing more than answering some simple questions and feeding disks into your computer when prompted by the Setup Wizard (unless, of course, you're installing via the handy CD-ROM). Just so you know what to expect, here's a rundown of some of the screens the Setup Wizard may send your way:

**Choose Directory**   From this screen, you can select a storage location on your hard drive for Windows 95. In most cases, you'll choose the default choice provided by the Setup Wizard (usually C:\WINDOWS).

**3.1**

### Are You Upgrading?

If you're upgrading to Windows 95, you might want to keep your existing version of Windows intact and install Windows 95 to a separate directory. The advantage of doing this is that you can always go back to your old Windows setup if you have problems with Windows 95. The disadvantage is that you have to reinstall all your Windows applications and re-create your program groups. If you want to try it, select **Other Directory**, select **Next >**, and then type in the new directory you want to use (say, C:\WIN95).

**Setup Options**   From this screen (see the following figure), you pick out the type of installation that suits your needs. Most people will select Typical, and that's the one you should probably use. However, you can also select Portable (if you're installing Windows 95 on a notebook computer), Compact (if you don't have enough hard disk real estate for the Typical installation), or Custom (if you really know what you're doing).

**User Information**   Enter your name and company name here. (If you're using Windows at home, you can leave the Company field blank. Or, even better, you can make up a silly name such as "Buy Or Dye Gift Shop and Hair Salon" or "Profane Gas Company." Why not? Believe me, Windows won't mind.)

*Use the Setup Options screen to tell Windows 95 what kind of installation suits your fancy.*

**Analyzing Your Computer** Use this screen to tell Windows 95 what kind of hardware you have. In the list of devices that appears, click on the ones you know are installed on your system.

**Windows Components** In this screen, choose which pieces of Windows 95 you want installed on your machine. To make your life easier, though, I'd recommend accepting the default option (namely, Install the most common components).

**Startup Disk** If your computer gives up the ghost and you're unable to start Windows 95, you (or a nearby computer guru) will need to do some troubleshooting. Your first task, however, will be to regain control of your wayward computer, and the best way to do that is with a "startup disk." In the Startup Disk screen, select the **Yes, I want a startup disk** option to get Windows 95 to create a startup disk for you. I highly recommend that you do this.

# A Few Post-Installation Chores

Once the Setup Wizard has finished copying all the files, it displays the Finishing Setup screen. Remove the last floppy disk from the drive and then select the **Finish** button. Setup restarts your computer and heads directly into Windows 95. After the program ruminates for a minute or two, it takes you through a few more tasks to make sure Windows 95 is ready to roll. The next few sections fill you in on the details.

## To Password or Not to Password?

When Windows 95 starts for the first time, you may eventually see a dialog box asking you to enter your "User name" and "Password" for logging on to Windows. (You'll see this only if your computer is part of a network.) Should you enter a password or not? Good question. The good thing about a password, of course, is that it prevents busybodies from snooping around your system. The bad thing about a password is that it's an extra step to go through every time you start Windows 95. (And if you forget your password, you won't be able to start Windows 95 at all!) Unless you've got some truly sensitive data on your computer, you're probably better off without a password. (Anyway, you can always add one later if you decide you need it.)

Once you've made your choice, you can proceed in one of two ways:

➤ If you don't care about a password, just type your name in the **User name** field and press **Enter**.

➤ If you think a password is a good idea, fill in both the **User name** field and the **Password** field. (When choosing a password, use a word that's easy to remember, but not easy for someone else to guess.)

### Can't Figure Out the Dialog Box?

If you're new to Windows and not comfortable with these dialog box things, you might want to pay a visit to Chapter 7.

In either case, click on the **OK** button or press **Enter** to continue. Windows 95 will ask you to confirm your password. (Yes, it does this even if you didn't give a password.) Retype your password in the Confirm new password field (or leave it blank if you're avoiding the password thing), and then select **OK**.

## Setting the Time Zone

The next dialog box that appears is called Date/Time Properties, and it's shown in the following figure. In this dialog box, you choose your time zone, as well as the current date and time. I'll show you how to set the time in the section in Chapter 18 titled "Doing Time with Date/Time." For now, just choose the appropriate time zone using one of the following methods:

➤ With your mouse, click on your location on the map.

➤ With the keyboard, use the arrow keys to select your time zone. (The left arrow and up arrow keys move west; the right arrow and down arrow keys move east.)

When you're done, select **OK**.

Are you wondering why the heck Windows 95 wants to know your time zone, anyway? Well, one of Windows 95's nice little touches is that it automatically adjusts your computer's clock for things like Daylight Savings Time. To do this, however, it needs to know your time zone.

*Use the Date/Time Properties dialog box to select your time zone.*

## That's All She Wrote!

Well, that just about does it. You'll eventually see a Welcome screen that gives you three options:

**What's New**   Select this button to get help on some of the new features of Windows 95.

**Online Registration**   Select this button to register your copy of Windows 95 with Microsoft.

**Close**   Select this button to close the dialog box.

# The Least You Need to Know

This chapter showed you how to get Windows 95 out of the box and onto your computer. Now that Windows is settled cozily into your hard disk, it's time to get to know your system's new tenant. The chapters in Part 2 give you a rundown on most of the basic Windows chores. We'll begin in Chapter 4 with a tour of the Windows 95 screen.

# Part 2
# Workaday Windows 95

*One of the great things about Windows 95 is what technoid types refer to as its "consistent interface." In English, this just means you'll be able to use a lot of the techniques you learn in a Windows application today in a different Windows application tomorrow. These techniques are things you'll be using day in and day out, and the seven chapters in this section cover just that.*

# Chapter 4

# The Lay of the Windows 95 Land

## In This Chapter

➤ Starting Windows 95

➤ The parts of the Windows 95 screen

➤ Mouse and keyboard basics

➤ Shutting down Windows 95

➤ A bird's-eye view of the Windows 95 landscape

As a stranger in the strange land of Windows 95, you'll want to get your bearings before lighting out for parts unknown. Well, you've come to the right place because that's exactly what this chapter's all about. Here we'll be taking in the big Windows 95 picture: the forest instead of the trees; the hills and valleys instead of the nooks and crannies. You'll also learn some valuable mouse and keyboard survival skills that'll stand you in good stead in the chapters to come. So, if you're ready (a few deep breaths might help at this point), let's get under way....

## Cranking Up Windows 95

The term "no-brainer" doesn't apply to very many computer-related tasks, but it certainly applies to starting Windows 95. Why? Because there is, quite literally, nothing to it. Once Windows 95 is installed, it'll start itself up automatically each and every time you turn on your machine. (What's that? Windows 95 isn't installed on your computer? You must have skipped Chapter 3. Just flip back a few pages to see what you need to do.)

While Windows 95 is pulling itself up by its own bootstraps, you may see all kinds of strange hieroglyphics on your screen. This gobbledygook can safely be ignored. (You can, if you'd like, give thanks to the deity of your choice that a happy life in no way depends on knowing what all that junk means.)

## Why It's Called "Booting" and Other Semi-Interesting Trivia

You've probably heard computer types talk about "booting" (or "reboot-ing") a computer. Although you might think this has something to do with punting the recalcitrant beast across the room, it's really just geek-speak for starting up a computer. I didn't just conjure up the image of Windows 95 pulling itself up by its own bootstraps out of thin air. I used it because that's pre-cisely where the term "boot" comes from. You see, Windows 95 is an *operating system*, and one of the main chores of an operating system is to load programs into your computer's memory. When you first fire up your computer, however, Win-dows 95 has to perform the slick trick of loading *itself* into memory. So, in a sense, it really is pulling itself up by its own proverbial bootstraps.

If you set up Windows 95 with a password (see Chapter 3 for more information on passwords), a box eventually appears on-screen asking you to enter your password. Type it in the **Password** field (for extra security, Windows 95 shows your typing as asterisks, instead of showing your actual password). If you make a mistake, press the **Backspace** key to wipe out the offending letters. When you're done, press **Enter**.

## When Windows 95 Finally Loads

When Windows 95 is finally ready, the Welcome to Windows 95 box appears, as shown on the next page. Read the handy little tip (which, understandably, may not mean anything to you at this early stage of your Windows 95 career), and press **Enter** or click on the **Close** button to get rid of the box. (The Welcome to Windows 95 box is an example of a *dialog box*. You'll learn all about them in Chapter 7.

*Windows' welcome mat: The Welcome to Windows 95 box appears when you first start Windows 95.*

The screen you're left with (see below) is the basic Windows 95 screen. It's actually kind of disappointing, isn't it? Heck, all that hoopla, all those installation disks, and *this* is all we get? Spartan doesn't even begin to describe it. However, this screen represents part of the Windows 95 philosophy: keep things simple and uncluttered to make it easier for people to figure out what they're supposed to do next.

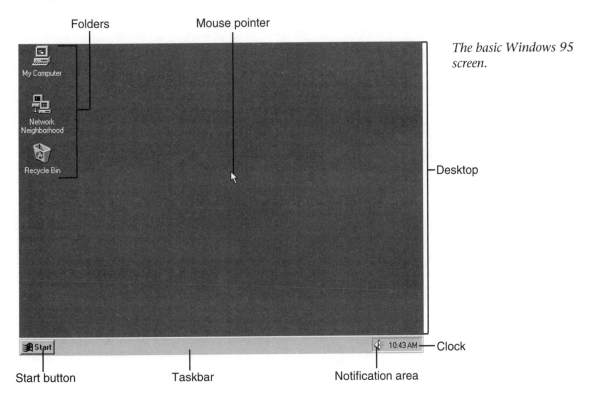

*The basic Windows 95 screen.*

However, the Windows 95 screen isn't completely barren; it does have a few knickknacks kicking around. The next couple of sections give you a quick rundown of the few things you *can* see.

# A Sea of Green: The Desktop

Ivory tower computer types like to invent metaphors for the way the rest of us use a computer. The idea is that more people will use a computer if using a computer is more like the way we do things in real life.

For Windows 95, the metaphor of choice is the humble desktop. The idea is that the Windows 95 screen is comparable to the top of a real desk in a real office or den. Starting a program is like taking a folder full of papers out of storage and placing it on the desk. To do some work, of course, you need to pull papers out of a folder and place them on the desk. This is just like opening a file within the program (it could be a letter, a spreadsheet, a drawing, or whatever). To extend the metaphor a little, most programs also come with *tools*, such as a ruler, a calculator, and a calendar, that are the electronic equivalents of the tools you use at your desk.

So, officially, the vast green expanse that takes up most of the screen real estate is the Windows 95 *desktop*, and it's where you'll do your work. (If you and green don't get along very well, changing to a different color or to a psychedelic pattern is no sweat. I'll tell you how in Chapter 23 in the "Doing Windows 95's Colors" section.)

**Missing Program Manager?** Are you Windows 3.1 users wondering what the heck happened to Program Manager? Sorry, but it's outta there, history, done like dinner, toast. With Windows 95, you'll do the vast majority of your program launching via the Start button (as explained in Chapter 5).

To get you going, the Windows 95 desktop starts off with a few items already visible. These are called *folders*, appropriately enough, and they appear in the upper-left corner of the screen. As you'll learn in Chapter 13, a folder is just a storage area. The number of folders you see depends on which components of Windows 95 you installed, but at the very least, you'll see the following two:

**My Computer** This folder contains visual representations of the various pieces of your computer: the floppy drives, the hard drives, the printer, and anything else that's attached to your machine. We'll check it out in more detail in Chapter 11.

**Recycle Bin** This folder is, literally, the Windows 95 garbage can. (You can make your own jokes about having a garbage can on top of your desk.) When you delete things from your computer, Windows 95 tosses them in the Recycle Bin. I'll take you through the full Recycling Bin rigmarole in Chapter 12 (see the section titled, "Tossing Files in the Recycle Bin").

### Storage—In the Trash?

Now wait just a cotton-picking minute! You said a folder was a storage area. Why the heck would Windows 95 store something I'm trying to get rid of? Good question. The answer is that it's not called the "Recycle" Bin for nothing. Suppose, for example, that you change your mind about the last thing you trashed, or that you accidentally toss out something important. In the old days (unless you had special software installed), the file was toast and you were out of luck. But with Windows 95's Recycling Bin, it's easy to just pluck the errant deletion out of the folder and restore it safely to its rightful place. (Check out Chapter 12 to get the details on all this.)

## Welcome to the Taskbar

The *taskbar* is the horizontal strip that runs along the bottom of the screen. It includes the Start button on the left, the notification area and clock on the right, and a blank area in between.

The *Start button* looks harmless enough, but it's actually a sort of "ignition switch" that gives you access to almost all of Windows 95. You'll be using it to do everything from launching programs to shutting down Windows 95 for the night. I'll talk more about the Start button in Chapter 5, in the section "The Start Menu: Your Windows 95 Launchpad" (although you'll also use it later on in this chapter when I show you how to quit Windows 95).

The *notification area* displays little pictures that tell you what's happening with your computer. When you're printing, for example, a picture of a printer appears in the notification area. If you have a sound card installed on your computer, a picture of a speaker appears (as you can see in the figure shown earlier).

The clock is obvious enough: it just tells you the current time. For more about the clock (such as how to display the date and how to set the time), head for Chapter 18 and read the section called "Doing Time with Date/Time."

The rest of the taskbar is blank right now, but it won't be for long. Once you start running programs (which I'll show you how to do in the next chapter), Windows 95 uses the taskbar to display a button for each loaded program. You can then use these buttons to quickly navigate between the programs.

# What's with This Mouse Thing?

Learning how to use a mouse just might be your most important Windows 95 survival skill. Why? Because most of Windows 95 is designed with the mouse in mind, and you'll find that using the mouse, you can accomplish most everyday tasks more quickly and easily. Does it require some superhuman level of dexterity? Nah. If you can use a fork without poking yourself in the eye, you'll have no trouble wielding a mouse.

The basic idea is simple: you move the mouse on its pad or on your desk, and a small arrow (the mouse pointer you saw earlier) moves correspondingly on the screen. By positioning the arrow on strategic screen areas and pressing the buttons, you can select objects, run programs, and alter the shape and size of windows. Not bad for a rodent!

## Basic Rodent Wrestling

Using a mouse is straightforward, but it does take some getting used to. Here's the basic technique:

1.  Turn the mouse so its cable extends away from you.

2.  Place your hand over the mouse in such a way that:

    ➤ The part of the mouse nearest you nestles snugly in the palm of your hand.

    ➤ Your index and middle fingers rest lightly on the two mouse buttons.

    ➤ Your thumb and ring finger hold the mouse gently on either side.

3.  Move the mouse around on its pad or on your desk. Notice that the mouse pointer on the screen moves in the same direction as the mouse itself.

### Mouse Potato

A person who spends too much time in front of his or her video screen. (This is, of course, the computer equivalent of a couch potato.)

## The Hard Part: Controlling the Darn Thing!

While moving the mouse pointer is simple enough, controlling the pesky little critter is another matter. New mouse users often complain that the pointer seems to move erratically, or that they run out of room to maneuver. To help out, here are a few tips that will get you well on your way to becoming a mouse expert:

➤ Don't grab the mouse as if you were going to throw it across the room (although there will be times when you'll be sorely tempted to do just that). A light touch is all that's needed.

➤ The distance the mouse pointer travels on the screen depends on how quickly you move the mouse. If you move the mouse about an inch very slowly, the pointer moves about the same distance (a little more, actually). However, if you move the mouse about an inch very quickly, the pointer leaps across the screen.

➤ If you find yourself at the edge of the mouse pad but the pointer isn't where you want it to be, simply pick up the mouse and move it to the middle of the pad. This doesn't affect the position of the pointer, but it does allow you to continue on your way.

## A Symphony of Mouse Movements

As you wend your way through this book, you'll find me constantly telling you to use your mouse to "point" at this, "drag" that, or "click" on something else. (If you get sick of all these instructions, you're well within your rights to say "Yeah, well click on *this*, buddy!") These are all run-of-the-mill mouse actions that'll soon become second nature to you. For now, though, they're probably not even third or fourth nature (or even in the top ten, for that matter), so let's see what they're all about:

*Point* means you move the mouse pointer so it rests on a specific screen location. For practice, point at the **Start** button in the lower-left corner of the screen. After a second or two, you'll see a little yellow banner that says "Click here to begin."

*Click* means you press and release the left mouse button. Note that you generally have to point at something before you can click on it. For example, if I say "click on the green and purple doodad," it means you should first point at the green and purple doodad and then click the button. Go ahead and click on the **Start** button. A whole menu appears on your screen. (This is called the Start menu, and we'll be checking it out in the next chapter. To send it back whence it came, click on an empty part of the desktop.)

*Double-click*, as you might expect, means to press and release the left mouse button twice quickly. This can be a bit tricky until you get the rhythm of it, so don't worry if Windows seems to be ignoring you. Again, you'll always point at something before you double-click on it. Itching to try an example? Try double-clicking on the time in the lower-right corner of the screen. If you do it right, a box titled Date/Time Properties appears. To get the goods on this box, light out for Chapter 18 and head for the section titled "Doing Time with Date/Time." For now, click on the **Cancel** button (or press the Esc key) to get rid of it.

### The Enlightened Double-Click

When I talk about the "rhythm" of a double-click, I'm talking about two distinct factors. First, there's the speed: the second click has to follow hot on the heels of the first, or Windows will think you're just doing two separate clicks. Second, there's the movement or, more accurately, the lack of movement: try your best not to jiggle the mouse between clicks. A properly executed double-click is a Zen-like combination of speed and stillness that requires patience and practice. Now here's the good news: the best Windows 95 program for practicing double-clicking (as well as most other mouse actions) happens to be a very addictive game called FreeCell. I'll tell you how to play it in Chapter 18 (look for the section called "Filling Your Free Time with FreeCell").

A *right-click* is similar to a regular click, except you quickly press and release the *right* mouse button. (If your mouse has three buttons, use the one on the far right.) As you'll see, when you right-click in Windows 95, a *shortcut menu* appears, giving you quick access to common commands. For example, right-click anywhere on the desktop to display one of these menus. Then click (the left button this time) on an empty part of the desktop to remove the menu.

*Dragging* the mouse has, fortunately, nothing to do with dressing funny. Instead, to drag means to point the mouse at a particular object, press and *hold down* the left mouse button, and then move the mouse. In most cases, the object you point at moves right along with the mouse pointer, so you'll generally use dragging to shift things from one spot and drop them on another (this is the "drag-and-drop" feature you may have heard about). It all sounds a bit vague, I know, but you'll be getting plenty of practice, believe me. In particular, you'll be dragging 'til you drop in Chapters 10 and 12.

# Windows Keyboarding for Non-Typists

Although a mouse is handy for many Windows 95 tasks, it's by no means essential. In fact, many Windows 95 commands have built-in keyboard shortcuts that can be real timesavers. Does this mean you have to become an expert typist to use Windows 95? Hardly. I've been using computer keyboards for years, and I wouldn't know what touch typing was if it bit me in the face.

Although there are a number of keyboard styles available, they all share a few common features. In the next few sections, I'll discuss a few of the keyboard's parts and explain how they relate specifically to Windows 95.

## Ctrl, Alt, and Those Strange Key Combinations

All keyboards also include Ctrl (it's pronounced *control*) and Alt keys (some newer keyboards have two of each). In Windows, you don't use these keys by themselves, but as part of *key combinations*. The Shift key often gets into the key combination act, as well.

For example, try pressing and holding down the **Ctrl** key, pressing the **Esc** key, and then releasing Ctrl. A menu of options sprouts from the Start button. (You'll learn about this menu in the next chapter.) This method of holding down one key while pressing another is called a *key combination* and is used extensively in Windows 95. (By the way, to remove the menu, just press **Esc** by itself.)

**Shortcut for Keyboard Shortcuts** It's going to be a real mouthful to say something like "hold down the Ctrl key, press the Esc key, and then release Ctrl" every time I tell you about a key combination. Instead, throughout this book, I'll simply write key combinations in the format *key+key* (as in Ctrl+Esc).

## The Esc Key

As you saw in the previous section, you were able to get rid of the Start menu by pressing the Esc key. In general, if you find yourself in some strange neck of the Windows woods and you're not sure what to do next, you can usually get back on more familiar turf by pressing the Esc key. (If that doesn't work, you can also try pressing the Alt+F4 key combination.)

## The Numeric Keypad

On each type of keyboard, the numeric keypad serves two functions. When the Num Lock key is on (there is usually a light on the keyboard that indicates when it is on), you can use the numeric keypad to enter numbers. If Num Lock is off, the keypad arrow keys (and other keys such as Home, End, Page Up, and Page Down) are enabled, and you can use them to navigate a document. Some keyboards (called *extended* keyboards) have a separate arrow keypad so you can keep Num Lock on all the time.

## Shutting Down Your Computer

When you've finished working with Windows 95 and are ready to turn off your machine for the night, you first need to exit Windows. Possibly the single most important thing to know about quitting Windows 95 is this: never, I repeat, *never* turn off your computer while Windows 95 is still running. Doing so could result in lost data, damage to important files, and accelerated hair loss. Having properly scared you into compliance, here are the steps to follow to shut down your computer:

1. Click on the **Start** button or press **Ctrl+Esc**. Windows 95's Start menu appears.

2. Click on the **Shut Down** option, or else press the up arrow key once to highlight the **Shut Down** option, and then press **Enter**. A dialog box entitled Shut Down Windows appears, as shown in the following figure. (This window is called a dialog box, and this is your first look at one. You'll be seeing plenty of them in your Windows 95 lifetime, so I've devoted an entire chapter—Chapter 7—to the ins and outs of using them.)

*When you shut down Windows 95, this dialog box appears to ask if you're sure.*

**A Faster Way**
If having to display the Start menu and select the Shut Down command seems like a lot of work just to exit, there *is* a quicker way: simply press **Alt+F4**. (This is one of those shortcut key combinations I told you about earlier.)

3. If you're sure you want to go through with it, click on the button that says **Yes**, or press **Enter**. (If you get cold feet at the last moment, you can abandon the shut down procedure either by clicking on the **No** button, or by pressing the **Esc** key.) Windows 95 takes a few seconds to prepare itself for bed, and then it displays a screen telling you it's okay to shut off your computer.

4. Turn off the computer and monitor.

## The Least You Need to Know

This chapter got you started with Windows 95. You learned how to get Windows 95 up and running, what the various parts of the screen were all about, how to use the mouse and keyboard, and how to exit the program. That's a lot! You might want to take five before moving on because the next chapter is where you start to make things happen in Windows 95.

# Chapter 5

# Making Things Happen in Windows 95

> **In This Chapter**
>
> ➤ Starting programs from the Start menu
>
> ➤ Getting the hang of the taskbar
>
> ➤ Techniques for switching between programs
>
> ➤ Windows to the rescue! How to use the Help system

As you might expect from that near-empty wasteland of a screen you see at startup, you have to do some digging to make Windows 95 do something. But where do you dig, how far down do you go, and how do you avoid the Windows equivalent of power lines, large rocks, and icky earthworms? What you need is a map that tells you how to get to all the good stuff in Windows 95, and that's just what this chapter is all about. I'll show you how to start programs and navigate between running programs, and I'll explain what this taskbar thing is all about.

## The Start Menu: Your Windows 95 Launchpad

Okay, Windows 95 is up and running, you've surveyed the landscape, and you're even learning to love that little plastic rodent. So far so good, but now what happens? Well, now it's time to shake Windows 95 from its slumbers and start making it earn its keep.

**Start** For starters (literally), let's check out the most obvious point of attack: the Start button. Go ahead and click on it to display the Start menu shown in the following figure. (Keyboardists can display the Start menu by pressing **Ctrl+Esc**. If you're using the crazy new Microsoft Keyboard—the one with the alphanumeric keys split down the middle and the postmodern, curvaceous, left-the-darn-thing-too-long-in-the-microwave-again look, you can also display the Start menu by pressing the key with the Windows logo on it.)

*Click on the Start button to display the Start menu.*

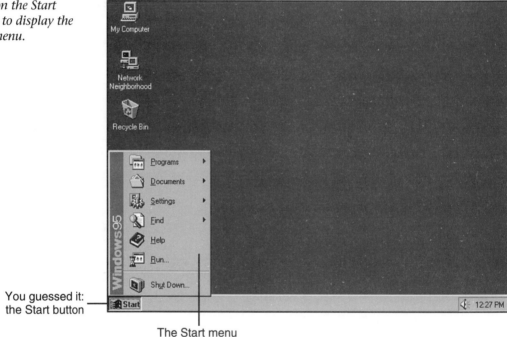

You guessed it: the Start button

The Start menu

The idea behind the Start menu is simple: it's a list of various things you can do with Windows 95. These "things" fall into three categories:

**Commands** A *command* is a feature that's built right into Windows 95 itself. For example, as you saw in Chapter 4, to quit Windows 95 you select the Start menu's Shut Down command.

**Accessories** The *accessories* are small programs that come as part of the Windows 95 package (some folks call these programs *applets*). As you'll see throughout this book, Windows 95 is loaded for bear with dozens of accessories for everything from word processing to dialing your phone.

**Applications** *Applications* are programs that are sold separately and have to be installed on your computer. In most cases, the installation procedure thoughtfully adds the name of the application to the Start menu. (However, if the name of one of your favorite applications doesn't appear on the Start menu, don't sweat it; I'll show you how to add it by hand in Chapter 23, in the section titled "Adding Items to the Start Menu.")

## Selecting Start Menu Items

To select an item from the Start menu, use either of the following techniques:

➤ With your mouse, click on the item you want to execute.

➤ With your keyboard, use the up and down arrow keys to highlight the item you want, and then press **Enter**. (As a shortcut, you can press the underlined letter in the item's name. For example, the *u* in the Shut Down command is underlined, so you could select Shut Down just by pressing **u**.)

> **A Point's as Good as a Click**
> Here's a tip that can save some wear-and-tear on your clicking finger: you don't have to click on a folder to open it. Instead, just point your mouse at the folder's name, and it opens automatically. The only time you really have to click is when you're selecting a program to run.

Notice that the top four Start menu items (Programs, Documents, Settings, and Find) have little arrows on the right? That means these items are *folders* that contain other items. For example, click on the **Programs** folder. Windows 95 opens the Programs folder and displays its contents in another menu that looks something like the one shown in the following figure. (Your menu may be different, depending on which Windows 95 options you've installed.) You can then select items from the new menu using the same techniques I outlined above. (We'll work through a concrete example in a sec.)

*The Programs item is a folder; when you click on it, Windows opens the folder and displays what's inside.*

Here's a summary of the items you get on the main Start menu:

**Programs**   Holds the various programs (accessories *and* applications) you can run from Windows 95.

**Documents**   Contains a menu of the last 15 documents you worked with in any of your applications. (In this sense, a *document* is any file you work with in a program. It could be a spreadsheet, a drawing, a letter, or whatever.) When you select a document from this folder, Windows launches the appropriate program and loads the document automatically. I'll talk more about this in Chapter 8's "Opening a Document from the Start Menu" section.

**Where, Oh Where, Have My Groups Gone?** Windows 3.1's Program Manager is history, so you may be wondering what happened to your program groups and all their icons. They're still around, but Windows 95 converted the groups into folders and stuck them inside the Programs folder.

**Settings**   Contains a few programs you can use to play around with various Windows 95 settings. We'll check out most of these settings later in the book.

**Find**   Contains tools that help you find things on your computer. I'll give you the details in Chapter 12, in the section "Finding File Needles in Hard Disk Haystacks."

**Help**   This command cranks up the Windows 95 Help system (which we'll talk about later on in this chapter).

**Run**   You use this command if the program you want to play with isn't listed in any of the Start menu folders. This isn't for the faint of heart, however. After selecting the command, you have to enter the disk drive where the program resides (e.g., **C:**), its folder (e.g., **\WP51\**), and then the name of the file that starts the program (e.g., **WP51.EXE**). Whew! Compared to the Start menu, that's some true, calluses-on-the-fingertips, manual labor.

**Shut Down**   As you saw in Chapter 4, this command tells Windows 95 that you've had enough for one day and want to return to the real world.

## Starting a Program: An Example

Let's add some flesh to all these Start menu bones by trudging through an example. The following steps show you how to launch WordPad, the word processing accessory that comes with Windows 95:

1. Open the Start menu by clicking on the **Start** button.

2. Select the **Programs** folder. Windows 95 displays another menu that contains the items inside the Programs folder.

3. Select the **Accessories** folder. Yet another menu appears, displaying a list of the items in the Accessories folder.

4. Select the **WordPad** item.

Once you select WordPad, Windows 95 takes a few seconds to load the program and then displays it (as shown in the following figure). Note that the taskbar sprouts a button for the program. I explain why you should care about this taskbar button in "Taking Windows 95 to Task: The Taskbar," on the following page).

Click on the Close button
to quit the program.

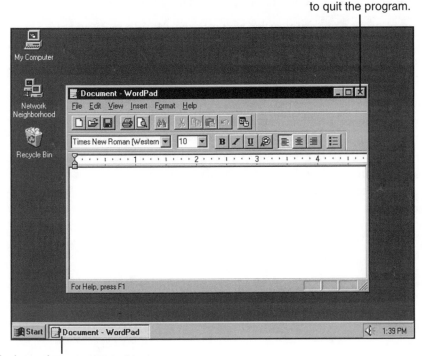

*Here's a picture of WordPad up and running.*

Each running program gets
its own taskbar button.

## Quitting a Program

When you're done with a particular program, you need to close it to clear your screen. There are actually a number of ways to shut down a running program, but the following three are the most common:

➤ With your mouse, click on the **Close** button in the upper-right corner of the program's window. The Close button is the one with the X.

➤ From the keyboard, press **Alt+F4**.

➤ Pull down the program's **File** menu and select the **Exit** command (or, more rarely, the **Close** command). I'll tell you how to work with pull-down menus in Chapter 6.

Depending on the program you're closing and the work you were doing with it, you might be asked if you want to "save" some files. I'll tell you how to handle this in Chapter 8, in the section called "Save Your Work, Save Your Life." (If you want, you can leave WordPad open while we discuss the taskbar in the next section.)

# Taking Windows 95 to Task: The Taskbar

When you started the WordPad program earlier, you saw that Windows 95 added a button for WordPad on the taskbar. What's the deal there? Well, with just one program open, there isn't much of a deal to speak of. No, the taskbar becomes useful only when you slap two or more programs onto the desktop at the same time.

*At the same time?* Sure. Windows 95 can handle the computer equivalent of walking and chewing gum at the same time. Specifically, it supports what the geeks call *multitasking*, which just means that Windows 95 is only too happy to let you run a whole passel of programs simultaneously. Why in the name of one-man bands would anyone need to run multiple programs at once? Isn't it hard enough just to use *one* program at a time? Actually, as you'll see in a second, even in the unlikely event that you have a dozen programs on the go, you really only work with one of them at a time. The idea is that you mess about in one program and then use the taskbar to switch to a different program when you need it. Here are some good reasons to take advantage of Windows 95's multitasking:

➤ You can set an operation in motion in one program and then switch to another program while the operation runs its course. The most common example of this is to start printing a document in, say, your word processor, and then switch to your spreadsheet program to crunch a few numbers.

➤ You might have a program that you use from time to time throughout the day. To avoid the tedium of continually starting and quitting the program, you can leave it open and switch to it when you need it.

➤ You might want to share information between two programs. Windows 95 lets you make a copy of, say, a chunk of text in one program, switch to a completely different program, and then insert the copy there. (This is explained in gory detail in Chapter 19.)

➤ If you're heavily into a game of FreeCell or DOOM (hey, we've all got to relax sometime, right?), you can quickly switch to a more corporate-looking program should the boss saunter into your office unannounced.

## The Technical Truth About Multitasking

Multitasking sounds like the cat's pajamas, but don't think you can just kickstart every program you've got and leave them running all day. The problem is that each open program usurps a chunk of Windows' resources. So the more programs you have running, the slower each program will be, including Windows. The number of applications you can fire up at any one time depends on how much horsepower your computer has, how much memory is installed in your system, and the availability of Windows 95's *system resources*. The system resources are small chunks of memory that handle things like the position of windows, the pattern of the desktop, and lots more. If the system resources become depleted, you won't be able to open any more programs. However, even a bare-bones Windows 95-capable computer should be able to get a few of the accessories going at once.

Okay, let's get down to brass tacks and check out how all this works. As you can see in the figure below, I've opened a second program—the Minesweeper game that comes with Windows 95. (To open this program on your computer, open the **Start** menu, select the **Programs** folder, the **Accessories** folder, and the **Games** folder—that's the last folder, I promise!—and then select **Minesweeper**.)

*Windows 95 with two programs running: WordPad and Minesweeper.*

The active program

Minesweeper appears to have lopped off a good portion of the WordPad window, but in reality, Windows 95 is just displaying Minesweeper "on top" of WordPad. (You'll see later that it's easy enough to place the WordPad window back on top of the pile.) In addition, the taskbar has changed in two ways:

➤ There's now a button for Minesweeper.

➤ The WordPad taskbar button no longer appears "pressed."

The taskbar tells us two things: which programs are running and which of those program is the "active" one. In this context, the active program is the one you're currently working in. (Technoid types say that such a program has the *focus*.) On the taskbar, the currently active program is shown with a "pressed" button.

If that was all the taskbar did, though, it would be a waste of precious screen real estate. No, the taskbar's true value comes through when you use it to switch between your open programs. All you have to do is click on the taskbar button for a program, and Windows 95 immediately brings that program to the foreground. For example, click on the **WordPad** button and see what happens. As you can see in the next figure, the WordPad window now appears on top of the Minesweeper window. Cool!

*To switch to WordPad, click on the WordPad button in the taskbar.*

Now the active program

Of course, you could also just use your mouse to click on the window you want. However, as you'll see later (in Chapter 10, to be exact), it's possible to enlarge a program's window so that it takes up the entire desktop. If you do that, you won't be able to see any of your other running programs, so the taskbar buttons become your best way to navigate all your programs.

### Overcoming Taskbar Crunch

One of the problems you'll run into is, once you've opened a few programs, Windows 95 shrinks the buttons so they can all fit on the taskbar. As a result, there are bound to be some buttons that show only part of the program name. To see the entire name, point your mouse at the button and let it sit there for a couple of seconds. Windows 95 then displays a small banner above the button that spells out the entire program name.

# More Methods for Switching Between Programs

As you'll see throughout this book, Windows 95 never gives you just one way to perform a particular task. No, that would be too simple (and using "Windows" and "simple" in the same sentences borders on the oxymoronic). Instead, Windows usually serves up several different methods and then watches us sweat trying to figure out which one to use. Switching between programs is no exception: there are, in fact, three other methods you can use.

➤ If you can see any part of a program's window, you can switch to the program by clicking inside the window. This is a handy technique if your programs are displayed in small windows (like Minesweeper's).

➤ From your keyboard, hold down the **Alt** key and tap the **Tab** key several times. Windows 95 displays the box shown in the following figure, and each time you hit Tab, it cycles through the names of your open programs. When you get to the one you want, release the Alt key, and Windows 95 switches to the program. This technique is useful if you don't have a mouse or if you have only two or three programs running. (In Windows circles, the Alt+Tab key combo is called the "cool switch.")

*Hold down Alt and tap the Tab key to cycle through the names of your open programs.*

**49**

➤ Hold down the **Alt** key and tap the **Esc** key several times. Again, Windows 95 cycles through the open programs with each press of the Esc key. In this case, however, you see the entire program window and not just its name. Use this technique if you forget what's in one or more windows and want to take a look before switching.

# Help! How to Get It

This book (a savvy and prudent investment on your part) will help you learn the most-used features of Windows 95 quickly and easily. But, as you've seen, my approach is purposefully not comprehensive, so there will be chunks of Windows 95 that you'll need some help with. Instead of plowing through the manual (shudder), you can use Windows' online Help system to get assistance on every aspect of the program with just a few keystrokes or mouse clicks. The rest of this chapter shows you how to use the Help system.

## Getting Help: The Basics

If you run into a problem with Windows 95, or if you simply find yourself in a strange part of town, you want to get help fast before panic sets in. Thoughtfully, the Windows programmers provided you with no less than four ways (see, I told you) to access the Help system:

➤ Press **F1** to get help that is *context-sensitive*. This means that the Help screen that appears is related to the Windows area you were in when you pressed F1. For example, when you're in WordPad, pressing F1 displays the Help Topics: WordPad Help window (see the following figure).

➤ Click on the **?** button in a dialog box and then click on something in the dialog box. This also accesses context-sensitive help: the help window that appears is related to the dialog box object you clicked on. (See Chapter 7 for more info on this.)

➤ Select the **Start** button and then select the **Help** command to get help on Windows itself.

➤ In most Windows applications, you can click on **Help** in the menu bar or press **Alt+H**. The Help menu that appears will have one or more commands for accessing different parts of the program's Help system.

*Pressing F1 in WordPad displays the Help Topics: WordPad Help window.*

# Displaying a Help Topic

When you invoke the Help system, the window that appears gives you a list of "books" that contain Help info. In the WordPad Help window, for example, there are books called "Working with Documents" and "Working with Text." To open one of these books, click on it and click on the **Open** button (or use your keyboard's up and down arrow keys to highlight a book and then press **Enter**).

When the book opens, several topics appear under it. To display one of these topics, click on it and click on the **Display** button (or, again, highlight the topic using the arrow keys and then press **Enter**). For example, opening WordPad's "Working with Text" book produces a whole slew of topics, including "Copying information between documents." Selecting the latter displays the Help text shown in the following figure. In addition to reading the displayed text, you can also perform any of the following actions:

➤ If you see a word in green text with a dashed underline, you can click on that word to display a definition of it. Press **Esc** when you're done reading the definition.

➤ Click on **Related Topics** at the bottom of the window to see a new Help window with info related to the current topic.

➤ Click on the **Back** button to see the previous Help topic.

➤ Click on the **Help Topics** button to return to the topics window.

➤ Click on the **Close** button to close Help.

*Selecting a Help topic displays a window like this one.*

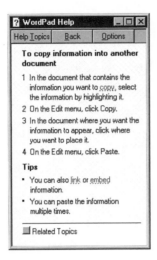

## Searching for a Help Topic

As handy as the Help system is, it can become a bit of a maze once you start jumping from topic to topic. To make it easier to find what you want, the Help system includes an Index feature that lets you search for a Help topic in an alphabetical list of topics, or simply type a key word or phrase. Here's what you do:

1. In a Help Topics window, click on **Index**.

2. Type the first few letters of the topic you want. For example, if you type **print**, Index moves to "print preview."

3. Click on the topic you want and then click on the **Display** button. The Help system displays the topic.

## The Least You Need to Know

This chapter showed you how to use Windows 95 to get programs off the ground, as well as how to juggle them once they're in the air. (Once you've got the hang of these basic techniques, you might want to pay a visit to Chapter 23 where, in the "Customizing the Taskbar and Start Menu" section, I show you how to modify the Start menu and the taskbar to suit your own style.)

Of course, starting a program is one thing, but actually getting something useful out of it is quite another. We'll take a big leap in that direction in the next chapter as we look at a few tools that enable you to take advantage of all the features and commands of any Windows 95 program.

# Chapter 6

# Your Click Is My Command: Menu and Toolbar Basics

## In This Chapter

➤ Learning about pull-down menus

➤ Using pull-down menus with a mouse and keyboard

➤ Working with shortcut menus

➤ Yet another menu: the Control menu

➤ Using toolbars to make your life easier

➤ Complete coverage of a few oh-so-handy tools that let you put the whip to Windows 95

In Chapter 5, you learned that you have to do some digging to discover the application nuggets and accessory trinkets you need to transform your computer from a doorstopper to a showstopper. However, you face a similar what-the-heck-do-I-do-now? problem once you've got a program up and running.

This chapter solves that problem by showing you how to uncover the features and commands in just about any Windows 95 program. Not only that, but we'll also look at a truckload of tools and techniques that'll make it easier to wield those tools you use the most. In other words, you'll learn how to control your programs instead of letting them control you.

# More Buried Treasure: Pull-Down Menus

As they say, life is full of surprises. One of my favorite surprises is lifting up the sofa cushions every few years and seeing what new collection awaits me. There is, of course, the usual assortment of flora and fauna: lint, crumbs, old Doritos, that kind of stuff. But you can also come across some buried treasure: coins, keys, a long-lost remote control—you name it.

The prospect of finding buried treasure is also what I like about the subject of this section: pull-down menus. These menus, which are normally hidden from view, contain all kinds of fun surprises, and they give you access to all the features of your Windows 95 programs.

## Desktop Metaphor Redux

Back in Chapter 4, I introduced you to the desktop metaphor used by Windows 95. I'm returning to this metaphor now because it's perfect for describing pull-down menus.

To get your work done, it's not enough to simply shuffle papers around all day (as tempting as that may be). You usually need to do something to those papers: write on them, staple them together, take numbers from them for your calculations, make cool airplanes, or whatever. To accomplish these tasks, you need the proper tools: a pen, a stapler, a calculator, and so on. With a few exceptions, you probably store most of these items in drawers instead of leaving them on top of your desk. (Unless, of course, you're one of those people who has to dig through layers of papers to see what kind of wood grain is on his desk.) When you need something, you just *pull* open the drawer (nudge, nudge) and select the item you want.

A pull-down menu in Windows 95 is just like a desk drawer. When you need to access a command in an application, you open the appropriate menu and select that command.

## Why You Pull "Down" Instead of "Up" or "Out"

Why are they called "pull-down" menus and not, say, "pull-on" menus? Well, because they're hidden inside a *menu bar*: the horizontal strip on the second line of most program windows. Selecting any of the items in a menu bar displays a menu of choices. For example, the following figure shows the Windows Explorer program with its View menu pulled down. (If you want to follow along, you can start Windows Explorer by opening the Start menu, selecting the **Programs** folder, and then selecting **Windows Explorer**. However, I won't be showing you how to use Explorer in this chapter. That'll have to wait until Part 3, "Navigating Your Computer with Windows 95.") The effect, you'll note, is as though you pulled the menu down from the menu bar. (See, sometimes this stuff actually makes sense! Besides, a "pull-on menu" sounds like something you'd wear when the Windows weather got a little chilly.)

Menu bar

The View menu
pulled down

*Selecting Explorer's View option pulls down this menu.*

# How to Use Pull-Down Menus with a Mouse

If you have a mouse, using pull-down menus is a breeze. All you do is move the mouse pointer into the menu bar area and then click on the name of the menu you want to pull down. For example, you simply click on **View** in Explorer's menu bar to pull down the View menu.

Once your menu is displayed, your next chore is to select one of its commands, and you do that just by clicking on the command. Depending on the command you select, one of three things will happen:

➤ **The command will run.** For example, Explorer's File menu has a Close command at the bottom; if you select that command, Windows runs the Close command and shuts down Explorer.

➤ **Another menu will appear.** For example, if you pull down Explorer's File menu and click on the New command, a new menu appears on the right. You then click on the command you want to execute from the new menu.

➤ **A dialog box will appear to ask you for more information.** For example, if you pull down Explorer's View menu and click on the Options command, a dialog box named Options appears. See Chapter 7 for details on using dialog boxes. (You can press Esc to get rid of the dialog box.)

## How to Use Pull-Down Menus with the Keyboard

Although a mouse makes it easy to use pull-down menus, there's no law against using your keyboard. In fact, the keyboard method may even be quicker because you don't have to reach all the way over to the mouse when you're typing on the keyboard. The secret to using pull-down menus from the keyboard is to look for the underlined letter in each menu bar option (they all have them). In Explorer, for example, look at the "F" in File and the "E" in Edit. These underlined letters are called the *hot keys*. (In geekier circles, they're also known as *accelerator* or *selection keys*.) How do they work? Simple: you just hold down the **Alt** key, press the hot key on your keyboard, and then release Alt. For example, to pull down Explorer's File menu, press **Alt+F**.

With the menu pulled down for all to see, select one of the menu commands by using the up and down arrow keys to highlight the command you want (a *highlight bar* moves up and down to mark the current command) and then pressing **Enter**. As I explained in the mouse section, depending on which command you select, one of three things will happen: the command will run, another menu will appear, or a dialog box will appear to pester you for more info.

### Bailing Out of a Menu

What do you do if you pull down a menu and then discover that you don't want to select any of its commands? You can remove the menu by clicking on any empty part of the program's window, or you can just pull down a different menu by clicking on the appropriate menu bar option.

From the keyboard, you have two choices:

➤ To get rid of the menu, press **Alt** by itself.

➤ To pull down a different menu, press **Alt** plus the letter of the new menu.

## Pull-Down Menu Doodads and Doohickeys

If you've pulled down a menu or two, you may have seen a few strange things in your travels. For example, did you notice that every command in a pull-down menu has one underlined letter? Or that some commands are followed by three ominous-looking dots? Or that still other commands also list a key or key combination? These are all perfectly normal pull-down menu features, and you can take advantage of some of these things to make your menu chores easier. The next few sections summarize these features.

## The Highlight Bar

As you move through a menu with your keyboard, a blue bar appears across the menu (see the figure below). This is called the *highlight bar*, and it indicates which command is current. As I've said, one way you can select a command is to press Enter when the command is highlighted.

*Some pull-down menu features.*

Check mark

Option mark

Highlight bar

Dimmed command

Ellipsis      Cascade menu

## Underlined Characters: More Hot Keys

Every command in a pull-down menu has one underlined character, which is called the hot key. Once you've displayed a menu, you can select any command simply by pressing its underlined letter on your keyboard. (For this reason, command hot keys are also known as *selection letters*.) In Explorer's View menu, for example, you can select the Options command simply by pressing O. (If you're itching to try this out, go ahead and open the **View** menu and press **O**. You'll eventually see a dialog box named Options. For now just press **Esc** to return to Explorer.)

### Hot Keys: Clear As Mud

*Techno Talk*

"Okay, let's get this straight: each menu bar option has a hot key, and to pull down a menu I have to hold down Alt and press the hot key letter; each menu *command* also has a hot key, but to select the command, I press the letter *without* holding down the Alt key. Is it just me, or is this confusing?" It *is* confusing at first, but it's just one of those arcane Windows things we have to live with.

# The Ellipsis (The Three-Dot Thing)

An ellipsis (...) after a command name warns you that a dialog box will appear when you select the command. A dialog box is a window a program uses to ask you for more information. As you saw in the previous section, selecting the View menu's Options command displayed the Options dialog box. See Chapter 7 for more details about dialog boxes.

# What You Can't Do: The Dimmed Commands

Sometimes certain menu commands appear in a lighter color than the others. (For example, check out the Line up Icons command in the View menu shown earlier.) These are called *dimmed commands*, and the dimming indicates that the command is not currently available. (It's the Windows equivalent of a "Gone Fishing" sign.) Generally speaking, if you see a dimmed command, it means that you must do something else with the program for the command to become available.

# Arrowheads (Menus, Menus, and More Menus)

In some applications, you'll see an arrowhead (▶) to the right of a menu command. This tells you that yet another menu will appear when you select this command. Explorer has several examples of the species. To see one, pull down the **View** menu and select the **Arrange Icons** command. A new menu appears on the right with several more commands related to arranging icons. These "submenus" are called *cascade menus*.

# Check Marks: Toggling Commands On and Off

Some commands operate like light switches: they toggle certain features of a program on and off. When the feature is on, a small check mark appears to the left of the command to let you know. Selecting the command turns off the feature and removes the check mark. If you select the command again, the feature is turned back on and the check mark reappears. Let's work through an example so you can see what I mean.

1. Pull down Explorer's **View** menu and take a look at the Status Bar command. You should see a check mark beside it. This tells you the command is "on" which, in this case, means that Explorer's status bar is displayed. (That's the gray area at the bottom of the Explorer window.)

2. Go ahead and select **Status Bar**. This turns off the Status Bar command, and as you might expect, the status bar disappears.

3. Pull down the **View** menu again. Notice that the Status Bar command no longer has a check mark beside it.

4. Once again, select **Status Bar**. This turns the command back on, and lo and behold, the status bar reappears at the bottom of the window.

## Option Marks: Selecting One Command Out of a Group

In addition to having features that can be toggled between two different states, some programs have features that can assume three or four different states. (I call them the "Three or Four Faces of Eve" features.) Explorer, for example, is designed to show you the contents of your computer, and it can display those contents in four ways: as large icons, as small icons, in a simple list, or in a list that gives the details of each item. (If you're not sure what all this means, don't give it a second thought. You'll get the full scoop in Chapter 11.)

To switch between these views, you choose from four commands on the View menu: Large Icons, Small Icons, List, and Details. Since these states are mutually exclusive (you can select only one at a time), you need some way of knowing which of the four commands is currently active. That's the job of the *option mark*: a small dot that appears to the left of the active command.

As an example, pull down the **View** menu and look for the option mark; you should see it beside the List command. Try selecting the **Large Icons** command and see what happens. Feel free to try out the other three commands as well. Notice that each time you pull down the View menu, the option mark appears beside the last command you selected.

## Shortcut Keys: The Fast Way to Work

Some menu commands also show a key or key combination on the right-hand side of the menu. These are called shortcut keys and they allow you to bypass the menus altogether and activate a command quickly from your keyboard. For example, if you pull down Explorer's **Edit** menu (see the following figure), you'll see shortcut keys listed beside the Cut command (Ctrl+X) and the Copy command (Ctrl+C), among others.

**Shortcut Key Confusion**
Confusingly, the shortcut keys work only when you don't have a menu displayed. If you press a key combination when a menu is pulled down, Windows 95 admonishes you with a beep and waits for you to do something sensible.

*Explorer's Edit menu has several commands with shortcut keys.*

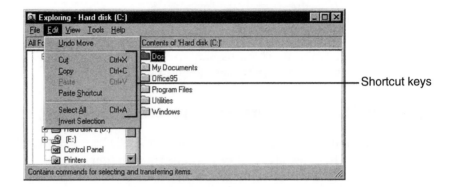

Once you've worked with your favorite Windows 95 applications for a while, you'll likely find that you often ignore the menus and just use the program's shortcut keys. It's simply a faster way to work. Some smart applications (such as Word for Windows 95) even let you create your own shortcut keys.

## Using the Control Menu

Besides the pull-down menus attached to the menu bar, each Windows 95 window also has a Control menu. You use the Control menu to manipulate certain features of the window, such as its size and position, or to close the window (see Chapter 10 for details). Before I show you how to display a Control menu, you need to know the difference between a program window and a document window.

A *program window* is the window that contains the entire program you're running. It includes the program's menu bar, its status bar (if it has one), and the area where you do your work in the program.

A *document window*, on the other hand, is a window within the program window, which usually contains a document you've created with the program. (Here, the term "document" is used in a generic sense to include anything you create with a program. So a document can be a spreadsheet, a database, a drawing, or a word processing document.) Why bother with document windows at all? Well, some applications enable you to display multiple documents at the same time, so you need separate windows for each document. You'll find, however, that most of the accessories that ship with Windows 95 don't let you open multiple documents, so they don't use document windows.

The figure below shows the Word for Windows program window with a document window inside it.

Click here to display the program window's Control menu.

Click here to display the document window's Control menu.

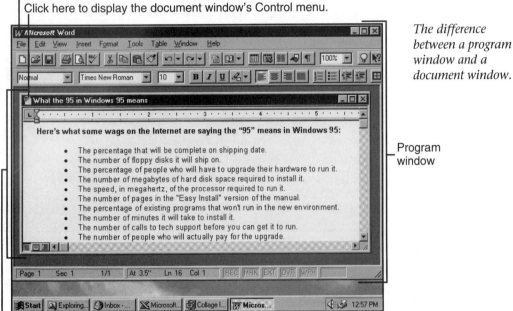

*The difference between a program window and a document window.*

Program window

Document window

Okay, now that we've got all that rigmarole out of the way, we can figure out how to display a Control menu:

➤ To display the Control menu for a program window, click on the icon in the upper-left corner of the program window. (You can also press **Alt+Spacebar**.) The following figure shows the Control menu for the Word for Windows program window.

➤ To display the Control menu for a document window, click on the icon in the upper-left corner of the document window (see the figure above). Keyboarders can also press **Alt+ –** (hyphen).

*The Control menu for Word for Windows' program window.*

Control menu

## Quick Access to Common Commands
## Part I: Shortcut Menus

Windows 95 boasts a new feature that gives mouse users a real bonus: shortcut menus. These menus display a brief list of commands related to a specific feature. All you do is place the mouse pointer over the feature and then right-click. When the menu appears, just click (the left button this time) on the command you want.

For example, right-clicking on the Recycle Bin displays the shortcut menu shown in the following figure. From this menu, you can select Open to open the Recycle Bin, Empty Recycle Bin to clean out the Recycle Bin's contents, or Properties to set some Recycle Bin options. (To get more details about what each of these commands does, set sail for Chapter 12 and read the section "Tossing Files in the Recycle Bin.") To get rid of the shortcut menu without selecting a command, click on an empty part of the desktop or press **Esc**.

*The shortcut menu that appears when you right-click on the Recycle Bin.*

# Quick Access to Common Commands
# Part II: Toolbars

In the bad old days of computers (way back in the '80s!), the only way to run a command in most programs was to press a key or key combination. Users complained, though, because not only was it hard to remember the proper keystrokes, but the hand contortions were crippling people for life.

In response to these complaints, the world's programming geniuses came up with pulldown menus and dialog boxes. These were a big improvement, but then people whined about having to wade through dozens of menus and windows to get to the command they needed. (You just can't please some people.)

So now we have *bars*. Whether they're called "power" bars or "tool" bars or "sushi" bars, they're all designed to give you push-button access to common commands and features. No unsightly key combinations to remember; no menu and dialog box forests to get lost in.

Windows 95 has jumped in with both feet by offering a toolbar with many of its accessories. To check one out, open Windows Explorer, pull down the **View** menu, and activate the **Toolbar** command. The toolbar appears just below the menu bar, as shown in the following figure.

Toolbar   Point at an icon to see its name.

*The Windows Explorer toolbar.*

The name of the icon is shown below it.

Most toolbar "tools" are buttons that represent commands you'd normally access using the pull-down menus. All you have to do is click on a button, and Explorer runs the command, no questions asked. For example, clicking on the Large Icons button is the same as pulling down the View menu and selecting the Large Icons command.

**63**

Okay, so which one is the Large Icons button? Ah, there's the rub. Most of those tiny pictures are pretty obscure, so icon-interpretation is quickly becoming one of the most coveted skills of the '90s. Fortunately, the Windows 95 programmers decided to have mercy on us all and included an easy method for identifying toolbar buttons. Just point the mouse at the button you're furrowing your brow over and wait a second or two. Eventually, you'll see a little yellow banner below the button that tells you the button's name (see the previous figure).

# The Least You Need to Know

This chapter showed you how to make Windows 95 programs toe the line. We first looked at pull-down menus and Control menus, which give you access to all of a program's features and commands. Then we looked at shortcut menus and toolbars, Microsoft's contribution to making our lives in the land of Windows 95 a bit cushier.

As you saw, however, just selecting a command isn't enough to set things in motion. Instead, lots of commands leave Windows wanting more feedback from you, so it displays a dialog box. You'll see dialog boxes of every shape, size, and description as you toil in Windows 95, and you'll need to know how to handle anything that's thrown your way. Therefore, my goal in the next chapter will be to work with you as you plumb the mysteries of these dialog box things.

# Chapter 7

# Talk to Me: Dealing with Dialog Boxes

## In This Chapter

➤ What is a dialog box?

➤ Getting around in dialog boxes

➤ Learning about dialog box buttons, boxes, and lists

➤ Working with Windows 95's Wizards

➤ Your field guide to dialog box flora and fauna

Communication is in. Everywhere you go people are "establishing a dialogue," "networking," or dealing with "interpersonal dynamics." Experts from all fields are appearing on sleazy daytime talk shows to remind us to "listen to each other" or risk a dysfunctional fate. One tiny, famous doctor tells us that "ze key to good zex is to communicate vis your partner."

Windows 95, being the hip, modern program that it is, is also getting into the act. As you work with Windows applications and accessories, endless little windows appear on your screen to prompt you for more information. These are called *dialog boxes*, and they're Windows' way of saying "Talk to me!" This chapter looks at these chatty little beasts and offers some helpful tips for surviving their relentless onslaught.

# Where Do They Come From?

Dialog boxes may sometimes seem to appear out of nowhere, but they generally show up after you select certain commands from an application's pull-down menu. Whether or not a dialog box appears depends on whether or not the application needs more info from you. For example, suppose you pull down a menu and select a command called Print. You'll probably see a dialog box something like the one in this figure.

*A dialog box you might see in response to a "Print" command.*

The program is telling you it needs more information. In this case, it wants to know which printer to use, which pages to print, how many copies you want, and so on.

# Some Dialog Box Basics

**Brace Yourself** You can always tell when a command will generate a dialog box by looking for three dots (...) after the command name. These three dots (an *ellipsis*) tell you that some kind of dialog box will appear if you select the command. This gives you a chance to psych yourself up for the ordeal to come.

Before we can delve any deeper into dialog boxes, we need to get a specimen on-screen. I'll be using dialog boxes from WordPad as examples throughout this chapter, so you may as well crank up WordPad now. (Open the **Start** menu, select the **Programs** folder, select **Accessories**, and then select **WordPad**.) To display the Print dialog box shown earlier, pull down the **File** menu and select the **Print** command.

The first thing you should notice about a dialog box is that it has several features in common with other windows that you've seen. For example, most dialog boxes have a title ("Print" in the previous example) and a Close button (the "X" in the upper-right corner). What's different, though, is what's inside. The various objects you see are called *controls* because you use them to control the way the dialog box works. Each control has a name that identifies it (such as Print to file or Number of copies).

**Techno Talk**

**Dialog Box Controls**

You'll notice that every time I refer to a dialog box control, the name appears in a special font. This is because Windows 95 uses some really long-winded control names, such as Verify backup data by automatically comparing files after backup is finished. It's easy to get lost in the middle of a name like that, and not know where it ends, so I'll use that special font to help you identify when I'm referring to a dialog box control.

Keep in mind that most dialog boxes like to monopolize your attention. When one is on the screen, you usually can't do anything else in the program (such as select a pull-down menu). Deal with the dialog box first, and then you can move on to other things.

## Getting Around in a Dialog Box

Later in this chapter I'll talk in nauseating detail about how the various dialog box controls operate. For now, though, you need to know how to cruise from one control to another. (This section applies only to keyboard users. Mouse maniacs do their control cruising on Easy Street because they navigate controls merely by clicking on them.)

The first thing you need to be able to figure out is which control is the *active control*. (This can be easy or hard depending on how many controls the dialog box has.) There are two things to keep your eyes peeled for:

➤ If the control displays text inside a box, the control is active either when the text is highlighted (which means the text appears as white on a blue background instead of the usual black on a white background) or when you see an insertion point cursor blinking on and off inside the box. For example, when you first display the Print dialog box, the text in the Name box is highlighted, indicating that the Name control is currently active.

➤ All other controls display a dotted outline around their name when they're active.

Think of these guidelines as "You are here" signs on a map, and keep them in mind as you move through the dialog boxes. There are two basic techniques you can use to move around:

➤ **Tab key**   Press the **Tab** key to move forward through the controls ("forward" means that you move either left-to-right or top-to-bottom, depending on how the dialog box is laid out). Press **Shift+Tab** to move backward. (Note that Tab may not highlight every control in the dialog box. To figure out why, see the section "Windows Does Multiple Choice: Option Buttons," later in this chapter.)

➤ **Hot keys**   Some control names have an underlined letter that acts as the control's *hot key*. This means you can select the control by holding down Alt and pressing the letter. In the Print dialog box shown earlier, for example, you could select the Number of copies control by pressing **Alt+C**.

To get the hang of these techniques, you really need to jump right in and get your feet wet. Feel free to use the Print dialog box for your experiments; simply moving around in the dialog box won't harm anything. As you leap around, make sure you can identify which control is active before you move on to the next one. When you're done, press **Esc** to close the dialog box without printing anything.

## Negotiating the New Tabbed Dialog Boxes

One common pet peeve among Windows users over the years is that you often have to wrestle with umpteen dialog boxes to get your work done. The complaining must have worked because the designers of Windows 95 decided to do something about the dialog box deluge. Their solution was to combine all related dialog boxes into a single, multipurpose dialog box. Now that doesn't mean you're going to see dialog boxes with billions of controls jumbled together willy-nilly. Thank goodness they were a little smarter about it than that. These multipurpose dialog boxes come equipped with *tabs* that work like the tabs in a notebook. Select one tab to see a particular set of controls; select another tab to see a whole new collection of controls.

Let's take a look at an example. Pull down WordPad's **View** menu and select the **Options** command to display the Options dialog box (shown in the following figure).

Select these tabs to see different sets of controls.

*The Options dialog box is an example of a tabbed dialog box.*

The tabs are the boxes that run across the top of the dialog box (Options, Text, Rich Text, and so on). When you first display the dialog box, the Word 6 tab is selected. To choose a different tab, click on it with your mouse. (If you prefer the keyboard, press **Ctrl+Tab** to cycle through the tabs from left to right or **Ctrl+Shift+Tab** to move through the tabs from right to left.) The following figure shows the controls that appear when you select the Options tab.

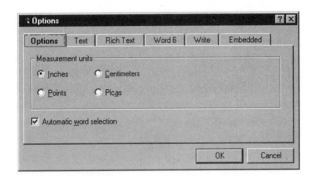

*If you select the Options tab, a whole new set of controls appears.*

### Getting Help in a Dialog Box

Most dialog boxes have a Help button in the upper-right corner (the question mark button to the left of the Close button). You can use this button to get a description of any dialog box control. To try it out, first click on the **Help** button. Your mouse pointer sprouts a question mark. Then click on the control you're puzzling over. In a few seconds, a brief description of the control appears on-screen. (No mouse nearby? No problem. Just highlight the control and press **F1**.)

# Dialog Box Gadgets and Gizmos

Now that we've dispensed with the preliminaries, let's look at some example dialog boxes and figure out what all those strange-looking controls are for. The next few sections give you the lowdown on each type of control.

## Setting Things in Motion: Command Buttons

All dialog boxes have at least one *command button*. They're called command buttons because when you select one, you're telling the program to execute the command written on the face of the button.

WordPad's Options dialog box, for example, has two command buttons: OK and Cancel (see the following figure). These are by far the most common command buttons, and you'll see them on the majority of dialog boxes you deal with. Here's what they mean:

Select **OK** when you've finished with the dialog box and want to put all your selections into effect. This is the "Make it so" button.

Select **Cancel** to bail out of the dialog box without putting your selections into effect. This is handy when you panic and realize that you're looking at the wrong dialog box or when you've made a mess of your selections. Think of this as the "Belay that last order" button.

*Some dialog box controls.*

To select a command button with a mouse, just click on the button. To select a command button from the keyboard, press **Tab** until the command button you want is active (its name is surrounded by a dotted outline), and then press **Enter**.

Here are some notes to bear in mind when working with command buttons:

➤ Many command buttons act just like the commands in pull-down menus: they might run a particular feature of the program, or they might even display *another* dialog box.

➤ Every group of command buttons has a default button that has a darker outline than the others (you need to look closely to see this). To select this button, just press **Enter** from anywhere in the dialog box. In the Options dialog box, for example, the OK button is the default.

➤ Instead of selecting the Cancel button, you can always cancel a dialog box either by pressing **Esc** or by clicking on the Close button (the X in the upper-right corner).

# Toggling Stuff On and Off: Check Boxes

The real world is constantly presenting us with either/or choices. You're either watching *Oprah* or you're not; you either like Bac-O-Bits or you don't. Windows handles these yes-or-no, on-or-off decisions with a control called a *check box*. The check box enables you to control whether or not a particular program setting or option is activated (checked) or deactivated (unchecked). In the Options dialog box shown earlier, for example, there are four check boxes: Toolbar, Format bar, Ruler, and Status bar. A check mark inside the box tells you the control is currently activated. If there's no check mark, the control is deactivated.

To toggle a check box on and off with a mouse, click on the box or on its name. To toggle a check box on and off from the keyboard, press **Tab** until the check box you want is active (its name is surrounded by a dotted outline), and then press the **Spacebar**.

# Windows Does Multiple Choice: Option Buttons

When I was in school, I hated multiple-choice questions for some reason. I guess I figured I could bluff my way through an essay question, but with multiple-choice, it's the law of the jungle: you're either right or wrong. I even had one perverse teacher who *subtracted* marks for wrong answers. (How do you tell your parents you got a *negative* score on a test?)

The Windows equivalent of the multiple-choice question is the *option button*. You're given two or more mutually exclusive choices, and you're allowed to pick only one.

The Word 6 tab in the Options dialog box (shown above) contains three option buttons: No wrap, Wrap to window, and Wrap to ruler. As you can see, an option button consists of a small circle with a label beside it that tells you what the option is. The currently selected option has a small black dot inside its circle. You'll also notice that most option buttons appear in herds. That is, they always appear together in a box called a *group*. (In our example, the group box is named Word wrap.) In each group, you can select only one option button.

How do you select an option button? If you have a mouse, simply click on the option you want (you can either click on the button itself or on the name). A black dot appears inside the circle when you select an option.

To select an option from the keyboard, you need to press **Tab** until one of the option buttons in the group is active (it's surrounded by a dotted outline). Then use the arrow keys to move through the group to the option you want. (In most cases, you'll use the up and down arrow keys to make your choice.)

# Typing Text in Text Boxes

A *text box* is a control in which you type text information, such as a description or a file name. A text box is active either when the text is highlighted, or when a blinking vertical bar appears inside the box. This blinking vertical bar is called the *insertion point cursor* or just *cursor*, for short.

Let's look at some text box examples. (If the Options dialog box is still displayed, select **Cancel** to get rid of it.) Pull down WordPad's **Format** menu and select the **Paragraph** command to display the Paragraph dialog box shown below. There are three text boxes in this dialog box: Left, Right, and First line.

*You use text boxes to type in text info.*

Text boxes

To use a text box with a mouse, click anywhere inside the box and then type in your text. To use a text box from your keyboard, press **Tab** until the text inside the box is highlighted, and then begin typing. If you make a mistake, you can use the left and right arrows to position the cursor appropriately and use the following techniques to make corrections:

➤ Press **Backspace** to delete the character to the left of the cursor.

➤ Press **Delete** to delete the character to the right of the cursor.

➤ If the entire text box is a mess, press **Alt+Backspace** to restore the original text and then start over.

## Watch Out for Highlighted Text Box Text!

When the text in a text box is highlighted, the next letter or number you press replaces the contents of the text box! If you don't want to replace all of the text, press the left or right arrow key to remove the highlight, position the cursor appropriately, and then start typing.

# Selecting from Mucho Choices: List Boxes

As you saw earlier, a check box essentially lets you choose between two options: having a particular feature on or off. Then I showed you option buttons, which usually give you a choice of three or four items. So what if you need to select from a dozen items, or a hundred? As you can imagine, a dialog box with a hundred option buttons to choose from would be a navigational nightmare.

To avoid such a diabolical dialog box fate, *list boxes* are used whenever you need to select from a relatively large number of items (such as fonts, file names, or Elizabeth Taylor's ex-husbands). A list box is about what you'd expect: a box that displays a list of items. There are three list box flavors that you'll come across in your Windows travels: a *regular list box*, a *combo box*, and a *drop-down list box*.

Let's start with the garden variety, *regular list box*. To see an example, pull down WordPad's **Insert** menu and select the **Date and Time** command. (Don't forget you first need to cancel the Paragraph dialog box if it's still on-screen from the previous section.) The Date and Time dialog box appears (see the following figure). The list box is the control named Available formats. Notice that Windows uses a highlight bar to show the currently selected item in the list.

*The Date and Time dialog box sports a plain vanilla list box.*

To select an item from a list box with your mouse, you can use either of the following techniques:

➤ If the item is visible in the list box, click on it.

➤ If the item you want isn't visible, use the *scroll bar* to display the item, and then click on it. (I explain how to use a scroll bar in the next section.)

To select a list box item with your keyboard, first press **Tab** until the list is active. (Unfortunately, figuring out when a list box is active isn't as easy as it is with the other controls.

You need to watch the list's highlighted item carefully as you poke the Tab key. The list is active when the highlighted item is surrounded by a dotted outline.) Then use the up and down arrow keys (or the Page Up and Page Down keys if the list is a long one) to highlight the item you want.

A *combo box* is a hybrid control that combines a list box and a text box. The idea is that you can select the item you want from the list box, or you can type what you want in the text box. An example will help make this clear. Shut down the Date and Time dialog box and then select the **Format** menu's **Font** command. WordPad displays the Font dialog box, as shown in this figure.

Combo boxes

*The Font dialog box has several combo boxes (and a couple of drop-down list boxes, for good measure).*

Drop-down list boxes

This dialog box has three combo boxes: Font, Font style, and Size. As you can see, the top section of each combo box is a text box, while the bottom section is a list box. You can choose the item you want either by scrolling through the list box (as described earlier) or by typing the name of the item in the text box.

Our final list box variety, the *drop-down list box*, normally shows only the currently selected item. (WordPad's Font dialog box has two examples of the species: the Color and Script controls.) To choose a different item, you "drop down" the list and then select the item you want just as you would in a regular list box. The following figure shows the Color list in its dropped-down state.

So just how does one go about dropping down a drop-down list box? It's easy:

➤ With your mouse, click on the downward-pointing arrow on the right side of the box.

➤ From the keyboard, press **Tab** until the drop-down box is active and then press **Alt+down arrow**.

**74**

*A dropped-down drop-down list box. (Try to say that three times fast.)*

### Easier List Box Navigation

Here's a tip that can save you oodles of time when you're mucking about with both regular list boxes and drop-down list boxes. Once the list box is active, press the first letter of the item you want. Windows 95 leaps down the list and highlights the first item in the list that begins with the letter you pressed. For example, if you drop down the Color list and press G, the highlight immediately moves to the Green item. If you press G again, the highlight moves to the Gray item.

## A Brief Scroll Bar Primer

You'll learn more about scroll bars in the next chapter, but I'll give you a brief introduction here so you'll be able to successfully negotiate list boxes with your mouse.

Some lists contain too many items to fit inside a box. When that happens, a *scroll bar* appears on the right-hand side of the box to make it easier to navigate the list. The box inside the scroll bar (called, appropriately enough, the *scroll box*) tells you where you are in the list. For example, if the scroll box is halfway between the top and the bottom of the scroll bar, you're approximately halfway down the list.

To navigate a list with the scroll bar, use the following mouse techniques:

**To scroll through the list one item at a time,** click on either the arrow at the top of the scroll bar (to move up) or the arrow at the bottom of the scroll bar (to move down).

**To jump quickly through the list,** click inside the scroll bar between the scroll box and the top (to move up) or between the scroll box and the bottom (to move down).

**To move to a specific part of the list,** drag the scroll box up or down.

## Putting the Spin on Numbers: Spinners

*Spinners* are controls that let you cycle up or down through a series of numbers. To see a spinner, pull down WordPad's **File** menu and select the **Print** command. In the Print dialog box that appears (see the figure shown on Page 66), the Number of copies control is a spinner.

**Spinner Ranges** Most spinners have a maximum and minimum value, and you can select any number within that range.

Each spinner has two parts:

➤ The box on the left is a text box you can use to type in the number you want (which is the boring way to do it).

➤ The right side of the spinner contains an upward-pointing arrow and a downward-pointing arrow. You click on the upward-pointing arrow to increase the number that appears in the text box. To decrease the number, click on the downward-pointing arrow. For some real fun, press and hold down the mouse button on one of the arrows and watch the numbers really fly!

## Values Without Numbers: Sliders

To help us enter values that have no intrinsic meaning (at least to non-nerds and other mere mortals), Windows 95 uses a control called a *slider*. The best way to describe a slider is to show you an example. Unfortunately, WordPad's dialog boxes don't use any sliders, so we'll have to look elsewhere.

To get to our slider example, select the **Start** button, select the Start menu's **Settings** folder, and then select **Control Panel**. In the Control Panel window, double-click on the **Keyboard** icon, or use your arrow keys to highlight **Keyboard** and then press **Enter**. The following figure shows the Keyboard Properties dialog box that appears.

*The Keyboard
Properties dialog box
uses sliders to let
you enter "values"
without numbers.*

This dialog box has three sliders: Repeat delay, Repeat rate, and Cursor blink rate. Let's take a look at the Cursor blink rate slider. (If you're wondering what the other sliders are for, you can turn to Chapter 24 and read the section "Customizing the Keyboard," to find out.) The Cursor blink rate slider is a ruler-like line with opposite values of Slow and Fast on either end. The idea is that you enter a "value" by moving the pointer (it's called the *slider bar*) either left (to get, in this case, a slower blink rate) or right (to get a faster blink rate). The insertion point cursor on the left gives you a visual indication of exactly what the new value does to the blink rate.

Mouse users operate sliders using the following techniques:

➤ To move the slider bar several notches in either direction, click on the slider between the slider bar and the edge of the slider.

➤ To move the slider bar to any particular position, drag it with your mouse.

You keyboarders have to press **Tab** until the slider is active (that is, it's surrounded by a dotted outline). Then use the left and right arrow keys to move the slider bar.

# Walking with Windows 95's Way Cool Wizards

Lots of Windows tasks are multistep rituals that allow no deviation from the norm. You have to perform the steps the right way in the right order, or Windows gets all huffy and refuses to play with you anymore. To spare us all from its mood swings and, even better, from having to memorize the correct rituals, Windows 95 delegates certain tasks to the care of various "Wizards." These Wizards take you by the hand and lead you through the appropriate steps for a task by asking you questions and providing places for you to enter your answers.

It's quite simple, really. Each Wizard displays a series of dialog boxes, and you use these dialog boxes to provide the information necessary to complete your chore. The dialog boxes use the standard controls that we've looked at in this chapter, including these command buttons that let you move between the various Wizard dialog boxes:

| | |
|---|---|
| **Next >** | Select this button to move on to the next dialog box. |
| **< Back** | Select this button to return to the previous dialog box. |
| **Cancel** | Select this button to bail out of the Wizard altogether. |
| **Finish** | Select this button to complete the task. (This button normally appears only on the last Wizard dialog box.) |

This figure shows an example of a Wizard dialog box. (You'll use the Add Printer Wizard in Chapter 9, in the section titled "Telling Windows 95 About Your Printer.")

*The Add Printer Wizard takes you through the otherwise-tedious task of installing a printer in Windows 95.*

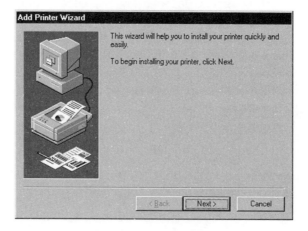

## The Least You Need to Know

This chapter showed you the ins and outs of using dialog boxes to communicate with Windows 95. Your Windows 95 education has now progressed far enough that you could actually crank up some programs and start working with them. In fact, that's just what we'll do in the next chapter. I'll take you through basic program chores such as opening and closing files, navigating documents, editing, and the all-important saving your work.

# Chapter 8

# Day-to-Day Document Drudgery

## In This Chapter

➤ Opening and saving a document

➤ Launching a document from the Start menu

➤ Navigating a document

➤ Editing a document

➤ A compendium of commonplace, nose-to-the-grindstone Windows 95 tasks and chores

It may sound strange to say, but Windows 95 is the reigning sex symbol of personal computing. Think about it: all those lush screens, the siren call of the seductive icons, the cheesecake graphics. This is one good-looking program.

But even sex symbols sometimes have to take out the garbage and feed the cat. In Windows 95, this means opening and closing documents, cutting and pasting text, and saving your work. These day-to-day chores are Windows 95 without its makeup on, and that's the subject of this chapter.

To get the most out of this chapter, you probably should follow along using an actual Windows 95 application. I'll be using WordPad, the word processor that comes with Windows 95, for my examples, but it doesn't matter a whole lot which one you use. Just make sure that the application has both File and Edit pull-down menus. If you'd like to use WordPad, you can fire it up by selecting the **Start** button, opening the **Programs** folder, opening the **Accessories** folder, and then selecting **WordPad**. (For information on actually using WordPad, though, you should head for Chapter 14.)

# First Things First: What the Heck Is a Document?

I've already talked about documents a couple of times, but I enjoy beating a dead horse as much as the next guy (metaphorically speaking, of course. No actual horses were harmed in the making of this book). To reiterate, Windows 95 uses the term *document* in its broadest sense. This means a document is anything you create using an application or one of the accessories. Here are some examples:

➤ A letter, memo, or even a novel created with WordPad.

➤ A logo or cartoon produced with Paint.

➤ A budget or mortgage analysis spreadsheet put together in a spreadsheet program.

➤ An inventory or sales database maintained by a database program.

➤ Anything created with any program, anywhere, anytime.

I think that just about covers everything!

Just to keep us all on our toes, Windows 95 also uses the term *file* to refer to a document. File is a broader term in that it refers to all the little chunks of information scattered about on your computer's hard disk, which includes not only your documents, but also the files that Windows 95 uses to start programs. You'll get the full scoop on files in Chapter 12. For our purposes in this chapter, though, I (impetuous bohemian that I am) will use the terms *document* and *file* interchangeably.

# Save Your Work, Save Your Life

When you start most Windows 95 applications, you usually see a new, blank document, ready and eager to receive your input. You have two choices at this point:

➤ You can work with the new document.

➤ You can open an existing document.

Since we're just starting out, I'm going to assume you want to work with the new document. I'll cover opening an existing document later in this chapter.

How you work with the new document depends entirely on which program you're in. In WordPad, for example, you type in text and add formatting to make it look good. In Paint, you create and color a drawing. Whatever you create, though, doesn't become a permanent entity on your computer's hard drive until you *save* it.

Most people learn the importance of saving documents the hard way. For me, it was a power failure that wiped out an entire morning's writing. Believe me, that kind of thing can make you old before your time. Why is saving necessary? Well, when you work with a new document (or with an existing document), you're actually making all your changes in the volatile confines of your computer's memory. When you shut off your computer (or if—groan!—a power failure forces it off), everything in memory is wiped out. If you haven't saved your document to your hard disk (which maintains its contents even when your computer is turned off), you lose all the changes you've made. Total bummer.

Fortunately, Windows 95 makes it easy to save your work. To save the document you're working on, pull down the application's **File** menu and select the **Save** command. If you've saved the document before, the program will take a second or two to make a copy of the document on your hard drive, and then you can continue working. Easy as shooting fish in a barrel.

 In WordPad and many other Windows programs, you can click on this toolbar button to save a document.

If you're saving a new document for the first time, though, you'll see the Save As dialog box, which is shown in the following figure. This dialog box wants to know two things:

**A Save Time-Saver** In most Windows 95 programs, you can select the Save command by simply pressing **Ctrl+S**.

➤ Where you want the document saved on your hard disk.

➤ What name you want to give to the file.

Current folder or disk drive

*Use the Save As dialog box to save your new documents.*

Contents of the current folder or disk drive

# Picking Out a Storage Location for the Document

The first thing you need to do is select a storage location for the document. From Windows 95's perspective, the storage location for a document has two components:

**A disk drive**   This is most likely your hard drive, but you're free to choose one of your floppy disks. (If you intend to select a floppy disk drive, you can avoid an error message by taking a second now to insert a floppy disk in the drive.)

**A *folder* on the disk drive**   A folder is a storage compartment on a hard drive or (more rarely) a floppy disk. They're called folders because you're supposed to think of your hard drive as a filing cabinet. In most filing cabinets, the contents are organized into separate folders; a hard drive's contents are also organized into folders. As you'll see, saving your documents in a particular folder makes it easy to find them later on.

(If all this folder foofaraw isn't clear in your mind right now, don't be too concerned. We'll be taking a closer look at folders in Chapter 11.)

**From Directories to Folders**   If you've graduated to Windows 95 from Windows 3.1, you should know that the *directories* you used in the old program are the same as the *folders* you'll be using from now on.

In the Save As dialog box, the Save in drop-down list displays the name of the current folder or disk drive. (If you're using WordPad, the current folder is usually Desktop, but it might also be Windows.) The large box below it shows the contents of the current folder or disk drive. In general, your task is to use the Save in list to select the disk drive and folder you want to use. Let's go through a specific example for WordPad.

I have a folder on my hard disk called My Documents that I use to store the documents I create. (You'll also have this folder if you've installed Office 95, the suite of applications from Microsoft. If you don't have this folder, I'll show you how to create one in Chapter 13, in the section called "Adding On: Creating Folders.") So I'll use the Save As dialog box to save my document in the My Documents folder. For starters, here's how I get to the My Documents folder:

1. Drop down the **Save in** list. (If you're not up on your drop-down list lore, head back to Chapter 7 to find out all you need to know.) The list that appears shows the disk drives on your computer, as you can see in the following figure. (Note that your list is probably different from mine.)

*Drop down the Save in box to see a list of your computer's disk drives.*

2. Select the drive you want to use to store the document. (This will usually be drive C: your hard drive.) The Save As dialog box displays all the folders available on the drive you selected. As you can see in the figure below, the My Documents folder is one of them.

Here is the My ⎯ Documents Folder

*When you select a disk drive, the Save As dialog box shows all the available folders on the drive.*

3. Select the **My Documents** folder either by double-clicking on it or by pressing **Tab**, using the down arrow key to highlight **My Documents**, and then pressing **Enter**.

Happily, you won't have to go through this rigmarole every time you save a new file. Most programs "remember" the most recent folder you worked with and will select it for you automatically the next time you're in the Save As dialog box. (Unfortunately, this only applies to the current session with the program. If you exit the program and then restart it, you have to reselect the folder.)

Okay, with the folder you want now selected, you can move on to the second stage: specifying a name for the document.

# Entering a Snappy Name for Your Document

Now we come to one of the all-time great features of Windows 95: the capability to use long, descriptive file names. If you're new to computers, you should thank your lucky stars that you never had to wrestle with the procrustean restrictions that were placed on file names by previous versions of Windows and DOS. In the old days, you couldn't create names any longer than eight lousy characters. (Plus, you could tack on a dot and a three-character extension.) As you can imagine, this led to the absurdity of names like 1STQBDGT.XLS and LTR2MOM.DOC. Ugly with a capital "Ug."

With Windows 95, however, those days are gone forever. Now we can bask in the luxury of file names that can be a whopping 255 characters long! Ah, the freedom! You can include spaces, too, so it's now possible to create names that are—gasp!—comprehensible to an ordinary human being. Here are some examples:

Fiscal 1995 - First Quarter Budget Spreadsheet

Letter to Mom (the one where I plead with her to send more money)

A Document with a Really Long-Winded and Rambling Name, Just for the Heck of It!

Other than the 255-character limit, the only other restriction you face is that you can't use any of the following characters:

\ | ? : * " < >

## What Do Older Programs Think of Long File Names?

The rub with long file names is that only programs written specifically for Windows 95 can take advantage of them. DOS programs and those meant to work with Windows 3.1 will scoff at your attempts to break through the old "8.3" file name barrier (8 characters for the file name and a 3-character extension).

So what happens if you create a document with a verbose name using a Windows 95 program, and then try to open that document in an older program? Well, the document will probably open just fine, but you'll notice that the file name has been knocked down to size. You see, Windows 95 actually keeps track of *two* names for each document: the long name and a shorter DOS-compatible name. The latter is just the first six characters of the long name (sans spaces), followed by a tilde (~), followed by a number. For example, a file named Fiscal 1995 - First Quarter Budget Spreadsheet would also use the DOS alias FISCAL~1.

Once you've decided on a descriptive name for the document, move to the **File name** text box and type in the name. (Some programs include a default name in the File name text box. WordPad, for example, uses Document. Make sure you delete this name before entering your own.)

Hey, you're almost done. For your last task, just select the **Save** button, and your document is safely stored on your hard disk.

# A Fresh Beginning: Starting a New Document

As I mentioned earlier, most applications display a new document when you first open them. In addition, you can open a fresh document anytime you want. All you do is pull down the application's **File** menu and select the **New** command or press Ctrl+N.

 You can also click on this button in WordPad's toolbar to run the New command. (Lots of other Windows programs include this button on their toolbars as well.)

# Reunited: Opening an Existing Document

Instead of opening a new document, you'll often want to work with an existing document that you saved previously. This means you have to *open* the document you want by pulling down the application's **File** menu and selecting the **Open** command. The Open dialog box appears (see the figure below).

**Faster Opening**
Pressing **Ctrl+O** in most Window 95 programs also runs the Open command.

In WordPad and many other Windows 95 programs, you can click on this button in the toolbar to display the Open dialog box.

*Selecting the File Open command displays the Open dialog box.*

As you can see, the Open dialog box bears a remarkable resemblance to the Save As dialog box you were slaving away in earlier. In this case, you use the Look in drop-down list to select the disk drive and folder that contain the document you want to open. Then you highlight the document you want to open and select the **Open** button.

# Opening a Document from the Start Menu

One of Windows 95's other handy features is its ability to open a document directly from the Start menu. You may have noticed that the Start menu includes a Documents folder. This folder maintains a list of the last few documents you opened, as shown in the following figure. To open one of these documents (and, of course, launch the program you used to create the document), select the **Start** button, open the **Documents** folder, and select the document you want.

*The Start menu's Documents folder keeps track of the last few documents you opened.*

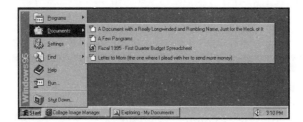

# The Strange But Useful Save As Command

Your application's File menu probably also includes a Save As command. This command is a lot like Save, except it enables you to save the document to a new name or a new location, which is useful if you need to create a new document that's very similar (but not identical) to an existing document. Instead of creating the new document from scratch, just open the existing document, make the changes, and then use the Save As command to save your changes as the new document. The old document remains as it was. When you select the Save As command, you see the same Save As dialog box that I showed you earlier.

# Closing a Document

Some weakling Windows 95 programs (such as WordPad) allow you to open only one document at a time. In such programs, you can close the document you're currently working on by starting a new document, by opening another document, or by quitting the application altogether.

However, most full-featured Windows 95 programs let you open as many documents as you want. Things can get crowded pretty fast, though, so you'll probably want to close any documents you don't need at the moment. To do this, activate the document you want to close, pull down the **File** menu, and select the **Close** command. If you made changes to the document, a dialog box appears asking if you want to save those changes. (Working with multiple documents in an application is an essential Windows 95 survival skill. Read Chapter 10 to learn the basics.)

# Using Scroll Bars to Navigate a Document

Depending on the program you're using, an opened document might appear in its own window, or it might appear as part of the program's window. In either case, you'll often find that the entire document won't fit inside the window's boundaries. When this happens, you need some way to move to the parts of the document you can't see.

From the keyboard, you can use either the basic navigation keys (the arrow keys, Page Up, and Page Down) or the special key combinations (which vary from application to application).

Mouse users, as usual, have all the fun. To navigate through a document, they get to learn a cool new skill: using *scroll bars*. Scroll bars are a lot like elevators. As you can see below, they sort of look like elevator shafts, and (like your favorite Otis device) they serve a dual purpose: they can tell you where you are and they can take you someplace else.

*The WordPad scroll bar.*

Up scroll arrow
Scroll box
Down scroll arrow
Scroll bar

**Keyboard Navigation Tips**

I've found a few key combinations that seem to work in many applications. For example, the Home key often takes you to the beginning of the current line, and the End key often takes you to the end of the line. Also, try Ctrl+Home to get to the beginning of the document and Ctrl+End to get to the end.

## Where Am I? The Scroll Bar Knows

Thanks to my innately lousy sense of direction (I've been known to get lost getting out of bed in the morning), I'm constantly looking at maps and street signs to make sure I'm where I'm supposed to be. This directional defect also carries over, unfortunately, into computers. Give me a file that has more than a couple of screens of information, and I'm toast. Fortunately, I have scroll bars to bail me out. The idea is simple: the position of the scroll box tells me my relative position in the document. For example, if the vertical scroll box is about halfway down, I know I'm somewhere near the middle of the document. So the scroll box is sort of like the floor indicator on an elevator.

## Can I Get There from Here? Navigating with Scroll Bars

The real scroll bar fun begins when you use them to move around in your documents. There are three basic techniques:

**Horizontal Scroll Bars**
You'll find these at the bottom of windows. Horizontal scroll bars work the same as vertical bars, except they let you move left and right in wide documents.

➤ To scroll up or down through the document one line at a time, click on the scroll bar's Up or Down scroll arrows.

➤ To leap through the document one screen at a time, click inside the scroll bar between the scroll box and the scroll arrows. For example, to move down one screenful, click inside the scroll bar between the scroll box and the Down scroll arrow.

➤ To move to a specific part of the document, drag the scroll box up or down.

## A Few Basic Document Editing Chores

You now know how to open a document, how to save it, and how to get around in it. What's missing? Oh yeah, you've got to do some work eventually! Of course, most of what you do in a document depends entirely on the application you're using, but let's look at a few basic skills that you can use in almost any program.

# Highlighting Text

Most documents have some sort of text in them that you can format (for example, add bold or underline to) or cut and paste. Before you can do any of these things, though, you need to *highlight* the text you want to work with.

To highlight text with a mouse, simply drag the mouse over the characters you want. *Dragging*, as you may recall, means to hold down the left mouse button and then move the mouse. In this case, you first position the mouse pointer ever so slightly to the left of the first character you want to highlight. Then you press and hold down the left mouse button and move the mouse to the right. As you do, the characters you're passing over become highlighted (instead of appearing black on a white background, they appear white on a black background; see the following figure). You can also move the mouse down to highlight entire lines. When you release the mouse button, your text remains highlighted.

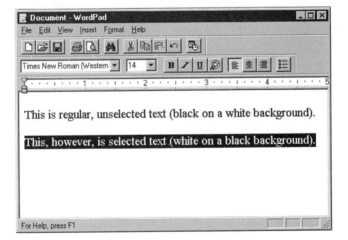

*Some selected text.*

To highlight with the keyboard, position the cursor to the left of the first character, hold down the **Shift** key, and then press the right arrow key until the entire selection is highlighted. Use the down arrow key (or even Page Down if you've got a lot of ground to cover) if you need to highlight multiple lines.

If you botch the highlight (it does take some practice) or if you decide not to work with the highlighted text, you can remove the highlight by clicking elsewhere in the document or by pressing one of the arrow keys.

**Accidentally Deleting Highlighted Text Is Really Easy**

If you highlight some text and then press a letter on your keyboard, you'll be dismayed to see your entire selection disappear and be replaced by the character whose key you pressed. (This also happens if you press a number or even the Enter key.) This is, unfortunately, normal behavior that can cause problems for even experienced document jockeys. To fix the problem, use the application's Undo command immediately (see "To Err Is Human, to Undo Divine," later in this chapter).

## Copying a Selection

One of the secrets of computer productivity is a simple maxim: Don't reinvent the wheel. In other words, if you've got something that works (it could be a picture, a section of text, whatever) and you need something similar, don't start from scratch. Instead, make a copy of the original, and then make any necessary changes to the copy.

Happily, most Windows 95 applications make it easy to copy. In fact, once you've highlighted what you want to copy, you simply pull down the application's **Edit** menu and select the **Copy** command. You then position the cursor where you want to place the copy (it could even be in another document or another application) and select the **Edit** menu's **Paste** command. A perfect copy of your selection appears instantly.

 This is the Copy toolbar button used in billions of Windows programs.

 This is the Paste toolbar button used in many Windows programs.

## Moving a Selection

If you need to move something from one part of a document to another (or from one document or application to another), you *could* do it by making a copy, pasting it, and then going back to delete the original. However, if you do this your colleagues will certainly make fun of you because there's an easier way. Once you've selected what you want to move, pull down the **Edit** menu and select the **Cut** command. Your selection disappears from the screen, but don't panic; Windows 95 is saving it for you. Position the cursor where you want to place the selection, open the **Edit** menu, and choose **Paste**. Your stuff miraculously reappears in the new location.

 This is the Cut toolbar button used in umpteen Windows programs.

## Deleting a Selection

Even the best typists make occasional typos, so knowing how to delete is a crucial editing skill. Put away the White-Out, though, because deleting a character or two is easier (and less messy) if you use either of the following techniques:

➤ Position the cursor to the right of the offending character and press the **Backspace** key.

➤ Position the cursor to the left of the character and press the **Delete** key.

If you have a large chunk of material you want to expunge from the document, you need to highlight it and press the **Delete** key. (Many applications also have Edit menu commands you can use to perform deletions; look for a command such as Delete or Clear.)

### Cutting versus Deleting

Okay, let's see if we've got this straight. If you cut something, Windows 95 removes it from the document; if you delete something, Windows 95 also removes it from the document. So what's the diff? Good question.

When you cut a selection, Windows 95 actually saves it in a special section of your computer's memory called the Clipboard. That's why it's easy to go to a different part of the document and issue a Paste command to move the text to the new location.

When you delete a selection, however, the text is gone for good (although, as you'll see in the next section, it's often possible to retrieve accidentally deleted text).

## To Err Is Human, to Undo Divine

At some point in your computing career, usually when you least expect it, you'll have the "uh-oh" experience. This occurs anytime you do something that you shouldn't have, such as consigning a vital piece of an irreplaceable document to deletion purgatory. Just so you're prepared, here are the symptoms: your life inevitably flashes before your eyes (and you remember where you lost that roller skate key in Grade 3), you start hallucinating (mostly distorted images of your boss saying "You're fired!"), and your stomach does backflips that would be the envy of any gymnast.

Fortunately, many Windows 95 applications now come with an Undo feature to get you out of these jams. The Undo command restores everything to the way it was before you made your blunder. (I've had some relationships where an Undo command would have come in *very* handy!)

To use the Undo feature, pull down the application's **Edit** menu and select the **Undo** command. (Depending on the action you're trying to reverse, the command may actually say something like "Undo Paste.")

 This is the Undo toolbar button in many Windows programs.

**Oodles of Editing Shortcuts** Almost all Windows 95 programs support the following keyboard shortcuts:

| | |
|---|---|
| Copy | Ctrl+C |
| Cut | Ctrl+X |
| Paste | Ctrl+V |
| Undo | Ctrl+Z |

In most applications, the Undo command works only on the most recent change you made. If you do anything at all after you make the mistake (such as type some text), you won't be able to reverse your mistake. For this reason, always select the Undo command immediately after your blunder. Having said all that, however, there are several applications (such as Microsoft Word for Windows and Excel) that offer a "multiple level" Undo. Check your application's documentation to find out if it's available and learn how to use it.

## The Least You Need to Know

Now that was a chapter! You learned all kinds of practical stuff from opening and saving documents to basic cut-and-paste techniques. Whew! The only routine chore we didn't cover was printing, and we'll tackle that in the next chapter.

# Chapter 9

# Windows 95 Printing Particulars

**In This Chapter**

➤ Basic printing steps

➤ Installing a printer in Windows 95

➤ Controlling your print jobs

➤ A peck of pickled printing points

I've suffered with various computers over the years, but one thing has remained constant: when I'm finished working, I need some physical, tangible proof that I really did *do* something, and that this stuff isn't just all smoke and mirrors. In other words, I've gotta see some hard copy. Fortunately, Windows 95 makes printing a relatively painless procedure. You set up your printer once, and all your Windows applications fall in line and use that same setup. In this chapter, I'll show you the basic printing procedure, and I'll cover how to install other printers and control your print jobs.

## Printing: The Basic Steps

The printing process provides a good example of the consistent Windows 95 interface I babbled on about back in Chapter 2. Although there are some small differences between applications, the basic steps are the same.

Before printing, make sure your printer is powered up, has plenty of paper, and is online. (*Online* means that your printer is ready, willing, and able to handle the blizzard of characters your program will be throwing at it. Most printers have some kind of Online button that you can press, just to make sure.) When your printer is ready for duty, return to your application, pull down the **File** menu, and select the **Print** command (or press **Ctrl+P**, which is the standard keyboard shortcut for displaying the Print dialog box in Windows programs.) You'll see a Print dialog box similar to the one shown below for the WordPad word processor.

 In most Windows programs (including WordPad), you can click on this toolbar button to bypass the Print dialog box and print the document directly.

*WordPad's Print dialog box.*

The options in the Print dialog box vary slightly from application to application. However, you'll almost always see three things:

➤ A drop-down list for selecting the printer to use. In WordPad's Print dialog box, for example, use the Name drop-down list to select the printer.

➤ A text box or spinner to enter the number of copies you want. In the WordPad Print dialog box, use the Number of copies spinner.

➤ Some controls for selecting how much of the file to print. You'll normally have the option of printing the entire document or a specific range of pages. (WordPad's Print dialog box also includes a Selection option button that you can activate to print only the text that's currently highlighted.)

When you've chosen your options, select the **OK** button to start printing (some Print dialog boxes have a Print button, instead). Keep your eyes peeled on the information area of the taskbar (the area to the left of the time). After a few seconds (depending on the size of the document), a printer icon appears, as shown in the following figure. This tells you Windows 95 is hard at work farming out the document to your printer.

The printer icon

*The printer icon tells you Windows 95 is printing.*

# Telling Windows 95 About Your Printer

In the nasty old DOS world, every program deals with the printer in its own special way. This sounds innocent enough, but it really means you have to perform some kind of printer setup for every program you use. Can you say "annoying"? Windows changes all that because its if-you-want-something-done-right-then-do-it-yourself approach to printing means that Windows itself handles all the printing chores. When you print from any Windows application, all the program does is pass everything over to Windows and say, "OK, you think you're so smart, *you* print the darn thing!"

This has two major advantages. First, it means that, as you saw earlier, the steps required to print something in Windows 95 are more or less the same for all programs. Second, it means that the only program that needs to know about your printer is Windows 95 itself. Your Windows applications couldn't care less; they're just along for the ride. So the upshot is that you only have to install your printer once—for Windows 95—and not for every program on your computer. Can you say "convenient"?

Printer installation is normally taken care of during the Windows 95 setup procedure. If you skipped that step or if you got a new printer for Christmas, you need to install your printer in Windows 95. This involves telling Windows 95 what kind of printer you have so it can copy the appropriate *printer driver* to your hard disk. (A printer driver isn't a chauffeur for your printer. Instead, it's a small program that translates the documents you print into some kind of gibberish the printer can understand.) Here are the steps to follow:

1. Select the **Start** button to open the Start menu, select **Settings**, and then select **Printers**. Windows 95 opens the Printers folder and displays it in the window shown in the following figure. (If you haven't installed a printer yet, your Printers folder will contain only the Add Printer icon.)

*The Printers folder shows the currently installed printers.*

2. Double-click on the **Add Printer** icon, or use the arrow keys to highlight it and then press **Enter**. Windows 95 calls up the Add Printer Wizard for duty.

3. The first dialog box just has a boring introductory message, so go ahead and select **Next >**. The Add Printer Wizard displays the dialog box shown in the following figure. (If, instead, the Wizard displays a dialog box asking you whether you want to install a "Local printer" or a "Network printer," select the **Local printer** option and select **Next >**. I'll talk about setting up a network printer in Chapter 22, in the section titled "Installing a Network Printer.")

*Use this Wizard dialog box to select the printer you have.*

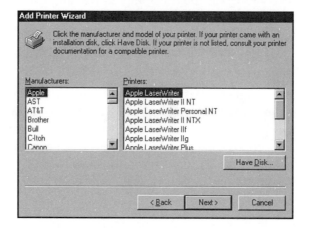

4. This dialog box lists dozens of printers that Windows 95 recognizes. In the **Manufacturers** list, select the manufacturer of your printer, and in the **Printers** list, select your printer model.

5. Select **Next >**.

6. If the printer driver file is already on your hard disk, the Wizard gives you the two choices described below. Make your choice and select **Next >**.

>    **Keep existing driver (recommended)**   This option is activated by default, which is fine because it's the one you'll choose 99% of the time.

>    **Replace existing driver**   If you're having trouble printing, one of the solutions you can try is reinstalling your printer in Windows 95 (as explained in Chapter 29 in the "Persnickety Printing Perplexities" section). In this case, you'll need to select the **Replace existing driver** option. If you're not having trouble printing, however, don't select this option because it may affect how your existing programs print.

7. The next Add Printer Wizard dialog box (shown in the following figure) asks you to specify which *port* to use with the printer (see the sidebar below for a short port report). Highlight the port to which your printer is attached and select **Next >**.

*This Wizard dialog box wants to know where your printer is attached.*

**The Printer Port Puzzle**

A *port* is the connection where you plug in the cable for a mouse, printer, or some other computer-related toy. If you're not sure which port is the correct one, check the printer cable connection at the back of your computer. Some thoughtful computer companies actually label their ports, so look for something like LPT1 (which is the port used by the vast majority of printers) or COM2. If there are no labels, your computer manual should tell you (provided, that is, you can make heads or tails out of all that geek-speak). If you're still not sure, just choose LPT1 and cross your fingers.

8. The next dialog box, shown in the following figure, prompts you to enter a name for the printer (you can either leave the suggested name as is, or you can enter a creative 32-characters-or-less name of your own), and it asks if you want the printer to be the *default* for Windows programs. (The default printer is the one that Windows programs use automatically when you run the Print command.) If this is the printer you'll be using all the time, select **Yes** and then select **Next >**.

9. Next, the Add Printer Wizard wonders whether or not you want to print a test page. It can't hurt, so make sure the **Yes** option is activated and then select **Finish**.

10. Unless the Windows 95 CD-ROM is still in your CD-ROM drive, Windows 95 will beep and ask you to insert one of your Windows 95 disks. Insert the appropriate disk (or the CD-ROM, if you have one) and select **OK**. Windows 95 copies the files it needs and then cranks out the test page.

*Use the Printer name text box to enter a clever name for your printer.*

11. Another dialog box appears asking you if the test page printed correctly. If it did (it may take a minute or so for the page to appear), select **Yes** to return to the Printers folder and see the icon for your new printer. If it didn't, select **No** to invoke the Help system's Print Troubleshooter. (I'll take you through Windows 95's Help Troubleshooters in Chapter 28's "Some Safe Mode Diagnostics" section.)

What do you do if your printer isn't on the Wizard's list of printers (the one you saw back in step 4)? You have three choices:

➤ Check your printer manual to see if the printer works like (or *emulates*) another printer. If it does, see if you can find the emulated printer in the list. For example, many dot-matrix printer models emulate printers from Epson and IBM. Similarly, many laser printer models emulate the Hewlett-Packard LaserJet printer.

➤ If your printer is a dot-matrix, select **Generic** for the manufacturer and **Generic/Text Only** for the printer. For a laser printer, select **HP** for the manufacturer and try the **HP LaserJet** printer.

➤ If your printer came with a disk, select the **Have Disk** command button (it's below the Printers list) and follow the Wizard's instructions.

## Changing the Default Printer

As you saw in step 8 in the previous section, you can designate a printer as the default for all Windows programs. If you install a single printer driver, that printer will, of course, be the default. If you install multiple printers (drivers), however, you may need to change which of them is the Windows default.

To do this, open the Printers folder (as described in the previous section) and try either of the following:

➤ Highlight the printer you want to be the default, pull down the **File** menu, and activate the **Set As Default** command.

➤ Right-click on the would-be default printer and then activate the **Set As Default** command from the shortcut menu.

## Selecting a Different Printer in an Application

When you print in a Windows application, the program always assumes you want to use the default printer as described above. If you want to print to a different printer, the Print dialog box should have a drop-down list that lets you choose which printer to use. (In WordPad's Print dialog box, for example, use the Name list.)

In some older programs, however, you'll need to either select the **File** menu's **Print Setup** command or select the **Printer Setup** button in the Print dialog box. In either case, a Print Setup dialog box appears, listing the installed printers. Select the one you want to use, and then select **OK**.

# Taking Control of Your Printing

When you tell a program to print a document, the program notifies Windows 95 that a print job is pending. To get you back to your application faster, Windows performs a nifty bit of trickery. It borrows the file, makes a copy of it, and then hands control back to the application. While you continue working, Windows 95 prints the copy of the file in the background (that's why you see the printer icon in the taskbar whenever you print).

Therefore, once you've sent a job to the printer, you normally don't have to bother with it again. Windows 95 just goes about its business behind the scenes—and it's usually best to leave it that way. However, there may be times when you want to cancel a print job or change the order in which the documents will print, and you need to stick your finger in the printing pie to do that.

## Opening the Printing Printer

If a print job you want to mess with is in progress, open the **Printers** folder and double-click on the printer you're using (or highlight the printer using the arrow keys and then press **Enter**). Windows 95 lists the print jobs in the order they were sent to the printer and shows the following info:

**Document Name**   The name of the document (duh).

**Status**   The current status of the print job. (*Spooling* means that Windows 95 is making the copy of the document that it will send to the printer.)

**Owner**  The username of the person who sent the document to the printer. The username matters only if you've set up Windows 95 for multiple users or on a network. (I'll tell you how to set up Windows 95 for multiple users in Chapter 22.)

**Progress**  How many pages have been printed and the total number of pages in the print job.

**Started At**  The time and date the document was sent to the printer.

## A Pause for the Cause: Pausing Printing

If you need to add paper to your printer or change the toner cartridge, you can tell Windows 95 to hold its printing horses. Open the printer window as described in the previous section, pull down the **Printer** menu, and then activate the **Pause Printing** command. This prevents Windows 95 from sending any more data to the printer. When you're ready to roll again, pull down the **Printer** menu and deactivate the **Pause Printing** command.

If you just want to pause a particular document, click on it (or use the up and down arrow keys to highlight it) and activate the **Document** menu's **Pause Printing** command. To resume printing, highlight the document and deactivate the **Document** menu's **Pause Printing** command.

## Bailing Out of Print Jobs

If you accidentally print the wrong document, or if you simply change your mind about printing it, deleting a file from the queue is no problem. To do so, open the printer window, highlight the appropriate file, open the **Document** menu, and select the **Cancel Printing** command.

If the whole printing process is a complete fiasco, you can cancel every print job by selecting the **Printer** menu's **Purge Print Jobs** command.

## The Least You Need to Know

This chapter gave you the lowdown on printing in Windows 95 and showed you how Windows' consistent interface makes printing a breeze. Speaking of breezes, is there a window open around here? In Windows 95, there is almost always a window open somewhere, so the next chapter tells you how to gain the upper hand on Windows' ubiquitous windows.

# Chapter 10

# The "Windows" in Windows 95

## In This Chapter

➤ Activating windows

➤ Moving and sizing windows

➤ Maximizing and minimizing windows

➤ Lots of fascinating windows lore

In ancient times, long before glass was in common use (and long before summertime air conditioning became *de rigueur*), people built their homes with holes in the walls to let in air and light. (Flintstones fans will know exactly what I mean.) Because these holes allowed the people to see out and allowed air in, they were called "wind eyes." Over time, people began covering these holes with glass and cheesy chintz curtains and the phrase "wind eyes" turned into the modern word "windows."

I tell you this seemingly pointless story by way of introduction to the subject of this chapter: the windows in Windows 95. In a sense, the old meaning of the word "window" fits quite nicely here. In Windows 95, you can "see through" a window to look at what's on your computer. But these windows also "let in" your input in the form of keystrokes and mouse clicks. It might help to keep all this in mind as you work with Windows 95's windows. Just remember that each window on the screen is a view of something on your computer and that you can "reach through" the window to make changes to what you see.

# The Parts Department: Anatomy of a Window

Before we pull out our digital machetes and start cutting our way through the thicket of Windows 95's windows, let's take a moment to get our bearings. In particular, there's a bit of unavoidable window lingo we need to get down, so we'll start with a quick lesson on window anatomy.

For openers, let's get a window specimen on-screen so we can do some poking around. We've used WordPad a few times already, so let's try something different this time: the Paint accessory. To prod Paint into action, select the **Start** button, open the **Programs** folder, open the **Accessories** folder, and select **Paint**. You'll soon see the Paint window on your desktop, as shown in the following figure. (Our look at Paint in this chapter will be superficial at best. To get the scoop on all the real Paint procedures, strike out for Chapter 15.)

*The Paint window and some of its nuts and bolts.*

Here's a quick rundown of the various window features in Paint (and just about every other Windows 95 program you're likely to trip over in your travels):

**Title bar**  This is the blue strip across the top of the window. The title bar usually shows two things: the name of the current document ("untitled" in the Paint window shown above) and the name of the program, separated by a dash. As you'll see later (in the section "Windows on the Move"), you can use the title bar to move a window with your mouse.

**Minimize button**   Of the trio of buttons in the top-right corner, the one on the left is the Minimize button. This button clears the window from the desktop without closing the program (as explained later on in the section "The Minimalist Approach: Reducing a Window to the Taskbar").

**Maximize button**   This is the center button of the three buttons in the top-right corner. This button enlarges the window so it takes up the entire desktop. (I talk more about this in the section "Taking It to the Max: Maximizing a Window.")

**Close button**   Of the three buttons in the top-right corner, the button on the right is the Close button. As I explained back in Chapter 5, this button shuts down the program.

**Border**   Most windows are surrounded by a thin border that you can use to change the size of a window with your mouse. This technique is explained in full in the section titled "Sizing Up Your Windows."

**Control menu**   The Control menu sports several commands that enable keyboard users to perform routine window maintenance. For a program window, press **Alt+Spacebar** to display the Control menu; for a document window, press **Alt+ –**.

### New Window Buttons in Windows 95

Veterans of the Windows 3.1 wars will note that Windows 95 has made some changes to the window buttons. Specifically, the Minimize and Maximize buttons look different, and the Close button is new. Personally, I'm not sure I like having the Close button right beside the Maximize button because, mouse-maladroit that I am, I often end up closing windows I wanted to maximize. Ah well, that's life in the big Windows 95 city, I guess.

# So Many Windows, So Little Space

Isn't there an old saying that talks about a person's greatest strength also being his greatest weakness? It's possible I just made it up, but in any case, it certainly applies to Windows 95. Why? Well, one of Windows 95's greatest strengths is that it enables you to work on multiple projects at the same time. This means you can have Paint running in one window, your word processor in another, a game of FreeCell in a third, and so on. And as if that isn't enough, Windows 95 also enables you to open multiple windows in a single application! So in your word processor, for example, you could have a window open for your letter to Mom, one for your shopping list, and one for your memo to the execs on the coast.

The problem with having all these open windows is that things can get real confusing, real fast. If you don't believe me, take a look at the screen in the following figure.

*Multitasking multitu-dinousness: opening just a few programs can quickly turn your screen into a true dog's breakfast.*

What a mess! And there are only a half dozen programs running in this picture. If your computer has enough memory, you could conceivably crack open a dozen programs or more. (Although *why* you'd want to do that I can't imagine.) What you need here are some simple techniques for managing windows before they get out of hand. Fortunately, Windows 95 offers a number of methods for regaining control of your screen. Throughout the rest of this chapter, I'll bring you up to speed on the easiest and fastest of these methods.

# Your Home Base: The Active Window

Anytime you find yourself with a bunch of windows on your screen, you can simplify your life immeasurably if you keep the following idea in mind: *You can work in only one window at a time*. In other words, no matter how many windows you may have open, the window you're currently slaving away in (it's called the *active window*, by the way) gives you its complete and undivided attention. You can, therefore, safely ignore everything else going on around it (or at least try to).

# Which Window Is Active?

With this in mind, the first stop on our window management tour will be to learn how to make a window active. How will you know when you've succeeded in making a window active? There are a few clues to watch for, and they're all illustrated in the next figure.

➤ The most obvious clue is the window's title bar. If the window is active, its title bar displays the title in white letters on a blue background. If it's an inactive window, the title appears in light gray letters on a dark gray background.

➤ The active program's taskbar button appears "pressed."

➤ An insertion point cursor or some other marker appears to tell you where you are in the program's document.

The title bar of an inactive window shows light gray text on a dark gray background.

The title bar of an active window shows white text on a blue background.

*How to tell the difference between an active and inactive window.*

The active window displays (in this case) an insertion point cursor.

The active window's taskbar button appears pressed.

## Activating a Window

I explained how to switch between windows in Chapter 5. However, a quick recap here won't hurt. To switch to a running application, use one of the following methods:

➤ Click on the program's taskbar button.

➤ Click anywhere inside the program's window, if you can see it.

➤ Hold down **Alt** and tap the **Tab** key repeatedly to cycle through the names of your running programs. When you see the name of the program you want, release Alt.

➤ Hold down **Alt** and poke the **Esc** key repeatedly to cycle through the windows of the open programs. When you get to the window of the program you're looking for, release Alt.

Activating a window is important, but it's only the first step towards gaining full control over how your windows appear on the screen. The rest of this chapter shows you a number of basic Windows 95 window-control techniques.

# Windows on the Move

One of the problems with having several windows open at once is that they have a nasty habit of overlapping each other. And what's covered up in a window is usually the information you want to see. (Chalk up another one for Murphy's Law, I guess.) Instead of cursing Windows 95's ancestry, you can try moving your windows around so they don't overlap (or so they overlap less).

If you use a mouse, you can move a window quite easily. First, using any of the techniques you learned earlier in this chapter, activate the window you want to move. Then point the mouse at the window's title bar and drag the window to its new location. (Recall that you drag something by pointing at it, holding down the left mouse button, and then moving the mouse.) As you drag, the window itself doesn't move. Instead, Windows 95 displays a dotted outline of the window border that moves with the mouse pointer, as you can see in the figure below. When the border appears to be in the position you want, release the mouse button. Windows 95 redisplays the entire window in the new position.

If you use a keyboard, follow these steps to move a window:

1. Activate the window you want to move.

2. Pull down the window's Control menu by pressing **Alt+Spacebar**.

3. Select the **Move** command. A dotted gray outline appears around the window border.

4. Use the arrow keys to move the window outline.

5. When the outline is in the location you want, press **Enter**, and Windows 95 redisplays the window in the new location. If you decide you don't want to move the window after all, you can press the **Esc** key at any time.

*When you drag the title bar, a dotted outline indicates the new position of the window border.*

A dotted outline of a window on the move.

## Sizing Up Your Windows

Another way to reduce window clutter is to change the size of the open windows. For example, you can reduce the size of less important windows and increase the size of windows in which you do the most work.

The secret to sizing is the window border. The idea is that you drag a section of the border (the top, bottom, left, or right side) with your mouse to create the new dimensions. Here are the explicit mouse steps:

1. Activate the window you want to size.

2. Point the mouse at the window border you want to adjust. For example, if you want to expand the window to the right, point the mouse at the right border. When the pointer is positioned correctly, it changes into a two-headed arrow.

3. Drag the border to the position you want. As you drag the mouse, Windows 95 shows a dotted outline of the new border position (see below).

*As you drag a window border, the new border appears as a dotted outline.*

Mouse pointer for sizing a window

4. Release the mouse button, and Windows 95 resizes the window.

5. Repeat steps 2–4 for any other borders you want to size.

**Two Sides at Once** If you want to size two borders at the same time, position the mouse pointer on the corner of a window border. When you drag the mouse, Windows 95 sizes the two sides that create the corner.

Diehard keyboardists need to follow these steps to resize a window:

1. Activate the window you want to size.

2. Pull down the window's Control menu by pressing **Alt+Spacebar**.

3. Select the **Size** command. A gray outline appears around the window border.

4. To select a border to size, press the corresponding arrow key. For example, to size the right border, press the right arrow key. The mouse pointer changes to a two-headed arrow.

5. Use the arrow keys to size the window outline.

6. When the outline is the size you want, press **Enter**. Windows 95 redisplays the window in the new size. If you decide you don't want the window resized, press **Esc** before you hit the Enter key.

108

# The Minimalist Approach: Reducing a Window to the Taskbar

You'll often find that you have some windows you know you won't need for a while. You could close them, move them out of the way, or make them smaller, but all that takes time, and our goal is always to make things as easy as possible. Fortunately, there's an alternative: you can remove a window from the desktop *without* closing it. This bit of window sorcery is called *minimizing* the window.

 If you use a mouse, you can minimize a window in no time at all by clicking on the window's **Minimize** button.

Minimizing a window takes a bit more effort if you're using the keyboard, however. In this case, you need to pull down the window's Control menu (by pressing **Alt+Spacebar**) and select the **Minimize** command.

In either case, the window disappears from the desktop, but its taskbar button remains in view. You can open the window again at any time by clicking on its taskbar button.

# Taking It to the Max: Maximizing a Window

To get the largest possible work area, you can *maximize* a window. This means that the window expands so it fills the entire desktop area (the taskbar, however, remains conveniently visible).

 To maximize a window with your mouse, all you have to do is click on the window's **Maximize** button.

To maximize a window keyboard-style, pull down the window's Control menu (by pressing **Alt+Spacebar**) and select the **Maximize** command.

# Back to Normal: Restoring a Window

When you maximize or minimize a window, Windows 95 is smart enough to remember the window's previous size and position. This makes it possible for you to easily restore the window to its former state.

With a mouse, you restore a window using one of these methods:

**If you minimized the window,** you can restore it by clicking on its taskbar button.

 **If you maximized the window,** Windows 95 changes the Maximize button to the Restore button. Simply click on the **Restore** button to return the window to its previous state.

From the keyboard, you need to do the following:

> **For a minimized window,** use either the **Alt+Tab** or the **Alt+Esc** key combination to select the window.

> **For a maximized window,** pull down its Control menu and select the **Restore** command.

# Letting Windows Do the Work: Cascading and Tiling

All this moving and sizing stuff is fine for people with time to kill, but the rest of us just want to get the job done and move on. To that end, Windows 95 has "cascade" and "tile" features that will automatically arrange your windows for you. (Sorry, keyboardists: these features are only available to mouse users.)

To cascade your windows, right-click on an empty section of the taskbar and select the **Cascade** command from the shortcut menu. This tells Windows 95 to arrange your open windows in a cool waterfall pattern, as shown in the following figure. This is good for those times when you want things nice and neat, but you don't need to see what's in the other windows.

*What the Cascade command does.*

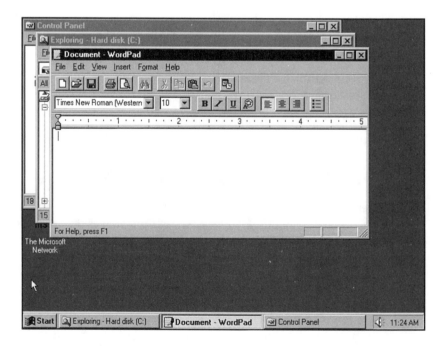

Tiling divides up your screen and gives equal real estate to each window. To try it out, right-click on an empty part of the taskbar and select either **Tile Horizontally** (to arrange the windows in strips across the screen, as shown in the following figure) or **Tile Vertically** (to arrange the windows in vertical strips). Either pattern enables you to work in one window and still keep an eye on what's happening in the other windows (you never know what those pesky devils might be up to!).

*The Tile Horizontally command gives each of your open windows an equal amount of screen space.*

If you'd prefer to clear off your desktop completely, you can minimize all of your running programs in one fell swoop by right-clicking on an empty part of the taskbar and selecting **Minimize All Windows** from the shortcut menu.

## Some Notes About Document Windows

So far in this chapter, we've concerned ourselves only with program windows. But lots of Windows 95 applications let you open multiple document windows, and this can also cause window clutter and navigation headaches. For example, the following figure shows how messy Microsoft Word can become with multiple documents on the go.

*Opening multiple documents in a single application can quickly get out of hand.*

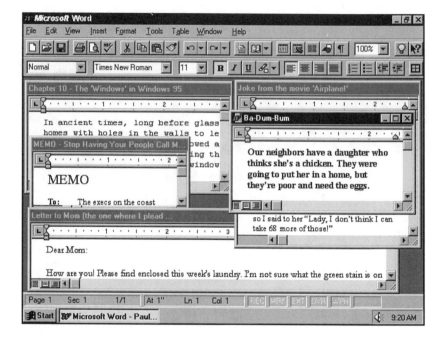

The good news is that most of the techniques you learned earlier for program windows apply equally well to document windows. In particular, you can move them, size them, minimize them, and maximize them. (Note that keyboard users access a document window's Control menu by pressing **Alt+–**.)

Virtually any Windows 95 application that lets you open multiple windows will have a Window pull-down menu. If you pull down the Window menu, you'll see a list of the open document windows at the bottom. To activate a window, simply select it from this menu. (You can also just click on the window if you can see it.) The Window menu will also probably have a few commands for arranging the document windows. Look for commands named Arrange, Cascade, or Tile, and try them out.

# The Least You Need to Know

This chapter gave you the lowdown on the windows that give Windows 95 its name. The emphasis was on gaining control over how your windows appear on your screen so you can reduce clutter and get more work done.

That ends our look at the various workaday Windows techniques. You now have all the know-how you need to successfully negotiate any Windows program, big or small. From here, most of our time together will be spent examining specific features of Windows 95.

# Part 3
# Navigating Your Computer with Windows 95

*Just because Windows 95 has us all singing rousing choruses of "Ding, Dong, DOS is Dead," doesn't mean we can get by without having to deal with some DOS-like maintenance chores. We still have to copy files, create folders, and format floppy disks. Fortunately, as you'll see here in Part 3, Windows 95 makes most of these routine tasks a walk in the park.*

NOW IF YOU WILL ALL JUST STEP TO THE RIGHT WE'LL BEGIN OUR TOUR. SIR, DON'T TOUCH THE HARD DRIVE.

# Chapter 11

# A Tour of Your Computer

## In This Chapter

➤ Files, folders, and disks explained (in English!)

➤ Getting to know the My Computer window

➤ Navigating your computer

➤ Checking out Windows Explorer

➤ A marvelous metaphor designed to knock some sense into all this file and folder fiddle-faddle

Most people who are new to Windows 95—and especially those who are new to computers in general—would rather have a root canal than deal with files and floppy disks and such. Let's face it, that kind of stuff can be just plain intimidating: all those strange, cryptic names and the confusing terminology. Shudder.

The good news, though, is that, thanks to Windows 95 and its My Computer and Explorer tools, these kinds of things don't have to be intimidating at all. Windows 95 tames the file and floppy disk beasts and makes otherwise-unpalatable chores (such as copying files) about as painless as they can get (or, at least, a step up from root canal). This chapter introduces you to both My Computer and Windows Explorer, gives you some plain English explanations of files, folders, and disks, and then shows you around.

# What Is the My Computer Window?

For the most part, Windows 95 does a pretty good job of shielding us from the harsh realities of the computer world. We have the Start menu to start our programs, we have pull-down menus, shortcut menus, and toolbars to access commands, and we have dialog boxes to talk to Windows 95. All very civilized, if you ask me.

With the My Computer window, this civil behavior is extended to normally uncivil things such as files and floppy disks. Dealing with such unpleasantries in DOS meant you had to jump through all kinds of techno-hoops just to find out what was on your hard drive, and then you had to peck out various bizarre and cryptic commands to get anything done. Just the opposite, My Computer maps out everything on your computer and presents it to you in an easy-to-digest visual format. Instead of entering unfathomable commands, you do things by simply selecting the appropriate pull-down menu commands or toolbar buttons. Easy as pie (really!).

**3.1**

### My Computer versus File Manager

If you've upgraded to Windows 95 from Windows 3.1, you may be wondering how My Computer compares with File Manager. Well, they're similar in that they both give you a visual map of what's inside your machine. There are, however, two main differences:

➤ My Computer opens up a new window every time you open a different folder or disk drive. File Manager, as you may recall, used the same window to display whichever disk drive or folder you were working in.

➤ My Computer shows you the contents of only the current drive or folder. There is no "directory tree" like you had in File Manager.

If you liked File Manager, you probably won't get along with My Computer very well. Instead, you'll probably prefer Windows Explorer, which I'll discuss later in this chapter.

Before we dive headfirst into My Computer's waters, let's take a step back and see if we can't make some sense of a few misunderstood fundamentals. Specifically, in the next few sections I'll give you some nontechnical explanations of files, folders, and disks.

# Getting a Grip on Files, Folders, and Disks

Remember the silly desktop metaphor I tried to pass off on you back in Chapter 2? Well, things are about to get even sillier as I (in true daredevil, throw-caution-to-the-wind, fashion) attempt to extend that metaphor to include your entire computer! Bear with me, here, because this exercise in metaphor-stretching should (I hope) give you a pretty good idea of what files and folders are all about, and it should make it easier for you to figure out My Computer (and the Explorer) later on.

## Your Computer: Just a Fancy Filing Cabinet

Okay, here goes (insert dramatic drumroll here): instead of thinking about just a desktop, let's expand our metaphoric view to include an entire office (or, if you home users prefer, a den). Any office worth its salt includes, of course, a filing cabinet, which is handy because that's just what I want you to think of your computer as. In particular, I want you to imagine a filing cabinet where each drawer represents a disk drive on your computer. The picture below shows what a typical computer might look like if it came back in the next life as a filing cabinet. As you can see, there are drawers for the 5$\frac{1}{4}$-inch floppy disk (drive A), the 3$\frac{1}{2}$-inch floppy disk (drive B), the hard disk (drive C), and the CD-ROM drive (drive D).

*Metaphor madness: if a computer is a filing cabinet, each disk drive is a drawer.*

## A Peek Inside the Filing Cabinet: Folders

So far so good. Now, what do you find if you open up a drawer in a typical filing cabinet? Folders, of course, lots of folders. Depending on whose filing cabinet you're dealing with (and how organized she is), you'll find folders for different customers, different projects, different employees, different strokes, different folks, well, you get the idea. The key is, though, that each folder contains only related information. If the first folder is for a customer named "H. R. Poopenscoop Dog Walking Service," everything in that folder has something to do with that company.

Disk drives, too, can have lots of folders. In this case, you can think of a folder as just a chunk of disk real estate set aside for storage. As with filing cabinet folders, computer folders usually contain only related items. In the picture shown below, the Hard Disk drawer has been opened to reveal four different folders: DOS, My Documents, Program Files, and Windows.

*Whether you open a filing cabinet drawer or a computer disk drive, you see lots of folders.*

## A Peek Inside the Folders: Files

**What Happened to Directories?** Windows 3.1 users and the old DOS diehards in the crowd may be wondering what in blue blazes happened to directories. They're still around, but Windows 95 now calls them *folders*.

What kinds of "related items" are we talking about folders containing? Well, let's head back to our old friend the filing cabinet. Most filing cabinet folders contain memos, invoices, letters, lists, contracts, artwork, and whatever else is related to the subject of the folder. The computer equivalents of these items are called *files*. A typical folder on a disk drive contains all kinds of files, which fall into three categories:

➤ Files that run your programs. They're called—surprise, surprise—*program files*.

➤ Files used by your programs once they're up and running. These are called *data files*.

➤ Files you create using these programs. These are the *documents* we talked about *ad nauseam* in the previous chapters.

But filing cabinet folders can contain other folders, as well. In my income tax folder, for example, I have a separate folder for each of my tax returns from the past few years. (It's a *very* depressing folder.) This folders-within-folders idea also extends to disk drive folders (you knew it would). For example, your hard disk includes a Windows folder that contains most of your Windows 95 files. But there are also several subfolders within the Windows folder. One of them, to give you a for instance, is called Start Menu; it includes the items you see when you open the Start menu.

So there you have it: disks, folders, and files explained in one easy-to-digest, no muss, no fuss metaphor. As you work with My Computer (and Explorer later on), try to keep these concepts in mind. They should help you out if (or perhaps I should say *when*) things become a bit overwhelming.

# Exploring the My Computer Window

Fine words butter no parsnips, as they say, (no, they really do)—so let's get the My Computer show on the road. Go ahead and double-click on the **My Computer** icon in the upper-left corner of the desktop. Windows 95 displays the My Computer window, as shown in the following figure (your window probably looks a bit different from mine).

*The My Computer window.*

What you're seeing here, essentially, are the drawers to your computer's filing cabinet! All your disk drives are shown as icons, and My Computer even throws in another couple of icons for good measure. (In the Windows 95 world, an *icon* is a picture that represents something else, such as a disk drive, a folder, or a file.) The following table shows some of the icons you're likely to see and what each of them represents.

## The My Computer Icons

| This Icon | Represents This |
|---|---|
| ![icon] | A 5¹/₄-inch floppy disk drive. |
| ![icon] | A 3¹/₂-inch floppy disk drive. |
| ![icon] | A hard disk drive. |
| ![icon] | A CD-ROM drive. |
| ![icon] | The Control Panel. (We'll be using the Control Panel to adjust the settings for your computer in lots of future chapters, but especially in Part 5.) |
| ![icon] | The Printers folder. |
| ![icon] | A garden variety folder. |

# Displaying My Computer from the Keyboard

Because the My Computer desktop icon is accessible only to mouse martins, the rodent-deprived in the audience may be thinking they're out of luck. Not so. There *is* a way to display My Computer with a keyboard, but it's not even close to being obvious.

First, display the Printers folder (!) by selecting the **Start** button, opening the **Settings** folder, and selecting **Printers**. Then, simply press the **Backspace** key and, just like that, the My Computer window appears! This may seem like deep voodoo now, but you'll see why it works later on in this chapter.

# Disk Driving: Selecting a Disk Drive

From here, checking out the contents of a particular disk drive is really easy:

➤ With your mouse, double-click on the drive icon.

➤ From the keyboard, use the arrow keys to highlight the drive icon, and then press **Enter**.

The following figure shows the window that appears when I select my hard disk (drive C). As you can see, I have six folders on my hard disk: Dos, My Documents, Office95, Program Files, Utilities, and Windows.

*The contents of my hard disk drive (drive C).*

## Folder Surfing: Looking in Folders

To see the contents of a folder, double-click on it, or use the arrow keys to highlight it and then press **Enter**. For example, try opening your Windows folder. A new window appears, similar to the one shown here.

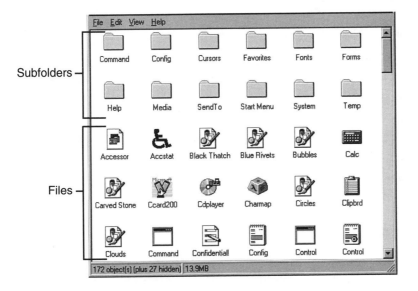

*The contents of my Windows folder.*

As you can see, the Windows folder contains even more folders (these are examples of the subfolders we talked about earlier), as well as all kinds of other interesting-looking icons. These are all *files*, and the icons indicate what type of files they represent.

Before you can work with a file (for instance, to rename it or to delete it), you need to select it. Easy money: just click on the file's icon with your mouse, or use your keyboard's arrow keys to highlight the icon.

**Cool Folder Navigation Tip**

First, some lingo: The folder/subfolder connection is often regarded as a sort of parent/child relationship because a subfolder is, in a sense, the "offspring" of the main folder. (I know, I know: the geeks who make up this stuff *really* need to get out more.) Anyway, if you open a subfolder and then decide not to stay, closing the window returns you to the parent folder. No big deal there. However, if you'd prefer to keep the subfolder window open, you can do that *and* return to the parent folder by pressing **Backspace**. (You could also just click on the parent folder's taskbar button.)

# Some Options for the My Computer Windows

To make My Computer a bit easier to manage, there are several options you can try out. The next few sections tell you all about them.

## Changing the File Display

By default, My Computer shows you just the name and icon for each folder or file. You can adjust this display to show more items or to show more detail about each item. Here are your choices:

➤ To show more folders or files in the current window, pull down the **View** menu and select either **Small Icons** (which displays the contents left to right and down the window) or **List** (which displays the contents in a vertical list).

➤ To see details such as the size of the file, the file type, and the date and time it was last modified, select the **View** menu's **Details** command.

## Sorting the Window Contents

My Computer normally shows your files in alphabetical order by name, which makes it easy to find the file you want. However, the View menu's Arrange Icons command displays a cascade menu that enables you to choose how the icons are arranged. In most cases, you have four commands at your disposal: **by Name** (the default sort order), **by Type** (to sort the files in alphabetical order by file type, which corresponds, roughly, to the three kinds of files we talked about earlier: program files, data files, and documents), **by Size**, and **by Date**.

Mouse users can also sort the contents of a My Computer window using the Details view. If you look at the screen of Details view, you see that the headings for each column are actually buttons. Clicking on one of these buttons sorts the contents according to the data in the column. (To reverse the sort order, hold down **Shift** while clicking on a column button.) For example, you can click on the Modified column's button to have Windows 95 sort the contents in descending order by date.

## Taming My Computer's Windows

One of the things I don't like about My Computer is that its windows multiply like rabbits. Every time you select a new drive or folder, a new window sprouts up. If you're doing a lot of work with your files and folders, the desktop can get overpopulated in a hurry. One way to prevent this is to tell My Computer to cool its jets and not display a new window with each new drive or folder. To give this a try, pull down the **View** menu and select the **Options** command. In the Options dialog box, make sure the **Folders** tab is selected, and then activate the following long-winded option button: **Browse folders by using a single window that changes as you open each folder**. Select **OK** to return to My Computer, and then try some folder hopping. My Computer recycles the same window each time you move to a different drive or folder.

## Another Approach: Windows Explorer

If you're more of a "big picture" kind of person, you may prefer to use Windows Explorer for all your folder and file fun and games. To understand why, let's get Explorer up to bat. Select the **Start** button to display the Start menu, open the **Programs** folder, and select **Windows Explorer**. You'll see a window like the one shown in the following figure.

Current folder or disk drive          Toolbar

*Windows Explorer lets you see disk drives and folders in one fell swoop.*

All Folders list    Contents list

To get the same view as the one shown in the previous figure, you may need to enlarge the window by clicking on the Maximize button—see Chapter 10. Also, if you don't see the toolbar, pull down the **View** menu and activate the **Toolbar** command.

The bulk of the Explorer screen is taken up by two list boxes: the All Folders list on the left and the Contents of... list on the right.

## Navigating the All Folders List

Explorer takes a tree-like view of your system. Tree-like? You mean yet *another* metaphor? Groan! Wait, work with me on this. Let's try an experiment so you can see what I mean. See the minus sign (–) to the left of My Computer in the All Folders list? Go ahead and click on that. (From the keyboard, press **Tab** until a highlight appears inside the All Folders list. Then use the up or down arrow keys to highlight **My Computer**, and press the minus key on your numeric keypad.) What we've done is simplified the All Folders list so that it looks like the one shown in the following figure.

*The simplified All Folders list.*

As you can see, the All Folders list shows the Desktop at the top of the list and has several other items branching off below it. (Well, okay, it's only semi-tree-like, but what the heck, it's close enough for my money.) Notice that the items branching off from Desktop are precisely the same items that appear on your Windows 95 desktop! Far out. The difference, though, is that if you highlight one of the items (by clicking on it or using the up or down arrow keys), its contents appear in, appropriately enough, the Contents list. Notice in this figure that I've highlighted the My Computer item. You can see in the

Contents list that the contents are exactly the same as they were in the My Computer window I showed you earlier. In other words, Explorer is just a different way of looking at the same thing.

To see how this difference can come in handy, click on the plus sign (+) beside the My Computer item. (Or highlight **My Computer** and press the plus key on your numeric keypad.) This returns you to your original Explorer view. Notice, though, that when Explorer opens My Computer, its contents appear in the All Folders list and they branch off from the My Computer item. This is the fundamental way you work with the All Folders list. To summarize:

> **To expand a branch**, click on the plus sign (+) to the left of the folder's name. (If the plus sign is too small a target, you can also double-click on the folder's name.) From the keyboard, use the arrow keys to highlight the item, and then press your numeric keypad's plus (+) key.

> **To collapse a branch**, click on the minus sign (–) beside the folder's name. (You can also double-click on the folder's name.) Keyboarders can use the arrow keys to highlight the item, and then press the numeric keypad's minus (–) key.

The advantage to this approach is that instead of opening all kinds of My Computer windows to get down to a folder or subfolder, you can just open up the appropriate "branch" in the All Folders list and then highlight it. The subfolders and files contained in that folder then appear in the Contents list.

One last thing to note: most of the options I told you about earlier for My Computer also apply to Explorer. In particular, you can display large icons, small icons, or file details in the Contents list, and you can sort the Contents list in various ways.

### Explorer: File Manager on Steroids

Fans of Windows 3.1's File Manager will probably feel right at home in Explorer. The layout is more or less the same, with directories (oops, I mean *folders*) on the left and subfolders and files on the right. As you'll see in the next couple of chapters, though, Explorer is more powerful, more flexible, and easier to use than File Manager.

# Which One Should I Use: My Computer or Windows Explorer?

Now that you've eyeballed both My Computer and Windows Explorer, which one should you use? That depends on what you need to do and how you prefer to do it. You'll probably have to work with each tool for a time to see which one feels right for you. Here's a quick summary that may help you decide:

Use My Computer if:

➤ You don't mind juggling multiple windows.

➤ You need to place a couple of folder or disk drive windows side by side for easy file copying or moving. (As you'll learn in Chapter 12, you can use your mouse to copy or move files from one My Computer window to another.)

➤ You're only interested in the small picture (what's inside a particular folder or disk drive).

Use Explorer if:

➤ You prefer to keep your desktop uncluttered with windows.

➤ Your computer is attached to a network and you need to access the other computers on the network.

➤ You need to access other desktop stuff such as the Recycle Bin and the My Briefcase folder. (I'll talk about Briefcase in Chapter 18, in the section titled "Taking Files on the Road with Briefcase.")

➤ You need to search a disk for a particular file. (Explorer has a Find feature, discussed in the next chapter, that lets you scope out lost files.)

➤ You want to get the big picture (everything that's available on your system).

# The Least You Need to Know

This chapter took you on a scenic tour of your computer using two not-unrelated Windows 95 tools: My Computer and Windows Explorer. I hope my computer/filing cabinet metaphor helped put some of this in perspective for you. I think it'll really help you get through the next two chapters as we turn our attention to actually working with files, folders, and floppy disks.

# Chapter 12

# Fooling Around with Your Files

## In This Chapter

➤ Copying and moving files

➤ Renaming and deleting files

➤ Searching for files

➤ Drag-and-drop demystified

➤ A slew of file maintenance shortcuts and speedups

➤ Various other nifty file techniques that are sure to impress your family and friends (at least those of them who are easily impressed)

In Chapter 11, I tried to sell you on the idea that your computer was like a filing cabinet full of folders. I told you to think of the files that inhabit your hard disk as being akin to the letters, contracts, and other papers you might find in a typical filing cabinet folder. In this chapter, you learn some basic secretarial duties, such as moving and copying files, deleting files, and searching for files. (Throughout most of this chapter, my instructions apply to both My Computer and Windows Explorer. Where there are differences, I'll point them out as we go along.)

# Making Copies of Files

In an office, photocopying memos, reports, and various parts of one's anatomy (after hours, of course) is a big part of the everyday routine. In your computer, you'll find that copying files, whether you're copying them from one part of your hard disk to another or between your hard disk and a floppy disk, will be one of your most common chores. This section shows you three ways to copy files: the old-fashioned way (using the Copy command), a faster way for hard-disk-to-floppy-disk copying (the Send To command), and the newfangled way (using something called "drag-and-drop").

## Copying Files with the Copy Command

Before you can copy a file, you need to select it, which you can do by opening the file's folder and highlighting the file. Go ahead and select a file—any file. Now pull down the **Edit** menu and select the **Copy** command. Hmm, nothing happened. Actually, it only *seems* like nothing happened. Windows 95, sneaky devil that it is, really did make a copy of the file, but it's storing the copy in a hidden part of your computer's memory. Fortunately, the mechanics of all this isn't something that need concern the likes of you and me, so we'll move on.

The next step is to select the folder or disk drive where you want to store the copy of the file. When you've done that, pull down the **Edit** menu and select the **Paste** command. Windows 95 takes the copy it made earlier and stuffs it into the folder. As it does, a window appears to show you the progress of the copy, as you can see in the figure below. (I'm a big fan of the animation that shows papers flying from one folder to another, because it looks just like those flying squirrels you often see in *National Geographic* specials.)

*The Copying window appears to let you know how the copy operation is proceeding.*

**This Ain't File Manager's Copy Command!**

When I first started using Windows 95, it threw me for a loop that I couldn't find a Copy command on the File menu of either Explorer or My Computer. I had to poke around for a bit before I realized that the Copy command is now on the *Edit* menu and that copying a file has become a copy-and-paste routine. Weird.

# An Easier Way to Copy Files to a Floppy Disk

A good chunk of your copying labors will involve sending files to a floppy disk to make backup copies of important data or for transportation to another machine. (Computer nerds, proving that at least some of them have a sense of humor, refer to transporting files via floppy disk as *sneaker net*.) Instead of trudging through separate Copy and Paste commands, you can toss a file onto a floppy in one easy step. All you do is highlight the file, pull down the **File** menu, and select the **Send To** command (or right-click on the file and select **Send To** from the shortcut menu that appears). As you can see in the following figure, selecting Send To produces a cascade menu that lists your floppy drives. Select the appropriate command from this menu, and Windows 95 sends the file to the floppy without further prodding.

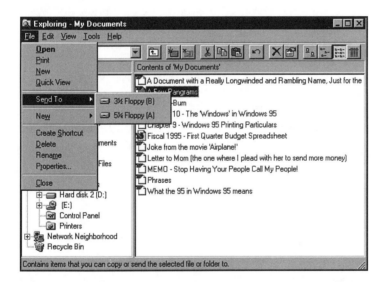

*The File menu's Send To command displays a list of your computer's floppy disk drives.*

## Don't Copy to a Floppy Without a Floppy!

Before you copy a file to a floppy disk, make sure you have a disk in the appropriate drive. If you don't, your computer makes a rude noise, and Windows 95 chastises you by displaying a dialog box with an error message. If you're not sure how to insert a floppy disk or which of your floppy disk drives to use, see Chapter 13.

# Drag 'Til You Drop: Yet Another Way to Copy

Now we turn our attention to the *drag-and-drop* method. It sounds like something you do when you get home after a hard day's work, but it's actually a cool mouse method for copying stuff from one locale to another. First, however, you need to arrange your windows appropriately:

➤ If you're using Explorer, make sure the Contents list shows the file you want to copy, and make sure the All Folders list shows the destination—the disk drive or folder to which you want to copy. (If you can't see the destination drive or folder, use the All Folders list's scroll bar to move up or down through the list until you see the destination you need. For a scroll bar refresher course, head back to Chapter 8 and read the section titled "Using Scroll Bars to Navigate a Document.")

➤ If you're using My Computer, you need to arrange two windows side by side. In one, display the folder that contains the file you want to copy, and in the other, display the destination—the folder or disk drive to which you want to copy. (Need a refresher course on arranging windows? Check out Chapter 10.)

With that out of the way, point your mouse at the file you want to copy, hold down the left mouse button, and (using your other hand, of course) hold down the **Ctrl** key. Now move the mouse towards the destination folder (this is the dragging part). As you drag the mouse, the pointer shows the file name and a little square with a plus sign (+) attached to it (see the figure below). The plus sign is Windows 95's way of telling you that you're copying the file.

A file in the process of being dragged

*When you drag a file, the mouse pointer shows the file name. The little square with the plus sign (+) tells you you're copying the file.*

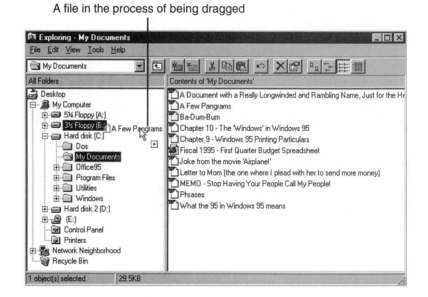

130

Move the mouse over the destination folder, release the mouse button (this is the dropping part), and then release **Ctrl**. Windows 95 copies the file to the destination as pretty as you please. (This is about as much fun as files get, so enjoy the moment while it lasts.)

# Moving Files from One Location to Another

When you copy a file, the original stays intact, and Windows 95 creates an exact replica in the new location. If you don't want to keep the original, however, you need to pack up the file and *move* it instead of copying it. Fortunately, moving stuff in Windows 95 doesn't require hunting down boxes and tape or hiring big, beefy guys to sweat all over your possessions. This section looks at two simpler methods you can use to move files.

## Using the (Yawn) Move Command

As you might expect, moving a file is quite similar to copying one. You highlight the file you want to move and pull down the **Edit** menu, but this time you select the **Cut** command. Again, nothing much happens except that the file's icon becomes a ghostly shadow of its former self. Then head to the disk drive or folder that'll be the file's new home, and select the **Edit** menu's **Paste** command. Windows 95 extracts the file from its original location and adds it to the destination.

## Using (Yea!) Drag-and-Drop

Moving files is easiest when you drag-and-drop them into their new locations. You use the same technique that I outlined for copying files (select the file by clicking on it with your left mouse button), with one important exception: instead of holding down the Ctrl key when you drag, you hold down the **Shift** key. (When you're dragging, notice that there isn't a little square with the plus sign; this is your clue that you're moving the file instead of copying it.) Once you've dropped the file, you can release the Shift key.

**You Need to Shift to Move**

**3.1**

If you're used to Windows 3.1, you'll have to get out of the habit of holding down the Alt key when you move a file with drag-and-drop, because Windows 95 has opted to use the Shift key, instead.

# A Slight Improvement on the Basic Drag-and-Drop Technique

Drag-and-drop is a handy way to sling files around on your computer. However, I do have one nit-picky complaint: I don't like having to remember to hold down Ctrl or Shift to designate a copy or a move.

**131**

To avoid this and keep drag-and-drop as a one-handed, all-mouse affair, Windows 95 also lets you use the *right* mouse button for drag-and-drop. Here's how it works:

1. Point your mouse at the file you want to copy or move, and then hold down the right mouse button.

2. Drag the file and drop it on its destination. When you release the right mouse button, a shortcut menu appears, as shown in the following figure.

*When you drag-and-drop a file with the right mouse button, this shortcut menu pops up.*

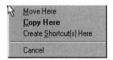

3. If you're copying the file, click on the **Copy Here** command. If you're moving it, click on **Move Here**, instead.

### Hopelessly Confusing Drag-and-Drop Drivel

Actually, there are times when you can copy or move files with drag-and-drop and avoid both holding down a key *and* using the right mouse button method. It's all a bit convoluted, but here goes nothing:

➤ If you're dragging a file to a *different* disk drive, Explorer assumes you're copying it. So, if you *are* copying the file, you don't have to hold down Ctrl. (If you're moving the file, though, you need to hold down **Shift**.)

➤ If you're dragging a file to another folder on the *same* disk drive, Explorer assumes you're moving it. So, if you *are* moving the file, you don't have to hold down Shift. (However, if you're copying the file, you need to hold down Ctrl.)

Confused? Me too.

# A File by Any Other Name: Renaming Files

If you don't like the name of a file, you can easily rename it to something you can live with. So, for example, if the file named Chitz in your Windows folder bugs you because you don't know what the heck a "chitz" is, you can rename it to, say, Chintz or Chits or Chi Chi Rodriguez. Renaming is easy; just use any of the following techniques:

➤ Highlight the file and select the **File** menu's **Rename** command.

➤ Highlight the file, and then click on the file again to edit the name. (Note, however, that you want to avoid double-clicking on the file. Click on it once to highlight it, wait a couple of beats, and then click on it again.)

➤ Highlight the file and press **F2**.

 Regardless of which method you choose, Windows 95 creates a text box around the file name, highlights the name, and throws in an insertion point cursor for good measure. Now you're free to edit the name just like you would any text in a text box. (If you need to learn more about how text boxes work, see Chapter 7's "Typing Text in Text Boxes" section.) When you're done, press **Enter** to remove the text box.

### Avoiding Wrong Steps When Renaming

When renaming your files, you need to watch out for a couple of things. First of all, remember that although Windows 95 is happy to accept long file names (up to 255 characters) with spaces in them, it chokes on names that include the following characters: \ | ? : * " < >.

Also, rename only those files that you've created yourself. Any other files on your computer are probably used by your programs, and those programs can be quite picky about what names these files have. If you mess around with the wrong file, your program may refuse to run altogether.

# Tossing Files in the Recycle Bin

In real estate, it's taken for granted that property values will always rise because nobody's making any more land. This is true in hard disk real estate, as well. As applications (especially Windows applications) become bigger and bigger, your hard disk becomes more and more cramped (remember how *huge* it seemed when you first got it?). This section shows you how to free up disk space by deleting files you no longer need. And, just in case you delete a vital file by accident, I'll also show you how to use the Recycle Bin to get a file back.

# Deleting a File

Okay, it's time to take out the garbage. Here are the steps you follow to delete a file:

1. Highlight the file you want to delete.

2. Pull down the **File** menu and select the **Delete** command. Windows 95 displays the Confirm File Delete dialog box (shown below) to ask if you're sure you want to go through with the deletion.

*Windows 95, ever paranoid, asks if you're sure you want to delete the poor file.*

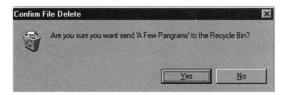

3. After giving the whole thing a second thought (and maybe even a third, just in case), select **Yes** to delete the file. (Alternatively, you can select **No** if you get cold feet at the last second.)

# Retrieving Files from the Recycle Bin

One of the sad realities of computing life is that sometime, somewhere, you'll accidentally delete some crucial file that you'd give your eyeteeth to get back. Well, I'm happy to report that you can keep your teeth where they are because Windows 95's Recycle Bin is only too happy to restore the file for you. (Actually, if the deletion was the last thing you did, you don't have to bother with the Recycle Bin. Just pull down the **Edit** menu and select the **Undo Delete** command.)

## Techno Talk
blah blah blah blah bl bl

## The Inner Mysteries of the Recycle Bin

Holy Lazarus! How the heck can the Recycle Bin restore a deleted file? Good question. You can get part of the answer by looking at the Recycle Bin icon on your Windows 95 desktop. It looks like a garbage can, and that's sort of what the Recycle Bin is. Think about it: if you toss a piece of paper in the garbage, there's nothing to stop you from reaching in and pulling it back out. The Recycle Bin operates the same way: it's really just a special, hidden folder (called Recycled) on your hard disk. When you delete a file, Windows 95 actually moves the file into the Recycled folder. So restoring a file is a simple matter of "reaching into" the folder and "pulling out" the file. The Recycle Bin handles all this for you (and even returns your file *sans* wrinkles and coffee grounds).

Your first step to retrieving a deleted file is to open up the Recycle Bin. If you're in Explorer, select **Recycle Bin** in the folder list. Otherwise, double-click on the desktop's **Recycle Bin** icon. Then highlight the file you want to undelete, open the **File** menu, and select **Restore**. The Recycle Bin instantly returns the file to its original location, safe and sound. (Insert sigh of relief here.)

# Making Life Easier: Selecting Multiple Files

So far, I've only shown you how to work with one file at a time. But if you've got, say, a dozen files to copy, even drag-and-drop can get old in a hurry. The solution is to select *all* the files you want to work with and then do the copy (or move, or delete, or whatever).

## Selecting Multiple Files, Mouse Style

With your mouse, there are three methods you can use to select multiple files:

➤ To select non-contiguous files in a folder (files that aren't displayed consecutively), hold down the **Ctrl** key and click on each file.

➤ To select contiguous files (several files in a row), click on the first file, hold down the **Shift** key, and then click on the last file.

➤ To select a group of files, "lasso" them with your mouse. Move the mouse pointer beside the first file (make sure it's not over the file's name or icon), and then drag the mouse down and to the right. As you're dragging, Windows 95 displays a dotted box, and every file that falls within that box becomes highlighted (see the figure below). When you've got all the files you need, release the mouse button.

*You can select a group of files by dragging your mouse over them.*

## Selecting Multiple Files, Keyboard Style

For dedicated keyboardists, here's how to select multiple files:

➤ To select every file in the current folder, press **Ctrl+A**.

➤ To select non-contiguous files (files not touching each other), use the arrow keys to highlight the first file, and then press and hold **Ctrl**. For each of the other files you want, use the arrow keys to highlight the file and then press the **Spacebar**. When you're done, release **Ctrl**.

➤ To select contiguous files (several files in a row), highlight the first file, press and hold down **Shift**, and use the arrow keys to highlight the other files.

# Finding File Needles in Hard Disk Haystacks

Today's behemoth hard disks can easily hold hundreds or even thousands of files. If you use your computer a lot, you know it's no sweat to add to this hard disk overpopulation by creating dozens of your own documents. So it's inevitable that you'll misplace the odd file from time to time. However, instead of wasting time scouring your folders, why not let Windows 95's Find program do the work for you?

Find is available from the Explorer window and from the Start menu. (Sorry, My Computer users, you can't get to the Find command from there.) Here are the two methods you can use to fire it up:

➤ Pull down Explorer's **Tools** menu, select **Find**, and then select the **Files or Folders** command.

➤ Select the **Start** button to display the Start menu, open the **Find** folder, and select the **Files or Folders** icon.

In either case, the Find window leaps onto the desktop (see the following figure).

*Use the Find program to scour your computer for a particular file.*

The first thing you need to do is use the Look in drop-down list to tell Find where you want it to snoop for the files. By default, the Look in box shows either the current Explorer directory (if you started Find from Explorer) or your hard disk (if you started Find from the Start menu). If you'd prefer to start your search from a different starting point, you have two choices:

➤ If you want to search in a particular disk drive, drop down the **Look in** box and select a drive from the list that appears.

➤ If you want Find to rummage through a particular folder, select the **Browse** button, choose the folder you want from the Browse for Folder dialog box that appears (it works just like Explorer's All Folders list), and then select **OK**.

Once all that's out of the way, you need to use the Named text box to tell Find the name of the file you want to track down. Fortunately, you don't have to type the entire name (a blessing if the file you're looking for has a lengthy moniker). Your best bet is to enter only one word or part of a word from the file name. (The problem with entering multiple words is that Find matches any files that contain one word *or* the other.)

When that's done, select the **Find Now** button. Find forages through the drive or folder you selected and displays its results in the box at the bottom of the window. From here, you can use the commands on Find's File and Edit menus to do what you will with the file. (If you want Windows 95 to go ahead and open the file's folder, select the **File** menu's **Open Containing Folder** command.) When you're done with Find, you can shut it down by selecting the **File** menu's **Close** command.

# Using the Open and Save As Dialog Boxes for More Convenient File Fun

If you're working in an application and need to perform one or two quick file maintenance chores (such as renaming or deleting a file), it often feels like overkill to have to crank up My Computer or Explorer, find the folder you want, and then run the necessary commands. Fortunately, Windows 95 gives you a more convenient way to handle these kinds of quickie tasks.

If the application is built specifically for Windows 95 (as are, say, WordPad and Paint) and you have a mouse, you can handle a good chunk of your file labors inside the program's Open and Save As dialog boxes. (We talked about these dialog boxes back in Chapter 8.) All you do is open either dialog box, find the file you want to work with, and then right-click on it. The shortcut menu that appears sports all kinds of file-related commands, including Send To, Cut, Copy, Delete, and Rename.

# Using Toolbars and Shortcuts for Faster File Fun

As you've seen, Explorer and My Computer make it easy to play around with the files on your computer. However, there are lots of faster ways to perform most of the techniques we've looked at. This section shows you how to use the toolbar, the right mouse button, and the keyboard to shift your file chores into overdrive.

As I explained back in Chapter 6, the toolbar gives you point-and-click access to a program's commands. You can also take advantage of the toolbar in Explorer and My Computer. The following table presents a summary of the file-related toolbar buttons and the keyboard equivalents you can use in these programs.

**Toolbar Buttons and Keyboard Shortcuts for Windows Explorer and My Computer**

| Click on this | Or press this | To do this |
|---|---|---|
| ✂ | Ctrl+X | Cut the highlighted file |
| 📋 | Ctrl+C | Copy the highlighted file |
| 📋 | Ctrl+V | Paste the cut or copied file |
| ↶ | Ctrl+Z | Undo the most recent action |
| ✕ | Delete | Delete the highlighted file |

## A Quick Click: The Shortcut Menus

You can usually get to a common command faster by right-clicking on an object to display the shortcut menu than you can by pulling down menus. Folders and disks also have shortcut menus that contain some common commands. In particular, you can use these menus to access the Find command and the Paste command.

# The Least You Need to Know

This chapter took you through several techniques for working with the files on your computer. Now that you've got files figured out, it's time to move on to a bigger game. In Chapter 13, we'll close out Part 3 by examining lots of useful techniques for monkeying around with folders and disks.

**138**

# Fiddling with Folders and Floppy Disks

## In This Chapter

➤ Creating new folders

➤ Copying, moving, and deleting folders

➤ More drag-and-drop shenanigans

➤ Painless facts about disks

➤ How to format a disk

➤ Creating a Windows 95 "startup" disk

➤ A font of file and floppy disk foolishness

This chapter closes the tour of your computer by showing you how to mess with folders and disks. We'll tackle such crowd-pleasing subjects as creating your own folders, performing routine maintenance on existing folders (moving them, renaming them, deleting them, and so on), formatting floppy disks, and creating a potentially life-saving Windows 95 "startup" disk.

# Adding On: Creating Folders

Remember that computer-as-a-filing-cabinet metaphor I threw at you back in Chapter 11? At the time, I mentioned in passing that the purpose of folders—real ones or computer ones—was organization. For a filing cabinet or hard disk to make sense and for you to be able to find things in it quickly, its folders should contain only related items.

The programs installed on your hard disk are probably already set up this way. When you install most programs, they take the liberty of creating a folder for themselves (the polite ones ask you first if it's okay), and then they install all their files in that folder.

You should follow their lead by creating some folders of your own and organizing your documents in the same way. You can create multiple folders and use each one to store only related documents. For example, you might create a Spreadsheet folder to hold your spreadsheet files, a Memos folder to hold your office notes, a Tirades folder to hold your letters to the editor, and so on. And, if several people have access to your computer (such as your spouse and kids), you could set up separate folders for each person.

The best way to do this is to create a new folder called, for example, My Documents (or perhaps Our Documents, depending on who's peering over your shoulder), and then add the other folders as subfolders under My Documents (or whatever). These, of course, are just suggestions. It is, after all, a free country, and you can organize your hard disk any way you darn well please.

## The Standard Way to Create a Folder

Okay, enough of the theory. Let's see just how you go about creating a folder. Before you add a folder, you have to decide *where* you want it:

➤ Do you want it to branch off from your hard disk? If so, you need to first open your hard disk window if you're using My Computer, or select the hard disk in Explorer's All Folders list.

➤ Do you want it to be a subfolder of an existing folder? In that case, you need to open the folder's window (if you're using My Computer) or highlight the existing folder in the All Folders list (if you're using Explorer).

Once you've selected the location, pull down the **File** menu, select **New**, and select **Folder**. Windows 95 adds a new folder and displays a text box in which you can enter a name for the folder (see the following figure). Folder names follow the same rules as file names: 255 characters max, and spaces are okay but the characters \ | ? : * " < > aren't. When you're done, press **Enter**, and your new folder is official.

*Windows 95 displays a text box for entering the name of your new folder.*

Enter a name for the new folder in the text box that appears.

# The Nonstandard Way to Create a Folder

Here's a scenario you'll probably stumble over umpteen times in your computing career: you create a new document in a Windows program and select the Save command to preserve your work. When you get to the Save As dialog box, though, you realize that you need to store this particular document in a new folder.

What's the solution? Well, you might think you have to trudge over to My Computer or Explorer, create the new folder, and then head back to the program and save your document in that folder. You *could* do that, but Windows 95 gives you an easier way. If you're using a program designed for Windows 95, you can create the folder right from the Save As dialog box! Here's how it works:

1. In the Windows 95 application you're using (such as WordPad), save a new document by selecting the **File** menu's **Save** command. (This procedure also works if you're saving an existing file to the new folder, in which case, you'd select the **File** menu's **Save As** command.)

2. In the Save As dialog box, select the folder or disk drive where you want the new folder to appear.

3. Click on the **Create New Folder** button, as shown in the following figure. Windows 95 adds the new folder and displays a text box for the folder's name.

*You can save oodles of time by clicking on the Create New Folder button in the Save As dialog box.*

The Create New Folder button

4. Type in a name for the folder and press **Enter**.

5. Select the new folder, enter a name for the document in the **File name** text box, and then click on the **Save** button.

# Copying and Moving Folders

The techniques for copying and moving folders are, mercifully, almost exactly the same as those for copying and moving files. And, as with files, you also have the choice of using the Edit menu commands or the drag-and-drop method.

## Copying and Moving with the Edit Menu Commands

**Shortcut Methods for Folders** Most of the shortcut methods for working with files that I showed you at the end of Chapter 12 work equally well when you're dealing with folders.

To copy a folder, select it, pull down the **Edit** menu, and select the **Copy** command. Then select the folder where you want the copy to appear, pull down the **Edit** menu again, and select the **Paste** command.

Moving a folder is similar. Begin by selecting it, pulling down the **Edit** menu, and selecting the **Cut** command. Then select the folder to which you want to move the original folder, pull down the **Edit** menu, and select the **Paste** command.

## Copying and Moving Folders Using Drag-and-Drop

Copying and moving folders is much more fun using the drag-and-drop method. As with files, you first need to make sure you can see both the original folder (the one you're copying or moving) and the destination folder.

To copy a folder, hold down the **Ctrl** key, drag the folder, and drop it on the destination folder. To move a folder, hold down the **Shift** key, drag the folder, and drop it on the destination folder.

If you don't want to bother with the Ctrl and Shift keys, use the right mouse button to drag the folder. When you drop it, a shortcut menu appears from which you can select either **Copy Here** or **Move Here**.

# Renaming Folders

If you don't like the name of one of your folders, go ahead and rename it. All you have to do is highlight the folder and use any of the following techniques:

➤ Select the **File** menu's **Rename** command.

➤ Click on the folder again to edit the name. (As with files, remember that you want to avoid double-clicking. Click on the folder once to highlight it, wait a couple of seconds, and then click on it again.)

➤ Press **F2**.

Windows 95 displays a text box so you can edit the folder name. Type the new name and press **Enter**.

> *Check This Out...*
>
> **Moving and Renaming Warning** Avoid moving or renaming folders created by your applications. Most programs are finicky: they expect to find their files in specific folders. Changing even a single letter of one of these folders can put an application in a huff and make it refuse to run. As with files, move or rename only folders you've created.

# More Recycle Bin Fun: Deleting Folders

If you no longer need one of the folders you've created, there's no sense letting it clutter up the Explorer or My Computer window. You may as well delete the thing and get it out of your life.

To delete a folder, highlight it and select the **File** menu's **Delete** command. Because deleting a folder is a fairly big deal, Windows 95 displays the dialog box shown in the following figure to ask if you're sure you want to go through with the deletion. If all looks well, click on the **Yes** button to get rid of the folder. Otherwise, you can click on **No** to bail out of the deletion. Whew—just in the nick of time!

*Windows 95 displays this dialog box to ask if you're sure you want to delete the folder.*

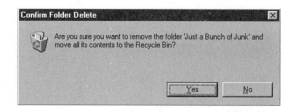

Just in case you're wondering: yes, you *can* bring back a folder from the dead. If the folder contained files, Windows 95 tossed them into the Recycle Bin. So all you have to do is head for the Recycle Bin, select the files that were in the folder, and run the **File** menu's **Restore** command. Windows 95 re-creates the appropriate folder and returns the files to their rightful place.

# Working with Multiple Folders

If you want to copy, move, or delete two or more folders, working with them all at once is no problem. To select multiple folders, use the same techniques that I outlined for selecting multiple files back in Chapter 12. Keep in mind, however, that you have to select your folders in Explorer's Contents list; you can't select multiple folders in the All Folders list.

# Types of Floppy Disks

We now turn our attention to floppy disks—those fun little plastic platters your kids have been using for frisbees. For starters, this section tells you about the different species of floppy disk that exist. (This is the kind of information you can use to impress your friends at parties.)

## Floppy Disk Sizes

Although the technowizards in the labs have been showing off a few weird-sized disks recently, your basic floppy disks come in the two sizes you see on the next page: $5^1/_4$-inch and $3^1/_2$-inch.

The $5^1/_4$-inch disks are usually black, and they come safely ensconced in a flexible plastic case. (The flexibility of the $5^1/_4$-inch disks is where the "floppy" in "floppy disk" comes from.) The $3^1/_2$-inch disks come in all kinds of designer colors. Their cases are quite sturdy, and they even have moving parts! They also fit nicely into a shirt pocket (if this doesn't feel like too nerdy a thing to do).

*5¹/₄-inch and 3¹/₂-inch disks.*

Which type of disk you use depends on the type of floppy disk drive (or drives) you have installed in your computer. If you're not sure, you can tell easily enough just by looking at the drive. If the opening is a little more than 5¹/₄-inches wide, it's a 5¹/₄-inch floppy drive. If it's about 3¹/₂-inches wide, it's a 3¹/₂-inch floppy drive. As you can see, this is not rocket science.

## The Capacity of a Floppy Disk

A slightly more subtle issue is the *capacity* of a floppy disk. A disk's capacity is simply the number of bytes of information the disk is designed to hold.

### What's a Byte?

A *byte* is a single character of information. So, for example, the phrase *This phrase is 28 bytes long* is, yes, 28 bytes long (you count the spaces, too). To make things really confusing, a *kilobyte* is equal to 1,024 bytes, and a *megabyte* is equal to 1,024 kilobytes. If you want to be hip, always say "K" instead of "kilobyte" and "meg" instead of "megabyte."

What's with this fetish for the number 1,024? You may be sorry you asked. You see, "kilo," as you may know, means "thousand," and it turns out that 2 to the power of 10 (2x2x2x2x2x2x2x2x2x2) is 1,024, which is close enough. Why *2* to the power of 10? Well, internally, computers can deal with only two states: on or off. A circuit has either a high current (it's on) or a low current (it's off). Amazingly, the world's computer geniuses have been able to create everything from Pac Man to Windows 95 out of these two simple states.

Don't be fooled by their sizes. You may think that since the 5¼-inch disk is bigger, that it holds more data. Actually the 3½-inch disk has a higher storage capacity. Both 5¼- and 3½-inch disks are available in two capacities: *double-density* and *high-density*. (Actually, the term "double-density" is relatively meaningless nowadays. It comes from the old days of computers—way back in the '80s!—when there were such things as "single-density" disks. Many people now refer to double-density disks simply as "low-density.") The following table summarizes the four most common floppy disk types.

### The Most Common Floppy Disk Types

| Disk Type | Storage Capacity |
| --- | --- |
| 5¼-inch double-density | 360 kilobytes (KB) |
| 5¼-inch high-density | 1.2 megabytes (MB) |
| 3½-inch double-density | 720 kilobytes (KB) |
| 3½-inch high-density | 1.44 megabytes (MB) |

Normally, the only way to tell whether a disk is high-density or double-density is to look at the disk's markings. For a high-density disk, look for the words "High-Density" (of course) or the letters "HD." For a double-density disk, look for "Double-Density" or "DD." If the disk has no markings at all, assume it's a double-density disk.

Which type should you use? Well, high-density disks are better because they can hold more info, but you should use them only if you have a high-density disk drive. The vast majority of computers shipped in the past two or three years are equipped with at least one high-density drive; so if your computer is fairly new, that's probably what you have. If you're not sure, your computer's manual ought to tell you. (You could also check out the machine's packing slip or receipt, if you still have either one.)

## Disk DOs and DON'Ts

Do:

➤ Place your 5¼-inch disks inside their protective covers when not in use.

➤ Label your disks so that, six months from now, you'll be able to figure out what they contain.

➤ Buy cheaper, no-name disks for everyday use.

➤ Buy top-quality disks for important needs, such as backing up your hard disk.

➤ Try to get out more.

Don't:

➤ Touch the magnetic surface of a disk.

➤ Expose a disk to direct sunlight or excessive temperatures.

➤ Place a disk near a strong magnetic or electronic source.

➤ Fold, spindle, or mutilate a disk.

➤ Use a pen or pencil to write on a label attached to a $5^1/_4$-inch disk (felt tip pens are okay).

➤ Try to remove a disk from a disk drive if the drive's light is still on.

➤ Take any wooden nickels.

# Formatting a Disk

You can't, of course, just stick any old piece of plastic in a disk drive and expect it to read and write information. Even official I-bought-it-at-the-local-computer-store floppy disks need to be initialized first so that information can be properly stored on the disk.

It's like the difference between a peg board and an ordinary piece of wood. Buying new disks (unless the box says they're "preformatted") is like buying a bunch of flat, feature-less pieces of wood. You can try all day to stick pegs in 'em, but they'll just fall off. What you need to do is "format" the wood with holes so you end up with peg board. *Then* you're in business. Floppy disks are the same way. Brand new disks are a bunch of flat, featureless pieces of plastic. You need to *format* each disk so it's capable of storing your files and documents.

Why aren't all disks preformatted? Well, most disks can be used with both DOS and non-DOS computers (such as Macintoshes), but different machines require different formats (think of peg boards with differently sized holes). So disk manufacturers simplify their lives by shipping their disks unformatted.

Fortunately, though, Windows 95 makes disk formatting a relatively painless affair. The following steps show you how to format a new disk or a used one:

1. Insert the disk you want to format in the appropriate drive.

2. Using Explorer or My Computer, select the drive. (If you're using Explorer, you need to select **My Computer** in the All Folders list and then highlight the drive in the Contents list. Strangely enough, Explorer won't let you format a floppy disk if you highlight it using the All Folders list.) If the disk has never been formatted, Windows 95 displays the following dialog box.

*If you try to select a drive that contains an unformatted disk, Windows 95 displays this dialog box.*

3. If the dialog box shown above appears, click on **Yes**. If it doesn't, pull down the **File** menu and select the **Format** command. (You can also right-click on the drive and select **Format** from the shortcut menu.) Windows 95 displays the Format dialog box, as shown here.

*Use the Format dialog box to set some formatting options.*

4. Fill out the following options in this dialog box:

   **Capacity**   Use this drop-down list box to select the proper capacity of the disk.

   **Format type**   For a new disk, select the **Full** option button. For a used disk, select the **Quick (erase)** option. (You can safely ignore the **Copy system files only** option.)

   **Label**   Fill in this text box (11 characters maximum) if you want to give the disk a name. This step is optional.

5. When you've set up your options, click on **Start** to get the formatting show on the road. When Windows 95 is done, it displays a dialog box full of incomprehensible data about the disk.

6. Click on **Close** to return to the Format dialog box.

7. Click on **Close** to return to Explorer or My Computer.

## The Quick (Erase) Option

When you're formatting a used disk, selecting this option is a real timesaver because it cuts the format time from a minute or so to a few seconds. Why would you want to format a used disk? Well, formatting can help protect you against computer *viruses*, those nasty programs that like to terrorize innocent machines. Most viruses are transmitted from computer to computer via floppy disks, so if you've inherited some old disks, the best thing to do is format each one to eradicate everything on the disk, including any viruses that may be lurking in the weeds. The only problem with the Quick (Erase) option is that it doesn't check the disk for damage. If you're dealing with a really old disk or if you've had problems with the disk, use the Full option instead.

# Creating a Startup Disk

The next time you start your computer, keep your eye on disk drive A. A few seconds after you throw the switch, the drive light should come on briefly. This means the drive is being set up for use, and once that's done, the light goes out again. A few seconds later, though, the light reappears. When the light comes back on, your system is looking to see if there's a floppy disk in the drive. If there is, the computer attempts to load Windows 95 from the floppy disk. If the disk contains the proper files—specifically, the Windows 95 *system files*—Windows 95 loads, but you'll see an **A:\>** prompt instead of the usual Windows 95 screen. This process is called *booting from a floppy*, and a disk with the Windows 95 system files is called a *startup disk*.

What good is such a disk? Well, it's possible that, thanks to a virus or a system crash, you could lose access to your hard drive. This would be bad news because Windows 95 normally uses your hard drive to start itself up when you turn on your computer. Therefore, no hard drive means no Windows 95, which means no work (or play, for that matter). If you have a startup disk, however, you just insert it in drive A and reboot your computer. Since the startup disk tells Windows 95 to boot from the floppy disk instead of the hard disk, you regain at least some control over your machine. You (or some nearby computer wiz) can then proceed to investigate the problem. Not only that, but the startup disk also contains some programs that you (or your troubleshooting guru) can use to diagnose the problem. For example, the startup disk includes the ScanDisk program (which I'll talk about in Chapter 17, in the section "Avoiding Hard Disk Hard Times: ScanDisk."

Is it hard to create a startup disk? Not at all. All you have to do is shuffle a couple of disks in and out of your computer, and Windows 95 takes care of all the dirty work. Here are the steps to follow:

1. Select the **Start** button, open the Start menu's **Settings** folder, and select **Control Panel**. The Control Panel window appears.

 2. Double-click on the **Add/Remove Programs** icon (or highlight it with the arrow keys and press **Enter**). This displays the Add/Remove Programs Properties dialog box.

3. Select the **Startup Disk** tab.

4. Click on the **Create Disk** button. Windows 95 displays a dialog box asking you to insert one of your Windows installation disks. (If you have the Windows 95 CD-ROM and it's still in the CD-ROM drive, you won't see this dialog box. Instead, Windows 95 eventually asks you to insert a disk in drive A. Skip to step 6.)

5. Insert the disk (or the Windows CD-ROM, if that's what you have) and select **OK**. After a few seconds, you're prompted to insert a disk in drive A.

6. Pick out a disk that doesn't have any files on it that you need (Windows 95 will obliterate all the current info on the disk), insert it, and select **OK**. Windows 95 chugs away for a minute or two while it creates the startup disk. When it's done, it returns you to the Add/Remove Programs Properties dialog box.

7. Click on **Cancel** to return to the Control Panel, and then select the **File** menu's **Close** command.

8. Remove the disk, attach some kind of label to it so you know what it is, store it in a safe place, and keep your fingers crossed that you never have to use it!

## The Least You Need to Know

This chapter told you everything you need to know about dealing with folders and floppy disks in Windows 95. It's all very practical information that's sure to come in handy as you work with Windows and Windows applications.

That ends Part 3 and your tour around your system with Explorer and My Computer. In Part 4, "Okay, Enough Gawking. It's Time to Get Some Work Done!," we'll turn our attention to the accessories that come as part of the Windows 95 package. First up: the WordPad word processor.

# Part 4
# Okay, Enough Gawking. It's Time to Get Some Work Done!

*Windows 95 is supposed to be "intuitive" and (ugh) "user-friendly," but it's taken us a full 13 chapters to figure out how to use it! Now, however, your investment starts paying off as we delve into the Windows 95 programs that you can use to, at last, get some work done.*

*Don't worry though: work won't be our only focus in these chapters (you know what they say about all work and no play). You'll find info on games, multimedia, drawing and painting, and other Windows 95 leisure-time activities.*

# Chapter 14

# Word Processing with WordPad

## In This Chapter

➤ Getting around in WordPad

➤ Editing text

➤ Formatting text and paragraphs

➤ Previewing documents before printing them

➤ A vast number of tips and tricks for getting the most out of WordPad

Almost everyone who uses a computer uses it to write something from time to time. It could be a letter to Mom, a memo to the honchos at HQ, or yet another attempt at the Great (insert nationality here) Novel. Most computer-based writing is handled by a *word processor*, which is a geekoid term for a program that lets you not only type in text, but also edit it and format it so it looks all nice and pretty.

WordPad is the word processor that comes free with Windows 95. Granted, WordPad may not have all the fancy-schmancy features you get in the more glamorous word processors (such as Word for Windows or WordPerfect for Windows), but it'll handle simple day-to-day chores, like memos, letters, résumés, or ransom notes, without a complaint. So unless you're a professional word jockey, WordPad will get the job done. This chapter gets you up to speed with this useful little writing tool.

# Taking a Look Around the WordPad Window

To start WordPad, select the **Start** button, open the Start menu's **Programs** folder, open the **Accessories** folder, and select **WordPad**. (What's that? You can't find hide nor hair of WordPad in your Accessories folder? Ah, then you need to install it on your computer. To find out how, travel ahead to Chapter 25 and read the section titled, "Adding and Removing Windows 95 Components.") The following figure shows the WordPad window and points out a few landmarks.

*The WordPad window.*

Here's a summary of the important features of the WordPad window:

**Toolbar** As described back in Chapter 6, you use a toolbar for one-click access to important everyday commands such as Open, Save, Cut, Copy, and Paste.

**Format bar** This is a variation on the toolbar theme. These buttons give you point-and-click service for many of WordPad's formatting commands. I'll talk about formatting later in this chapter in the sections "Sprucing Up Your Text" and "Getting Your Paragraphs Just So."

**Ruler** You use the ruler for setting tabs, indenting paragraphs, and changing margins. The left edge of the ruler (at 0 inches) represents the left margin, and the right edge (at 6 inches) represents the right margin.

**Typing area** This is the vast white expanse that takes up the bulk of the WordPad window, and it's where your document text will appear.

**Insertion point cursor** The text you type always appears to the right of this blinking vertical line.

**3.1** **WordPad Can Out-Write Write Any Day!**

If you've been using Write, the word processor that came with Windows 3.1, you'll *love* WordPad. Why? Well, let's just say that if WordPad and Write had an arm wrestling match, WordPad would win hands-down (no pun intended) every time. I mean, right off the bat you can look at the handy toolbar and format bar, and you just *know* WordPad is easier to use. It also includes some nice features (such as the capability to preview your documents before printing them) that Write could only dream about.

# The Ol' Hunt and Peck: Entering Text in WordPad

Unlike with some of today's big-bucks word processors, you don't need a degree in rocket science to get up and running with WordPad. Once you've loaded the program (and, if necessary, opened a file you've saved before), you can simply go ahead and start pounding out your deathless prose. Each character you type appears beside the insertion point cursor, and the cursor then leaps ahead to show you where your next character will appear.

If you're used to typing with a typewriter, you may be tempted to press the Enter key when you approach the end of a line. No way, José! You don't have to bother, because WordPad handles that chore for you. No guff. You see, when you hit the end of a line, WordPad automatically dispatches the cursor to the beginning of the *next* line. Even if you're smack in the middle of a word, WordPad automatically trucks the entire word to the start of the next line. (This handy feature is called *word wrap*, in nerdspeak.) The only time you need to press Enter is when you want to start a new paragraph. Hey, this ain't no Selectric!

# Can I Get There From Here? Navigating a Document

For the terminally verbose, WordPad can handle tome-like documents as large as your computer's memory will allow. When your writings become several pages or more in length, however, you'll need some way to navigate them quickly. If you use a mouse, you can move the cursor by clicking on the appropriate text inside the window. To move to other parts of the document, use the scroll bars to leap giddily from page to page. (Need a scroll bar refresher course? Head back to Chapter 8 and re-read the section "Using Scroll Bars to Navigate a Document.")

From the keyboard, you can use the techniques outlined in the following table to navigate a document.

## Handy WordPad Navigation Keys

| Press... | To move... |
| --- | --- |
| Left arrow or right arrow | Left or right one character |
| Ctrl+left arrow or Ctrl+right arrow | Left or right one word |
| Home or End | To the beginning or end of a line |
| Up arrow or down arrow | Up or down one line |
| Ctrl+Page Up or Ctrl+Page Down | To the top or bottom of the window |
| Page Up or Page Down | Up or down one screen |
| Ctrl+Home or Ctrl+End | To the beginning or end of the document |

# Some Text-Selection Tricks

When editing and formatting a WordPad document, you often need to select a group of characters or lines to work with. Because selected text appears as white letters on a dark background, this is also called *highlighting* text.

**Formatting?**
Formatting a WordPad document involves altering the look of your text to make the document more effective or more presentable. For example, you can make a word **bold** so it stands out from the crowd, *or you can change a phrase to italics* to add emphasis. Formatting your documents gives them a real professional look.

I showed you some basic methods for highlighting text back in Chapter 8 (in the "Highlighting Text" section), and these techniques will stand you in good stead for most text-selection chores. But WordPad also has a few other tricks you can stuff up your word processing sleeve:

**To select a word,** double-click on it.

**To select a line,** click inside the narrow strip of white space to the left of the line (that is, between the line and the WordPad window's left border).

**To select a paragraph,** double-click to the left of the paragraph. If you're feeling athletic, you can also select a paragraph by *triple*-clicking anywhere inside the paragraph.

**To select the entire document,** hold down **Ctrl** and click anywhere inside the narrow strip of white space to the left of the document text.

Now that you know how to select text, you're ready to add formatting. The next few sections show you how to use formatting to dress up your WordPad prose so it looks respectable.

# Sprucing Up Your Text

When you get to Chapter 21, you'll find out all about *fonts*. "Font" is a catchall term that refers to the formatting of your document text. I'll save the details for Chapter 21, but the following figure shows a WordPad document with a few font examples.

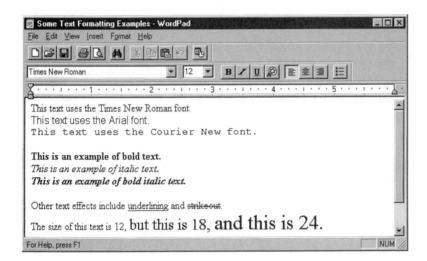

*Some of the ways you can format your WordPad text.*

Here are the WordPad steps you plow through to format text with a particular font:

1. Select the text you want to format using the techniques described earlier.

2. Pull down the **Format** menu and select the **Font** command (or right-click on the selection and then choose **Font** from the shortcut menu). WordPad displays the Font dialog box, as shown in the following figure.

*Use WordPad's Font dialog box to add all kinds of fancy formatting to your text.*

**157**

3. Use the controls in the Font dialog box to pick out the various font options you need. As you make your selections, watch the Sample box to see what havoc you'll wreak on your text.

4. When you've finished playing, select **OK**. WordPad returns you to the document and reformats the selected text.

### Formatting New Text

Instead of typing some text and then going back to format it, you can apply some formatting options to new text. First, position the insertion point where the new text will appear. Launch the Font dialog box, make your formatting selections, and then return to the document and start typing. WordPad displays the new text using the formatting you selected. To return to your normal text formatting, display the Font dialog box again and reset the options you adjusted earlier.

If you just want to throw a little bold or italic at a word or two, it's a bit of a hassle to fire up the Font dialog box every time. (Lazy? Moi? Well, maybe a little.) To make your text formatting tasks go faster, WordPad offers all kinds of shortcut methods.

For mouse mavens, the following table lists the format bar buttons you can use to fancy up some text quickly.

### Format Bar Buttons for Formatting Text

| Click on... | To get... |
| --- | --- |
| Times New Roman ▼ | A list of fonts |
| 10 ▼ | A list of font sizes |
| **B** | **Bold** |
| *I* | *Italics* |
| <u>U</u> | <u>Underline</u> |
| 🎨 | A list of colors to apply to your text |

For keyboard connoisseurs, the following table summarizes some shortcut key combinations you can use.

### Shortcut Key Combos for Formatting Text

| Press... | To get... |
| --- | --- |
| Ctrl+B | **Bold** |
| Ctrl+I | *Italics* |
| Ctrl+U | <u>Underline</u> |

# Getting Your Paragraphs Just So

Although the content of your documents is important, how the documents look on the page is equally (if not more) important. Why? Because in these busy times, people will simply ignore (or trash) a document if it looks cramped and uninviting.

To avoid this fate, use WordPad's paragraph formatting options to make yourself look good on paper. To try them out, first place the cursor in the paragraph you want to format. (If you want to format multiple paragraphs, select the text for each paragraph.) Then select the **Format** menu's **Paragraph** command to display the Paragraph dialog box, as shown in the following figure. (You can also coax this dialog box onto the desktop by right-clicking on the paragraph and selecting **Paragraph** from the shortcut menu.)

*Use the Paragraph dialog box to format your paragraphs.*

The Paragraph dialog box contains the following controls:

**Left**   Use this text box to control how far (in inches) the paragraph is indented from the left margin. For example, if you enter 1, the paragraph is indented one inch from the left margin; entering .5 indents the paragraph one-half inch.

**Right**   Use this text box to control how far the paragraph is indented from the right margin.

**159**

**First line**   Use this text box to control how far the first line (and only the first line) of the paragraph is indented from the left margin.

**Alignment**   Use this drop-down list to adjust the alignment of the paragraph's lines. If you select **Left**, all lines in the paragraph are aligned with the left margin; if you select **Right**, all lines in the paragraph are aligned with the right margin; if you select **Center**, all lines in the paragraph are centered between the margins. As the following table shows, you can also pick out an alignment using the format bar.

## Format Bar Buttons for Aligning Paragraphs

| *Click on...* | *To get this alignment...* |
|---|---|
| ▤ | Left |
| ▤ | Center |
| ▤ | Right |

Just so you have some idea of what the heck I'm talking about, the following figure shows examples of the paragraph formatting options.

*WordPad's paragraph formatting options.*

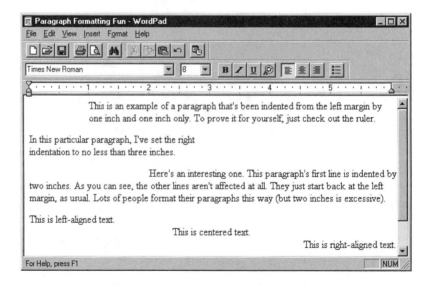

# Setting Tab Stops

Documents look much better if they're properly indented and if their parts line up like soldiers on parade. One easy way to do this is to use tabs instead of spaces whenever you need to create some room in a line. Why? Well, a single space can take up a different amount of room depending on the font, the type size, and so on. So your document can end up looking pretty ragged if you try to use spaces to indent your text. Tabs, on the other hand, are meticulously precise. When you press the Tab key, the insertion point moves ahead to the next tab stop, no more, no less. (If you don't have any tab stops set, pressing Tab moves the insertion point ahead exactly half an inch.)

However, if you don't like the tab stops currently set in WordPad, don't just boycott tabs altogether; change 'em! After all, you're the one who's running the show around here. You'll need to make your way through the following steps to set your own Tab stops.

1. Place the insertion point inside the paragraph you want to format. If you want to set the same tab stop for multiple paragraphs, select them all. (Keep in mind, too, that if you set some tab stops for the current paragraph, each new paragraph you create below it will also use the same tab stops.)

2. Pull down the **Format** menu and select the **Tabs** command. The Tabs dialog box appears, as shown in the following figure.

Enter the new tab position here.

Tabs you've already set appear here.

*Use the Tabs dialog box to set up one or more tabs for the current line.*

3. In the Tab stop position text box, enter a location for the tab stop. For example, if you want the tab stop to be one inch from the left margin, enter **1**.

4. Click on the **Set** button, and WordPad adds the tab to the list.

5. If you're feeling gung-ho, repeat steps 3 and 4 to enter any other tabs you want to set.

6. When you've had just about enough, select **OK**. WordPad adds the tab stops to the document and displays them in the ruler.

**Faster Tab Stops**

Instead of entering tab stop positions blindly in the Tabs dialog box, WordPad gives you a way to set your tabs visually. As usual, place the cursor in the paragraph you want to work with; then move your mouse into the ruler, point at the position where you want your tab stop, and click. A tab stop appears instantly. If the tab isn't quite in the right spot, just drag it to the left or right with your mouse. To get rid of a tab, drag it off the ruler.

# Finding Lost Text in Humongous Files

Finding a particular word or phrase is usually no problem in small WordPad files. But, as your competence with WordPad grows, so will your documents. When you start dealing with 10- and 20-page documents, finding what you need becomes a real "Where's Waldo?" exercise.

To help out, WordPad has a Find feature that does the searching for you. To try it out, pull down the **Edit** menu and select the **Find** command (or press **Ctrl+F**). The Find dialog box appears, as shown in the following figure.

 You can also fire up the Find command by clicking on this button in the WordPad toolbar.

*Use the Find dialog box to search for a word or phrase in your document.*

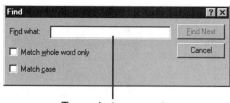

Type what you want to look for here.

In the Find What text box, enter the word or phrase you want to locate. You can also refine your searches by using the two check boxes provided:

**Match whole word only**   WordPad normally tries to find partial matches for your search text. For example, if you enter **waldo**, WordPad finds *Waldorf*, *Gottwaldov* (a city in the Czech Republic), and, of course, *Waldo*. If *Waldo* is all you want, activate the **Match whole word only** check box, and WordPad ignores partial matches.

**Match case**    Activate this check box to make WordPad's searches *case-sensitive*. For example, if you enter **Curt** as your search text and you activate this check box, WordPad ignores the word *curt* and finds only the name *Curt*.

**Continuing the Search**    Once you're back in the document, you may realize you have to locate another occurrence of the search text. Instead of going through the hassle of the Find dialog box, you can continue the search by selecting the **Edit** menu's **Find Next** command (or you can simply press **F3**). WordPad remembers the last word(s) you were searching for.

When you're ready to go, click on the **Find Next** button. If WordPad finds the text, it highlights it in the document's typing area. If that's not the occurrence of the text you're looking for, keep clicking on **Find Next** until you find it. When you do, click on the **Cancel** button to return to the document. If WordPad can't locate a match, a dialog box appears to tell you it has finished searching the document.

# Finding and Replacing Text

A slightly different kettle of fish involves finding text and *replacing* it with something else. For example, you might want to change each occurrence of *Ave.* to *Avenue* or some occurrences of *affect* to *effect* (yeah, I have a hard time remembering which is which, too).

To do this, pull down the **Edit** menu and select the **Replace** command (or press **Ctrl+H**). The Replace dialog box that appears is almost identical to the Find dialog box you saw earlier. As before, enter the text you want to locate in the **Find what** text box. In the **Replace with** text box, enter the replacement text. You now have two ways to proceed:

➤ If you know you want to replace every occurrence of the search text with the replacement text, click on the **Replace All** button. WordPad trudges through the entire document, finding and replacing as it goes. When it's done, it displays a dialog box to let you know. Select **OK** to return to the Replace dialog box, and then select **Close** to return to the document. (You'll need to exercise a bit of caution before using the Replace All feature willy-nilly. For example, suppose your search text is *ave* and your replacement text is *avenue*. Since *ave* may also match *avenge* or *average*, Replace All changes these words into the nonsensical *avenuenge*, and *avenuerage*.)

➤ If you want to replace only *certain* occurrences of the search text, click on the **Find Next** button. Whenever WordPad finds an occurrence you want to replace, click on the **Replace** button.

# Some Notes About a Few Basic WordPad Chores

Back in Chapter 8, I took you through a few routine tasks that are more or less the same in most Windows applications. Thankfully, most of the techniques you learned in that chapter are also readily applicable to WordPad. However, WordPad does have a few minor quirks you should know about:

➤ To make our lives more complicated, every word processor has its own format for the documents it creates. The format WordPad uses is the same as that used by Microsoft's high-end word processor, Word for Windows 6.0. So when you run the Open command, WordPad's Open dialog box shows only those documents that conform to the Word for Windows 6.0 format. If you want to open a different type of document (such as a straight text file), you need to use the Open dialog box's Files of type drop-down box, which lists various other document types.

➤ If you select the File menu's New command, WordPad displays the New dialog box. Here, WordPad wants to know what kind of document you want to create: Word 6 (the normal WordPad type, and the type you'll use most often), Rich Text (a special text file that lets you add formatting), or Text Only (a pure text file that can't contain any formatting).

➤ WordPad has a Print Preview feature that can save you lots of time (and paper). What Print Preview does is give you a bird's-eye view of your document so you can see if your formatting looks the way you want it to. To give it a go, pull down the **File** menu and select the **Print Preview** command.

 Clicking on this toolbar button also displays the Print Preview window.

➤ The WordPad window can display only one document at a time. If you need to copy or move a chunk of text between two WordPad documents, just start up a second copy of WordPad and open the other document in it. Then cut or copy the text from the original WordPad window, switch to the second window, and paste it. See Chapter 10 for instructions on switching between open applications.

# The Least You Need to Know

This chapter gave you a basic introduction to WordPad, Windows 95's not-overly-powerful-but-hey-whaddya-want-for-nothing word processor. We covered all the must-know word pro tasks, including entering text, navigating a document, formatting text and paragraphs, setting tab stops, and finding and replacing text. So go out and land that fat publishing contract and spend your lavish advance on something completely self-indulgent, because that successful writing career is now surely just around the corner.

# Chapter 15

# The Art of Windows 95: The Paint Program

**In This Chapter**

➤ Navigating the Paint window

➤ Drawing lines, boxes, circles, and other funky shapes

➤ Drawing freehand lines

➤ Editing your drawings

➤ More ways of reliving your youth than you can shake a stick at

If you enjoyed finger painting when you were a kid, you'll get a kick out of Paint, Windows 95's drawing program. Oh sure, you can use it for practical stuff like logos, charts, and whatnot, but to my mind, Paint's real reason for being is sheer fun. Think about it: all you do is select a "tool" to work with and then just wiggle your mouse around the screen. Magically, you get all kinds of cool shapes and patterns. Throw in a few colors and a dash of imagination (or just plain silliness) and you have a recipe for hours of entertainment (and—bonus!—your fingers stay nice and clean).

## Powering Up Paint

When the creative urge hits, you can start Paint by selecting the **Start** button, opening the Start menu's **Programs** folder, opening **Accessories**, and then selecting **Paint**. (If Paint is nowhere to be found in your Accessories folder, you need to install it on your system. The section titled "Adding and Removing Windows 95 Components" in Chapter 25 gives you the goods on installing Windows 95 accessories.) Eventually, the Paint window shown in the following figure appears.

*Your Windows 95 canvas: the Paint window.*

### Paint: A New and Ever-So-Slightly Improved Paintbrush

If you're a fan of Windows 3.1's Paintbrush accessory, you'll be happy to know that Paint carries on the tradition. In fact, the two programs are almost identical, although Paint does bring a few improvements to the easel. For example, some of the tools have a few more options to try out, and the Zoom command is a bit more flexible. The one thing that Paint lacks is probably the one thing nobody will miss: keyboard support.

## A Look Around the Paint Studio

As you can see, the Paint window is chock-full of artistic goodies. Let's take a close look at the various toys you can play with:

**Tool Box**   This section contains the various "tools" you use to create or edit your drawings. You get a Pencil, a Brush, an Airbrush, an Eraser, and all kinds of utensils for drawing lines and shapes. I'll show you how to wield each tool as you work (or should I say *play*) in this chapter. Don't even think about memorizing which Tool

Box tool is which. If you draw a blank (sorry about that), just point your mouse at the Tool Box button in question. In a second or two a small banner appears to tell you the name of the tool.

**Tool styles**   Some of the tools give you a selection of styles so you can add some variety to your drawings. When you select one of these tools (such as the Brush tool or the Line tool), the available styles appear in the area below the Tool Box.

**Color Box**   This section shows the available colors and patterns you can use for drawing or filling shapes. Think of this as your own personal 28-box of Crayola crayons (sans that icky flesh-colored crayon) that never need sharpening.

**Current colors**   These two boxes display the currently selected foreground color (the top box) and background color (the bottom box). What do I mean by *foreground* and *background* colors? Well, that's actually a tough question to answer! It really depends on which tool you're using, so I'll pass the buck and just explain everything as we go along. To select a new foreground color, click on one of the color rectangles in the Color Box. To select a new background color, right-click on a color.

**Drawing area**   This is the large blank area that takes up most of the Paint window. The drawing area is your Paint canvas: it's where you'll be doing the actual drawing and painting that leads to the creation of your digital masterpieces. It is, in short, the place where all the fun happens.

# Drawing with Paint

The best way to approach Paint is simply to have a good time fooling around with the various tools, styles, and colors. Go on, let loose; toss off those inhibitions, free yourself from the shackles of adult responsibilities, and allow yourself to revert to a more immature, to-heck-with-it-I'm-going-to-be-at-one-with-my-inner-child state. (You may want to close the door for this.)

Once you're suitably juvenile, you can pick a tool and start playing. However, there *is* a basic four-step method you'll use for each tool:

1. Select the tool you want to work with by clicking on it in the Tool Box.

2. Click on one of the available tool styles (if the tool has any, that is).

3. Select a foreground and background color from the Color Box.

4. Move the pointer into the drawing area and draw the shape you want. (As you'll see, the specifics of the drawing process vary from tool to tool.)

The next few sections flesh out these generic steps by showing you how to wield specific tools.

# A Note About Bailing Out of Your Mistakes

Before we get started, you should probably know how to get rid of the botched lines and mutinous shapes that inevitably appear when you're learning to use each tool.

**Don't Forget to Save!** When you draw something just right, you should save your work right away (by pulling down the **File** menu and selecting the **Save** command, or by pressing **Ctrl+S**). Once you've saved the drawing, if you mess things up, you can get back to the saved version by closing the drawing and then opening it again. (To close, select the **File** menu's **New** command; in this case, make sure you select **No** when Paint asks if you want to save your changes.)

Using any of Paint's tools requires that you hold down one of the mouse buttons while drawing. If you make a mess during the drawing, you can start again by simply clicking the other mouse button *before* you release the button you're using.

What if you've already finished drawing the shape? No problem. Just select the **Edit** menu's **Undo** command (or press **Ctrl+Z**). In fact, Paint can handle up to three levels of Undo. So, if you need to, you could wipe out the last three shapes you created by selecting the Undo command three times. What happens if you've got more stray shapes to get rid of? (My, you *are* messy, aren't you? Maybe you should just tell everyone the drawing is *supposed* to look like that.) Happily, Paint comes with a couple of erasers that can expunge any wayward lines or colors. See the section "Erasing Parts of a Drawing" later in this chapter.

If the drawing is a total disaster, you can start over by selecting the **Image** menu's **Clear Image** command (or by pressing **Ctrl+Shift+N**).

## Drawing Lines

The simplest drawing element is probably the straight line, so (as you might expect) it's the easiest to use of Paint's drawing tools.

 Begin by clicking on the Line tool in the Tool Box.

Now click on one of the line widths displayed below the Tool Box and then select your colors.

Move the pointer into the drawing area (as you do, the pointer will change to a crosshair; this is perfectly normal behavior) and position it where you want the line to start. Press and hold the left mouse button, drag the pointer until the line is at the angle and length you want, and then release the mouse button. (Mouse Refresher Course—Dragging 101: Remember that dragging the mouse means holding down one of the mouse buttons and moving the mouse at the same time.) If you want the line to appear in the current foreground color, use the left mouse button to drag the pointer; if you prefer the current background color, use the right mouse button.

**Keeping Lines on the Straight and Narrow**
To draw a perfect horizontal or vertical line, or to draw your line at exactly a 45-degree angle, hold down the **Shift** key while dragging the mouse.

## Drawing Rectangles and Circles

You can use rectangles, circles, ellipses, and rounded rectangles (along with lines) to create most of the basic shapes in your drawing. The Paint tools you use to create these shapes are, not surprisingly, the Rectangle, Ellipse, and Rounded Rectangle tools.

The Rectangle tool

The Ellipse tool

The Rounded Rectangle tool

To use any one of these tools, click on the tool in the Tool Box, and then click on one of the three border styles that appear at the bottom of the Tool Box.

Next, click on your foreground and background colors. (I'll explain how the colors work with these tools in a sec.)

Then move the pointer into the drawing area and position it where you want the shape to start. Drag the pointer toward what will be the opposite side of the shape until the object is the size and shape you want. Then release the mouse button.

The colors that Paint uses for the shape depend on which style you selected, which mouse button you drag with, and what mood Paint is in that day:

**Perfect Circles and Squares**
To draw a perfect square or circle, hold down the **Shift** key while dragging the pointer.

**Border only**   This style draws only the border of the shape. If you left-drag (click the left mouse button and drag the mouse), the border appears in the current

**169**

foreground color; if you right-drag (click the right mouse button and drag the mouse), the border appears in the current background color.

**Border and fill**   This style draws a border and fills it with a color. If you left-drag, the border appears in the foreground color, and the fill appears in the background color; right-dragging applies the background color to the border and the foreground color to the fill.

**No border**   This style leaves off the shape's border and draws only the fill. If you left-drag, the fill appears in the current background color; if you right-drag, the fill appears in the current foreground color.

Got all that? No? Well, not to worry; there's plenty of time before tomorrow's pop quiz.

## Drawing Curves

For your nonlinear moods, Paint has a Curve tool you can use to draw wavy lines. It's actually a bit tricky to use, so you may need to play around with it a bit. Here are the steps to follow:

1. Click on the **Curve** tool, click on the style (you get the same choices you saw earlier for the Line tool), and select the color you want to use.

2. Position the pointer where you want the curve to start.

3. Drag the mouse until the line is the length you want and then release the button. (As with the Line tool, drag with the left button to use the foreground color or drag with the right button to use the background color.)

4. Drag the mouse again to curve the line. For example, if you drew a horizontal line in step 2, you can drag the mouse down to curve the line downwards. Similarly, you can drag the mouse up to curve the line upwards. When you've got the curve you want, release the button.

5. If you want to add a second curve to the line, drag the mouse again and release the button when you're done.

## Drawing Polygons

*Polygon* may sound like a parrot that's flown the coop (here, I'll save you the trouble: "Groan!"), but it's really just a highfalutin mathematical term for a collection of straight lines that forms an enclosed object. (A triangle is a common example of a polygon.) Follow these steps to create a Paint polygon:

1. Click on the **Polygon** tool, click on the style (you get the same choices that you saw earlier for the Rectangle and Ellipse tools), and select the color you want to use.

2. Move the pointer into the drawing area and position it where you want the polygon to start. The pointer changes to a cross.

3. Drag the pointer (using the left button for the foreground color or the right button for the background color) until the first side is the length and angle you want.

4. Release the mouse button.

5. Position the pointer where you want the next side to end.

6. Click a mouse button, and Paint draws a line from the end of the previous line to the pointer.

7. Repeat steps 5 and 6 to define the other sides of the polygon. To finish the shape, connect the last side with the beginning of the first side.

## Drawing Freehand Lines

As you've seen, Paint makes it easy—some would say *too* easy—to draw lines, circles, and polygons. To become a true Paint artiste, or just to have some real fun, try using the Pencil tool or the Brush tool to draw freehand lines.

 Begin by clicking on the **Pencil** tool or the **Brush** tool.

 If you choose the Brush tool, you can also choose from one of the dozen different styles that appear at the bottom of the Tool Box.

Next, you can select a foreground and background color for each tool.

Move the pointer into the drawing area and position it where you want to start drawing. (If you're using the Pencil, the pointer changes to a pencil; if you're using the Brush, the pointer changes to the style you selected.) Then just drag the pointer, and a line follows your every twitch. (As usual, you left-drag to display the line in the foreground color and right-drag to display the line in the background color.) When you're done, release the mouse button.

## Filling Shapes with Color

What do you do if you create, say, a rectangle using the "border only" style, and then later decide you'd like the rectangle filled with a particular color? Or suppose you create an enclosed area with the Pencil or Brush and would like to fill it in with a color.

 The solution to these Paint problems is the Fill With Color tool. As its name implies, the Fill With Color tool fills in any enclosed shape with whatever color you select.

It's really easy to use, too: just click on the **Fill With Color** tool in the Tool Box, and then click anywhere inside the shape. If you left-click, Paint fills the shape with the current foreground color; if you right-click, Paint uses the current background color.

### Sometimes Fill With Color Does Too Good a Job

Before foisting the Fill With Color tool on a shape, make sure the shape is completely enclosed. If it's not—even if there's just the tiniest gap— Fill With Color's color leaks out and fills in any enclosed area that surrounds the original shape, which usually means the entire drawing area! Argh! This will happen more times than you think, so it's important to know what to do. After counting to ten or chanting your mantra or doing whatever it is you do to calm yourself, immediately select the **Edit** menu's **Undo** command (or press **Ctrl+Z**). Then return to the shape and close the pesky gap that caused the leak. (For best results, you may need to magnify the shape. See the section "A Zoom with a View," later in this chapter.)

## Using the Airbrush Tool

The Airbrush tool (as its icon shows) is actually more like a can of spray paint. This is useful for satisfying those graffiti urges without breaking the law.

Click on one of the three Airbrush styles (these define the size of the "spray") and then click on your colors.

Move the mouse pointer into the drawing area (the pointer changes to a spray can) and hold down a mouse button to start spraying. You know the drill by now: hold down the left button for the foreground color or the right button for the background color. Simply drag the pointer around the drawing area, and you're an instant graffiti artist.

## Adding Text to a Drawing

Paint is mostly for your right brain, but if your left brain wants to get in on the act, you can use the Text tool to add text to a drawing. Here's what you do:

1. Click on the **Text** tool, click on either the opaque or transparent style (the following figure shows an example of each style), and then click on your colors.

*You can add text to your drawing using either an opaque or transparent style.*

Opaque style
Transparent style

2. Position the pointer where you want the text to start and drag the mouse to create a box large enough to hold the text. When you release the mouse button, an insertion point cursor appears inside the box.

3. If this is the first time you've used the Text tool, a Fonts toolbar appears (see the following figure). If you don't see the Fonts toolbar, right-click on the **Text** box and select **Text Tool** from the shortcut menu.

*Use the Fonts toolbar to format your text.*

4. Use the drop-down lists and buttons on the Fonts toolbar to establish a format for your text. (To find out more about fonts, pay a visit to Chapter 21.)

5. Type your text. When you're done, click on the **Text** tool again.

# Cutting, Copying, and Pasting Drawings

You can apply the cut and paste techniques that I described in Chapter 8 to Paint drawings; however, there are some extra steps involved. The next couple of sections explain everything you need to know.

## Selecting Parts of a Drawing

If you need to cut or copy a piece of a drawing (to paste either elsewhere in the drawing or, perhaps, in a different program altogether), you first need to select the image you want. Paint gives you two tools to do the job: the Select tool and the Free-Form Select tool.

 The Select tool

 The Free-Form Select tool

Use the Select tool to select a rectangular area of the drawing. Click on the tool and move the pointer to the upper-left corner of the area you want to select. Drag the mouse until the box encloses the area you want to work with, and then release the mouse button.

Use the Free-Form Select tool to select any area that's not rectangular shaped. After clicking on the tool, move the pointer into the drawing area and drag the mouse around the area you want to select. Release the button when you've completely outlined the area.

**Check This Out...**

**Pasting into Another Drawing** Paint, like WordPad, doesn't let you work with more than one document at a time, so if you need to paste some or all of one drawing into another Paint drawing, just start up a second copy of Paint and open the other drawing in it. You can cut or copy the image from the original Paint window, switch to the second window, and paste it. See Chapter 10 for instructions on switching between open applications.

## Pasting Cut or Copied Images

Once you've cut or copied your selected image (by using the Edit menu's Cut or Copy commands), you need to paste the image.

With text, as you may recall, you first position the cursor where you want the new text to appear. However, Paint doesn't have a cursor. So when you select the Edit menu's Paste command, the image appears in the upper-left corner of the drawing. To position it, move the mouse pointer inside the image, and then drag the image to the location you want.

## Erasing Parts of a Drawing

Because it takes a little time to get used to the Paint tools, you'll probably have a number of stray lines and shapes that you don't want in the finished drawing. Fortunately, you can use Paint's Eraser tool to remove any rogue elements.

Actually, Eraser is two tools in one: a normal eraser and a color eraser.

As a normal eraser, the Eraser tool does pretty much what you'd expect: it wipes out everything in its path. (This is not a tool to be wielded carelessly!)

Select the eraser width from the styles that appear at the bottom of the Tool Box. If you have a lot to erase, pick a wider shape; if you want fine control, pick a thinner shape.

Move the pointer into the drawing area and position it near where you want to start erasing. (The pointer changes into a box.) Drag the pointer to start erasing, and everything in the path of the box is erased. (Technically, everything in the path of the box is replaced by the current background color.) When you're done, release the mouse button.

What's the Eraser tool's other personality—the color eraser—all about? Well, suppose you want to preserve the outlines of a drawing but wipe out the color that fills it, or suppose you want to replace one color with another. These sound like tricky operations, but the color eraser can do the job without breaking a sweat.

You use the color eraser just as you do the eraser, except that you right-drag the eraser box. When you drag the tool over your drawing, it replaces anything it finds in the current foreground color with the current background color.

# A Zoom with a View

For fine detail work, Paint lets you "zoom" in on a section of a drawing. This magnifies the drawing so you can get a closer look at a particular section. At the maximum magnification (a whopping 800%), you can even see the tiny individual elements (the *pixels*) that make up a Paint picture.

**Techno Talk**

**Pixel Perfect**
The elements that comprise a picture are called *pixels* ("pixel" is a combination of the term "picture elements"). A typical Paint image has pixels arranged in 640 columns and 480 rows, which totals more than 300,000 pixels!

To try this out, click on the **Magnifier** tool and then click on a magnification from the choices that appear at the bottom of the Tool Box. When you move the mouse into the drawing area, the pointer changes into a box. Move the box over the area you want to magnify, and then click. Paint zooms in, as shown in the following figure. The little Thumbnail window shows the normal view of the magnified area so you can keep things in perspective. (If you'd prefer not to see the Thumbnail window, open the **View** menu, select the **Zoom** command, and deselect the **Show Thumbnail** command in the cascade menu.)

*The Zoom tool in action.*

Thumbnail window

Select a magnification option.

You can work on the drawing normally in this view because almost all the other tools are available (the Text tool is the only exception). When you've finished, click on the **Zoom** tool and then click on the **1x** style to return to the normal view.

There are actually a couple of other methods you can use to zoom in and out:

➤ Pull down the **View** menu, select the **Zoom** command, and then select **Large Size** from the cascade menu. (Or you can bypass the menus altogether by simply pressing **Ctrl+Page Down**.) This command magnifies the drawing by 400%.

➤ Select the **View** menu's **Zoom** command, and then select **Custom** from the cascade menu. In the Custom Zoom dialog box that appears, select one of the zoom percentages, and then select **OK**.

➤ Pull down the **View** menu, select the **Zoom** command, and then select **Normal Size** from the cascade menu. (Or you can press **Ctrl+Page Up**.) This command returns you to the regular view.

# Getting a Bigger Picture

Instead of seeing less of your drawing, you may prefer to see more of it. This section lets you in on a few Paint techniques for seeing the big (or, at least, bigger) picture.

To expand the picture so it takes up the entire screen, pull down the **View** menu and select the **View Bitmap** command (or press **Ctrl+F**). To return to Paint, click the mouse or press any key.

Alternatively, you can give yourself more elbow room by hiding certain elements of the Paint window:

➤ To hide the Tool Box, deselect the **View** menu's **Tool Box** command (or press **Ctrl+T**).

➤ To hide the Color Box, deselect the **View** menu's **Color Box** command (or press **Ctrl+A**).

➤ To hide the status bar, deselect the **View** menu's **Status Bar** command.

If you'd prefer to keep the Tool Box and Color Box on-screen, you can still create more room by dragging them out of their normal locations. (Be sure to use the margins surrounding the tools or color squares to drag each box.) As you can see in the figure below, this turns the boxes into "floating" windows that sit on top of your drawing.

Use the margins surrounding the tools or color squares to drag each box.

*To see more of your drawing, move the Tool Box and Color Box anywhere you like.*

## The Least You Need to Know

This chapter showed you how to have all sorts of fun with Paint, Windows 95's drawing program. Most of the tools take a bit of getting used to, but even your experiments will probably be a lot of fun! Unfortunately, I didn't have the space to get into some of Paint's wilder features. The Image menu, in particular, is a rich source of wow-your-friends special effects. Feel free to try out the Flip/Rotate, Stretch/Skew, and Invert Colors commands on your own.

# Chapter 16

# Working with a Net: Using Microsoft Backup

**In This Chapter**

➤ Starting Microsoft Backup

➤ Going through the backup steps

➤ Understanding backup sets

➤ Restoring backed up files

➤ Real-world backup tips and strategies designed to help you sleep better at night

These days, there's no shortage of books and magazine articles that list all the possible ways your hard disk can crash. Computer veterans seem to delight in telling war stories about hard disks going down for the count, rogue programs running amok, lightning storm meltdowns, and—more and more often—vicious, disk-trashing viruses that give no quarter to your valuable data.

All these stories lead us to one inescapable conclusion: our precious files are at risk and they need our protection. Fortunately, protecting data doesn't mean investing in an arsenal of semi-automatic weapons and heavy artillery. No, all that's needed is to make backup copies of your data at regular intervals. Now here's the good news: Windows 95 comes equipped with its own backup artillery (oops, I mean accessory) called Microsoft Backup. This chapter takes you through the Backup basics.

# Up an' at 'Em: Starting Backup

As you'll see later on, the Backup program makes backing up your data a relatively painless procedure. You just select the files you want to back up, and the program dutifully copies them to floppy disks. Then, if any disaster occurs, you can use Backup to restore your data safe and sound from the disks. For now, though, let's uncrate Backup so we can get a good look at it.

To start Backup, first open the Start menu by selecting the **Start** button. Then open the **Programs** folder, the **Accessories** folder, and the **System Tools** folder. Take a second or two to catch your breath, and then select **Backup**. (Is panic setting in because Backup is nowhere in sight in your System Tools folder? Don't worry: you just need to install it from your Windows 95 disks. Leap ahead to Chapter 25 and read the section titled "Adding and Removing Windows 95 Components" to find out how it's done.)

When Backup comes up, you see the Welcome to Microsoft Backup dialog box, shown in the following figure. This otherwise-useless dialog box just gives you a not-very-complete overview of the whole backup process. Unless you want to read this drivel every time you crank up Backup, activate the **Don't show this again** check box and select **OK**.

*The Welcome dialog box gives you a backup summary that's a few geese shy of a gaggle.*

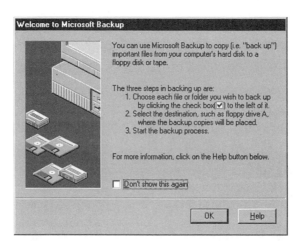

Backup rummages around in your system for a couple of seconds, and then it displays a dialog box (shown in the following figure) telling you it has created a "full backup set" named Full Backup Set (how imaginative). You gotta love it: you just started the program a few moments ago, and already it's throwing some jargon in your face. Here's the quickie explanation: a *backup set* is a collection of files selected for backup (it also includes a couple of other things as well, as you'll soon see). A *full backup set* is a backup set that includes every file on your hard drive. So why don't they just say "everything on your hard drive"? Ah, technogeeks: you can't live with 'em, and you can't (unfortunately) live without 'em.

*Some not-even-close-to-comprehensible mumbo-jumbo about backup sets.*

With that out of the way, activate the **Don't show this again** check box and select **OK** so you won't be pestered by this dialog box again. If you don't have a tape drive installed on your system, another dialog box will appear to let you know that.
Select **OK** to move on.

At last, you end up at the Backup window shown in the following figure. As you can see, it looks a lot like the Explorer window, with a folders list on the left and a contents list on the right.

*The Microsoft Backup window.*

# Backing Up Is Hard to Do: Here's How to Make It Easier

Before getting down to business, you need to ask yourself which files you want to include in the backup. Your first inclination might be to use the infamous Full Backup Set that the Backup program mentioned earlier, just to be safe. The problem with this approach is that even a small hard disk contains enough data to fill a couple of dozen floppy disks. Believe me, shuffling that many disks in and out of your machine every time you do a backup will get old *really* fast. "Sorry, I'd like to do a backup, but I have to delouse my Rottweiler."

Instead, we need to take a "real-world" approach to backups:

➤ The problem with a full backup is that it includes all your program files (the ones that run your applications). Presumably, however, you have these files on disk somewhere, so why include them in a backup? If worse comes to worst, you can always reinstall your programs (and even Windows 95 itself, if necessary).

➤ If you're going to leave out your program files, however, you should seriously consider making backup copies of your program disks. You only have to do it once, and you probably only have to do it for your most important programs.

## Copying Disks Is (ugh) a DOS-Only Deal

For some bizarre reason, neither Explorer nor My Computer have commands that will make copies of floppy disks. Go figure! I'm sorry to have to report that to get the job done you have to run a *DOS* command. Shudder.

But, hey, a person's gotta do what a person's gotta do, right? So here's how it works: first start a DOS session by displaying the Start menu, opening the **Programs** folder, and selecting **MS-DOS Prompt**. When you get to the C:\WINDOWS> prompt, insert the disk you want to copy in the floppy drive. Now enter the following command: **diskcopy *drive: drive:*** (where *drive* is the letter of the floppy drive you're using) and press **Enter**. For example, if the disk is in drive A, type **diskcopy a: a:** and press **Enter** (note that there's a space between the two "a:" thingys). DOS then displays a series of instructions for you to follow. When it's done, type **exit** and press **Enter** to get the heck out of there.

➤ All the energy you put into backing up should go toward protecting your documents because, unlike your programs, these are usually irreplaceable. To make life easier, you should create separate folders to hold only your documents (as described back in Chapter 13). Then you only have to back up those folders.

➤ Take advantage of Backup's two different backup types: full and incremental. *Full* backs up all the files you select; *incremental*, on the other hand, backs up only those files that have changed since the last full backup, which can really cut down on the number of files involved. Your overall backup strategy might look something like this:

1. Perform a full backup of all your documents once a month or so.

2. If you do most of your work in one or two programs, do a full backup of these programs' documents every week or two.

3. Do an incremental backup of modified files every couple of days (although you might think about backing up your really important documents every day).

➤ If, after all this, you still have a few dozen megabytes or more to back up, forget floppies altogether and invest in a tape drive. They're a little pricey, but they can hold hundreds of megabytes of data, and they do it all while you're doing lunch.

# Backup's Five-Step Procedure

The first dialog box you saw told you that backing up requires three steps, but that's not quite true. "Oh, great, now Windows is lying to me. And after all we've been through together!" It's sad, but true, because it can actually take as many as five steps when you're just starting out:

1. Select the files you want to back up.

2. Select the type of backup (full or incremental).

3. Select the drive you want to use for the backup.

4. Save your backup set.

5. Start the backup.

The next few sections take you through the details for each step.

## Step 1: Selecting the Files to Back Up

I mentioned earlier that the Backup window resembles the Explorer window. There's one important difference, however: in the Backup window, all the disk drives, folders, and files have a check box next to them, as you can see in the following figure.

*To make backup selection easier, Backup displays check boxes beside your drives, folders, and files.*

Click here to select an entire drive.

Click here to select an entire folder.

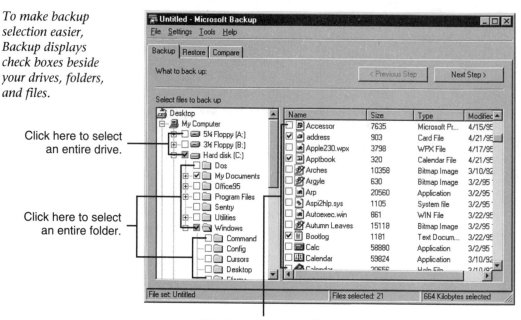

Click here to select a file.

The general idea is that you activate the check box for each drive, folder, and disk you want to include in the backup. (You activate the check boxes either by clicking on them, or by highlighting the disk, folder, or file and pressing the **Spacebar**.) Here are the specifics:

➤ To back up all the files on a disk drive, activate the disk drive's check box.

➤ To back up all the files inside a folder, activate the folder's check box. (For example, see the My Documents folder in the figure shown above.) Now you see why it's so convenient to include all your documents in a single folder.

➤ To back up a file, activate the file's check box.

## Why the Grayed Check Boxes?

If you take a close look at the figure shown above, you'll notice that the check boxes for Hard disk (C:) and the Windows folder have a gray background. The gray tells you that only some of the disk's or folder's contents have been selected for backup.

## Step 2: Selecting the Type of Backup

As I said earlier, Backup can perform two kinds of backups:

**Full**   Backs up all the files you selected in step 1.

**Incremental**   Of all the files you selected in step 1, this backs up only those files that have changed since the last full backup.

To select the backup type you want to use, pull down the **Settings** menu and select the **Options** command. In the Settings - Options dialog box that appears, select the **Backup** tab (see the figure below). Choose either the **Full** or **Incremental** option button, and then select **OK**.

*Use the Backup tab to choose either a Full or an Incremental backup.*

## Step 3: Selecting the Backup Destination

Once you've selected all the documents you want to back up, select the **Next Step >** button. Backup redisplays the window as shown in the following figure. You use this window to highlight the drive or folder where you want to place the backup copies of your documents. You'll usually select a floppy disk drive or a tape drive (if you have one). Note, as well, that the < Previous Step button is active in this window. You can use it to go back and make adjustments to your file selections at any time.

*Use this window to specify where you want your documents backed up.*

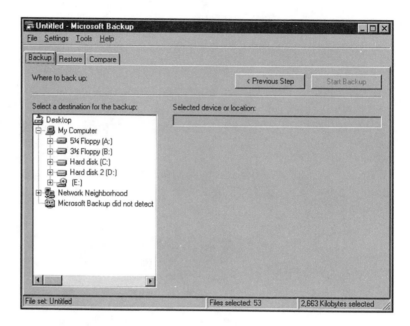

## Step 4: Saving Your Backup Set

Together, the files you selected in step 1, the backup type you selected in step 2, and the destination you selected in step 3 make up your *backup set*. Because this is a combination you'll likely use quite often, it's a good idea to preserve your selections by saving your backup set.

To do that, pull down the **File** menu and select the **Save** command (or press **Ctrl+S**). In the **File name** text box, enter a descriptive name for the backup set (such as Documents only - incremental), and then select **Save**.

**Reusing a Backup Set**
Once you've saved a backup set, reusing it in the future is easy. Just select the **File** menu's **Open File Set** command, select the backup set in the Open dialog box that appears, and then select **Open**.

## Step 5: Doing the Backup Thing

Well, at long last, we're just about ready to roll. Here are the steps to follow to back up your data:

1. Place a floppy disk in the drive you selected.

2. Select the **Start Backup** button. Backup displays the Backup Set Label dialog box, as shown in the following figure.

3. Your files aren't backed up individually. Instead, they're combined into a single file, and that file is backed up. Use the Backup Set Label dialog box to enter a name for this file, and then select **OK**.

*Use this dialog box to enter a name for the backup file.*

Enter a name for the backup set here.

4. If the disk you're using is full, Backup asks if you want to erase the data. If that's not what you want, remove the disk and insert another one. Select **Yes** when you're ready to go. The Backup dialog box appears to keep you posted on the progress of the backup (see the figure below).

*This dialog box shows you how much of the backup has been completed.*

5. Depending on the number and size of the files you selected, Backup occasionally prompts you to enter more disks. When it does, insert the new disk and select **OK**. When you're done with a disk, you should label it for future reference (e.g., Backup Disk #1).

6. Backup displays a dialog box to let you know when it's finished. Select **OK** to return to the Backup dialog box, and then select **OK** again to return to the Backup window.

# Backup DOs and DON'Ts

Here are a few more hints and suggestions to make backing up easier and safer:

Do:

➤ Decide on a backup strategy and stick to it. Otherwise, you'll fall victim to one of computerdom's strictest laws: hard disks only crash when they contain priceless, irreplaceable data that isn't backed up.

➤ Use backup sets to configure the program quickly.

➤ Run the ScanDisk program before a major backup to look for any problems. (For the lowdown on using ScanDisk, read the section in Chapter 17 titled "Avoiding Hard Disk Hard Times: ScanDisk.")

➤ Have your pet spayed or neutered.

**Don't:**

➤ Use 5$^{1}$/$_{4}$-inch disks if you don't have to. With high-density 3$^{1}$/$_{2}$-inch disks, you not only get a little more data on each disk, you also get the added safety of a sturdy case.

➤ Keep all your backup disks in one place. If a thief happens upon them, you'll be out of luck. Some folks go as far as keeping a copy in an offsite location such as a safety deposit box.

➤ Use low-priced, no-name disks for your backups. Stick with high-quality disks, and you'll sleep better at night.

➤ Be lazy or put it off. Back up your files now!

# Restoring Your Data

If some unforeseen disaster should occur, you'll need to restore your data from the backups. Here are the steps to follow:

1. Start Microsoft Backup, as described earlier in this chapter.

2. In the Backup window, select the **Restore** tab.

3. Insert the first floppy disk from the backup set.

4. Use the **Restore from** list to select the floppy drive. The name of the backup set should appear in the box on the right side of the window (see the following figure).

5. If there are multiple backup sets, select the one you want to use.

6. Select the **Next Step >** button. The window changes to show the folders and files in the selected backup set.

7. Use the check boxes to choose which folders or files you want to restore.

8. Select the **Start Restore** button. Backup restores the files.

9. Backup displays a dialog box to let you know when it's finished. Select **OK** to return to the Restore dialog box, and then select **OK** again to return to the Backup window.

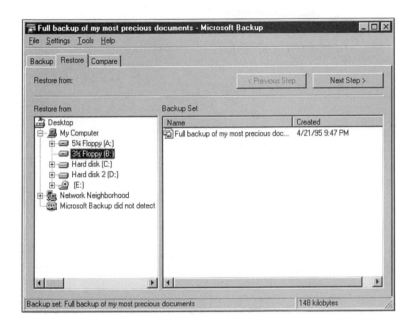

*Use the Restore screen to select the backup file that contains the files you want to restore.*

# The Least You Need to Know

This chapter showed you how to use Microsoft Backup to achieve the peace of mind that comes when you know your precious data is safe and sound. As a reminder, here's a recap of the basic five-step backup procedure:

1. Select the files you want to back up.

2. Select the type of backup (full or incremental).

3. Select the drive you want to use for the backup.

4. Save your backup set.

5. Start the backup.

To put your worried mind even more at ease, the next chapter presents a few more of Windows 95's system tools, a couple of which can scope out and repair problems on your hard disk.

# Routine Maintenance: The System Tools

As we work with our computers, we usually focus on just the external appendages that we can readily eyeball: the mouse and keyboard, the monitor, maybe a floppy disk or two. But the old phrase "It's what's inside that counts" has no more apt a subject than that big beige box squatting impassively on your desk. An internal tour of your machine would reveal some crucial digital anatomy, including the processor that runs the whole show (that's the *386*, *486*, or *Pentium* everyone's always talking about), the memory chips that give your programs room to roam, and the cooling fan that keeps everything from melting into a silicon puddle.

But, for my money, the most critical component inside my computer's case is by far the hard disk. Processors process, memory chips remember, and cooling fans cool, and each one can be replaced or upgraded without a moment's thought. But the hard disk is where you store your program and document files. Without a hard disk, you have no way to run Windows 95 and all its applications, and your computer becomes simply a two-thousand-dollar paperweight.

This chapter focuses on three tools that help you get the most out of your precious hard disk. ScanDisk watches your hard disk for signs of trouble, Disk Defragmenter keeps your files and folders shipshape, and DriveSpace performs the impressive feat of effectively doubling the size of your hard disk!

**Check This Out...**

**Installing the Tools** As you work through this chapter, if you find that one or more of these programs aren't installed on your system, you'll need to load them from your original Windows 95 disks (or the Windows 95 CD-ROM). Flip to Chapter 25 and read the section "Adding and Removing Windows 95 Components" to find out how it's done.

# Avoiding Hard Disk Hard Times: ScanDisk

Computers are temperamental, finicky beasts that often seem all too eager to act strangely or to give up the ghost altogether. Most computer components can be easily (albeit expensively) replaced if they head south. But if your hard disk goes haywire, you may lose irreplaceable data (you might lose a few hairs, too, and gain a shiny, new ulcer).

Of course, as a responsible practitioner of the arcane art of computing, you *do* perform regular backups of your documents, right? I thought so. However, replacing a hard disk, reinstalling and reconfiguring your programs, and then restoring your data from the backups is a real pain in the you-know-what. To put it off for as long as possible, you can use Windows 95's ScanDisk accessory to give your hard disk regular checkups.

When you have a physical exam, your family doctor pokes you and prods you and generally gives you the once-over. In the same way, ScanDisk performs a battery of tests on your hard disk to make sure it's up to snuff and that there are no chinks in its electronic armor. If it finds any minor problems, ScanDisk lets you know and offers to fix them for you on the spot. If it finds a more serious problem, the program warns you that hard disk failure is, if not imminent, at least a possibility in the near future.

## Getting ScanDisk Started

As you'll see, the great thing about ScanDisk is that it's so easy to use. For now, though, let's just get it started. Begin by selecting the **Start** button to display the Start menu.

Then open the **Programs** folder, open the **Accessories** folder, and open the **System Tools** folder. Select **ScanDisk**, and you'll see the ScanDisk window shown in the following figure.

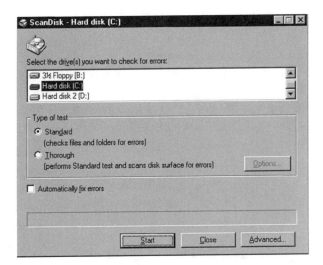

*Use the ScanDisk window to select a disk and get the show on the road.*

### Avoid DOS 6's ScanDisk and Other "Disk Doctors"

DOS 6.2 came with its own version of ScanDisk, but you should avoid it like the plague. Why? Because the DOS ScanDisk won't be able to figure out some of the Windows 95-specific stuff on your hard disk, and it may report errors where none exist (or, even worse, try to fix them!). You should also steer clear of similar utilities from other companies—such as the Norton Disk Doctor—that were designed in the pre-Windows 95 era.

## Selecting a Disk to Scan

ScanDisk's Select the drive(s) you want to check for errors list is where you choose the drive or drives you want to check. The program automatically selects the hard disk where Windows 95 is installed, but you can select another hard disk (if you have one) or even one of your floppy disks.

To select another disk, just highlight it in the list. (If you're going to select a floppy disk, first make sure there's a disk in the drive.)

## Selecting the Type of Test

ScanDisk is no mere one-trick pony. It is, in fact, fully capable of performing not one, but *two* types of tests: Standard or Thorough. Which of the two you choose depends on how much time you have to kill, how patient you are, and how paranoid you are about your hard disk having a nervous breakdown.

The **Standard** test runs various checks to ensure the integrity of your hard disk's files and folders. It shouldn't take more than a few seconds to perform this test. The **Thorough** test delves deeper and checks not only your hard disk's files and folders, but also the surface of the hard disk itself. Depending on the size of your hard disk, this test can take 15 minutes or more.

Which one should you choose? Well, if you've never run ScanDisk before, you should probably run a Thorough test just for the extra peace of mind it'll bring. After that, you could set up a ScanDisk schedule (assuming, of course, you're a schedule setter-upper type of person). For example, you could run a Standard test every day and run a Thorough test once a week.

**Check This Out...**

**Use ScanDisk If Windows 95 Crashes and Burns** Windows 95 was designed to be more robust and to crash less often than its previous incarnations. However, if Windows 95 does go wonky on you, reboot your computer and run a Standard ScanDisk test when you get back to Windows 95. This should weed out any lingering bad effects from the crash.

## Scanning a Disk with ScanDisk

Okay, you're almost ready for action. Your last remaining chore is to decide if you want ScanDisk to automatically fix any errors it finds. This is handy if, for example, you want to perform the lengthy Thorough test and you'd like to head off to a three-martini lunch while it's running. To have ScanDisk fix any errors, activate the **Automatically fix errors** check box.

To commence the ScanDisk checkup, select the **Start** button. ScanDisk begins nosing around in your hard disk's private parts and displays its progress at the bottom of the window. If ScanDisk finds a problem (and you didn't tell it to fix errors automatically), a dialog box appears that gives you several options. In the example shown in the following figure, ScanDisk has found some "lost file fragments" (aw, how sad) and wants to know what to do with them.

In this case, it's best to just chuck these fragments. So select the **Discard lost file fragment(s) and recover disk space** option and select **OK**. If you're really not sure what to do, you could try selecting the **More Info** button to display a dialog box with a few more facts. (Select **OK** when you're done with this dialog box.) If that still doesn't help, just select **OK** and let ScanDisk figure things out for itself.

*ScanDisk displays a dialog box like this one when it finds an error.*

When ScanDisk's labors are complete, it displays the Results dialog box to let you know what happened. This dialog box is jam-packed with stats and numbers that are sure to warm the cockles of nerdy hearts everywhere. Nod your head knowingly and select **Close** to return to the ScanDisk window.

# Putting Your Hard Disk Affairs in Order with Disk Defragmenter

You can use Windows 95's Disk Defragmenter program to *defragment* the files on your hard disk. Defragmenting sounds pretty serious, but it's just Windows 95's way of tidying up a messy hard disk. It puts your files in order and does a few other neat-freak chores. (Don't worry though: Disk Defragmenter doesn't change the contents of the files, and they'll still appear in the same places when you look at them in Explorer or My Computer.)

## A Plain English Explanation of Defragmenting

Why bother with this arcane defragmenting business? Well, imagine, if you will, a particularly disorganized household where, say, the cutlery and dishes are scattered throughout the house. The knives are in the basement, the spoons are in the den, the plates are out on the porch, and so on. Imagine how long it would take you to set the table for dinner if you had to run around to all these different locations to get what you needed. Obviously, storing these items in one place (the kitchen, silly) would reduce table-setting times to a fraction of what they were before.

Defragmenting does the same thing for your files. You see, Windows 95 is, to be blunt about it, a real pig. When it stores files on your hard drive, it often just throws them anywhere it can find space. This is a simple way to work (Windows 95 can be a bit dim at times, so it likes to keep its life as simple as possible), but it often means that pieces of your files are scattered willy-nilly around your hard disk. And the more pieces there are, the longer it's going to take to load the file the next time you want to use it. After a while, this can get so bad that your hard drive slows to a crawl.

## Clusters, FATs, and Other Useless Terminology

Windows 95 stores hard disk files in fixed-sized chunks called *clusters*. The size of each cluster depends on the disk, but 4,096 bytes and 8,192 bytes are typical sizes. Because most files are larger than 4,096 (or even 8,192) bytes, each file is divided into many different clusters.

Windows 95 keeps track of all the clusters on a disk by means of the *file allocation table* (or FAT for short). When Windows 95 needs to store a file, it looks at the FAT to determine where the empty clusters are, and then just starts storing clusters wherever it can find room. So it ends up putting part of the file here, another chunk there, and so on. The result is a *fragmented* file. Disk Defragmenter's job is to rearrange everything so that each file's clusters are reunited.

# Doing the Defragmenting Thing

Before you use Disk Defragmenter, you need to do a little preparation yourself:

➤ As described in Chapter 12, you should delete any files from your hard disk that you don't need. Defragmenting junk files only slows down the whole process.

➤ Check for hard disk errors by running Windows 95's ScanDisk program as described earlier in this chapter. You should probably run a Thorough test just to be safe.

When you've done these preliminary chores and are ready to use Disk Defragmenter, follow these steps:

1. Display the Start menu, open the **Programs** folder, open the **Accessories** folder, open the **System Tools** folder, and select **Disk Defragmenter**. The Select Drive dialog box appears so you can select the drive you want to defragment.

2. Use the **Which drive do you want to defragment?** drop-down list to choose a drive, and then select **OK**. Disk Defragmenter analyzes the fragmentation of your files, and if it's not too bad, it displays the dialog box shown in the following figure.

*Disk Defragmenter lets you know if your hard disk isn't too messy.*

3. If you want to go ahead with the defragment, select **Start**. Disk Defragmenter starts tidying up your hard disk and displays a dialog box that lets you view its progress.

4. If you'd like to see a visual representation of the Disk Defragmenter's labors, select the **Show Details** button. The window that appears looks something like the one shown below. To find out what all those squares mean, select the **Legend** button.

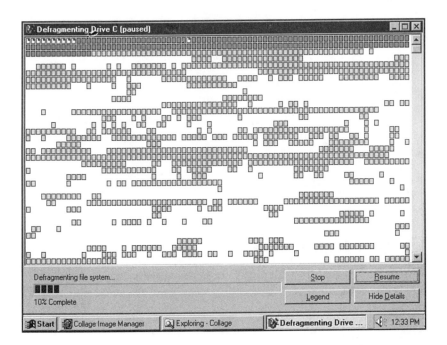

*Select the Show Details button to watch Disk Defragmenter do its thing.*

5. When Disk Defragmenter finally finishes its chores (it may take 10–15 minutes depending on the size of your disk, how cluttered it is, and how fast your computer is), your computer beeps, and a dialog box appears to tell you the "defragmentation" is complete and ask if you want to defragment another drive. If you do, select **Yes**. Otherwise, select **No** to exit Disk Defragmenter.

## How Often Should I Defragment?

How often you defragment your hard disk depends on how often you use your computer. If you use it every day, you should run Disk Defragmenter about once a week. If your computer doesn't get heavy use, you probably only need to run Disk Defragmenter once a month or so.

# Doubling Disk Space with DriveSpace

Although hard disks have been getting bigger over the years, they haven't kept pace with the ever-fatter programs developers have been throwing at us. As a result, we have a new corollary to Murphy's Law: No matter how huge your hard disk seems today, you'll wish it were twice that big six months from now.

But hey, why wait six months when you can nearly double the size of your hard disk right now? If you have Windows 95, you can do just that with the gnarly new DriveSpace program.

"Double the size of my hard disk?!" Well, okay, DriveSpace doesn't actually make your hard disk twice as big. Instead, it uses something called *disk compression* to make all the files on the disk take up less room. In most cases, DriveSpace can coerce the files into taking up about half the space they normally do. This means you can store twice as much data on the hard disk, so its size is effectively (if not actually) doubled.

The real trick, though, is that you can still use your files as though nothing has ever been done to them. They still have the same names, and they still appear in the same folders. They look the same, act the same, and, for all intents and purposes, *are* the same.

## How Does Disk Compression Work?

Disk compression sounds like real pie-in-the-sky stuff, but it actually works. If you'd like to know how it performs its magic, here's a look at DriveSpace's inner workings.

Disk compression is based on an obscenely complex mathematical algorithm (called the Lempel-Ziv algorithm) that searches a file for redundant character strings and replaces them with small tokens. Let's look at a simple example. Consider the following phrase:

> *It was the best of times, it was the worst of times, it was the age of wisdom, it was the age of foolishness.*

To compress this quotation, the program starts at the beginning and looks for at least two consecutive characters that it has already seen. In this case, the first such match is the *t* and the following space at the end of the word *best*. This matches the *t* and the space that follows at the end of *It*. So the program replaces the match with a token, as shown here. (I've used an asterisk to represent the various tokens.)

> *I\*was the bes\*of times, it was the worst of times, it was the age of wisdom, it was the age of foolishness.*

Not very impressive so far. But the program chugs along finding small redundancies (for example, the *es* in *times* matches the *es* seen earlier in *best*), and then it hits the jackpot:

larger phrases such as *it was the*, *of times*, and *age of* are repeated and can all be replaced by tokens. In the end, you end up with something that looks like this:

*I\*\*\*b\*\*\*\*\*\*wors\*\*\*\*\*\*w\*dom\*\*\*\*\*\*fool\*hn\*s.*

It looks weird, but it's less than half the size of the original. To decompress such data, all the program has to do is translate the tokens back to their original form. This is all handled by a mathematical formula, and it's quite safe.

## Taking DriveSpace for a Test Drive

What DriveSpace does is complicated, but, fortunately, using the program isn't. As you did with Disk Defragmenter, you should do some preliminary chores before starting:

➤ Use Explorer or My Computer to toss out any junk files hanging around.

➤ Run a Thorough ScanDisk test to weed out any drive errors.

➤ Back up your important documents just in case some natural disaster occurs in the middle of the procedure. (For the basics of Backup, see Chapter 16.)

When you're all set, display the Start menu, open the **Programs** folder, open the **Accessories** folder, open the **System Tools** folder, and select **DriveSpace**. After a second or two, the DriveSpace window appears so you can pick out the drive you want to work with.

Use the Drives on this computer list to select the drive you want to compress, then pull down the **Drive** menu and select **Compress**. DriveSpace examines the drive and displays the Compress a Drive dialog box that gives you an estimate of what the drive's new capacity will be. As you can see in the following figure, in this case DriveSpace increases the capacity of my hard disk from about 232 megabytes to about 436 megabytes—yep, almost double.

*You'll see a dialog box like this one if your hard disk size is 256 MB or less.*

Techno Talk
blah blah
blah bla
ah bl
b

## Some Technical Mumbo-Jumbo About How DriveSpace Handles Larger Hard Disks

If the size of your hard disk is greater than 256 megabytes, DriveSpace gets a little more complicated. When DriveSpace compresses your hard disk, it doesn't just shrink each file separately. Instead, it combines all your files into one monster file and compresses that. This file is called a *compressed volume file* (or CVF, for short). If you open up, say, Explorer, you won't see the CVF, however. Instead, you'll just see the normal contents of your hard drive.

If your hard disk is larger than 256 megabytes, however, DriveSpace has to divide the disk into a compressed part (the CVF) and everything else (the uncompressed part). In Explorer, the CVF appears as drive C, and the uncompressed part (which is called the *host drive*) appears as drive H. (Actually, if the host drive has less than 2 megabytes of free space, it won't appear in Explorer at all.)

Select the **Start** button in the Compress a Drive dialog box, and another dialog box appears asking if you're sure you want to compress the drive. (This dialog box also gives you the option of backing up your files.) If you're sure, select **Compress Now**. DriveSpace checks the drive for errors (yours should pass with flying colors because you've already run ScanDisk) and then starts compressing. When it's done (it takes quite a while for larger hard disks), you're returned to the DriveSpace window.

# The Least You Need to Know

This chapter showed you how to wield three of the Windows 95 system tools. You learned how to use ScanDisk to perform a checkup on your hard disk, you saw how Disk Defragmenter can keep your hard disk's hatches battened down, and you learned how to increase the capacity of your hard disk with DriveSpace.

The next chapter continues our look at the multitude of Windows 95 accessories as I tell you about Notepad, Calculator, and even a couple of games: FreeCell and Minesweeper.

# Chapter 18

# Everything But the Kitchen Sink: More Accessories

> **In This Chapter**
>
> ➤ Working with Notepad and Calculator
>
> ➤ Setting your system's date and time
>
> ➤ Using Briefcase to tote files around
>
> ➤ Keeping your affairs in order with Calendar and Cardfile
>
> ➤ Spending some quality leisure time with FreeCell and Minesweeper
>
> ➤ A veritable Windows 95 accessories extravaganza

One of the first things I learned in my freshman Economics class (besides the fact that I was lousy at economics) was that there's no such thing as a "free lunch." So far, we've proved that the economists are wrong. Windows 95 users get a free lunch that's a multi-course meal. We've ingested WordPad, Paint, and Backup, as well as the system tools ScanDisk, Disk Defragmenter, and DriveSpace. That's a lot, but I hope you still have a little room for a few more treats. In particular, this chapter serves up eight—count 'em, eight—more accessories to whet your appetite: Notepad, Calculator, Date/Time, Briefcase, Calendar, Cardfile, FreeCell, and Minesweeper. Bon appétit!

Depending on how Windows 95 was installed on your machine, one or more of these programs may not appear on your Start menu. That's not a problem, though, because you can easily add them from your original Windows 95 disks. You can find the instructions for doing so in Chapter 25, in the section "Adding and Removing Windows 95 Components."

# Performing Text File Tasks with Notepad

Back in Chapter 14, you learned how to wield WordPad's word processing tools. But not all the documents you come across will have (or need) fancy character and paragraph formatting. Many documents are pure text files, which means they contain only the letters, numbers, and symbols you can peck out on your keyboard. Although you can use WordPad to work with these simpler document specimens, it's probably overkill. Therefore, Windows 95 comes with an accessory that's designed specifically for text files: Notepad.

## Getting Notepad Up and Running

To get Notepad on the desktop, first select the **Start** button to display the Start menu. Then open the **Programs** folder and the **Accessories** folder, and select **Notepad**. The figure below shows the Notepad window that appears.

*Notepad's window redefines "Spartan."*

There's not much to see, is there? That's in keeping with Notepad's nature. It's just a simple tool for making quick edits to text-only documents. No one expects you to use it to write your next novel.

## Some Notepad Notes

The austere layout of Notepad's window is matched by its frugal collection of commands and features. Check out the File and Edit menus, for example, and you'll see that, for the most part, they contain only the standard commands available in most programs: New, Open, Save, Save As, and Print on the File menu; Undo, Cut, Copy, Paste, and Delete on the Edit menu. Yawn. (I covered all of these commands back in Chapter 8.)

However, Notepad is not without its unique features and quirks, the most important of which I've summarized in the following list.

➤ Notepad assumes the documents you'll be opening are text files with names that end with .TXT. There are, however, lots of text files that don't have this extension. To see these other files in the Open dialog box, select the **All Files (\*.\*)** option in the **Files of type** drop-down list.

➤ One of Notepad's biggest limitations is that it chokes on documents that are over a certain size. If you try to open such a file, you'll see the dialog box shown below. In this case, you'll probably want to select **Yes** to open the file in WordPad.

*Some documents are too big for Notepad's britches.*

➤ The File menu's Print command doesn't display a Print dialog box. Instead, it just fires the document right to the printer without even so much as a how-do-you-do.

➤ If you hit the right edge of the window as you're typing, Notepad may not wrap your text onto the next line. It'll just keep you on the same line for a thousand characters or so! To avoid this bizarre (and annoying) behavior, pull down the **Edit** menu and activate the **Word Wrap** command.

# Figuring Out Calculator

Forget your fingers! Windows 95 gives you an easier way to add things up: the Calculator. To crank it up, display the Start menu, open **Programs**, open **Accessories**, and select **Calculator**. In no time flat, you see the Calculator window shown in the figure below. As you can see, Calculator looks just like your basic calculator. It won't do rocket science, but it's good for simple operations such as addition, subtraction, multiplication, and division.

*The standard view of the Calculator window.*

## Working with Calculator

Using Calculator is a no-brainer. You just click on the appropriate numbers and operators, and then click on the equals sign (=) to see the answer in the readout below the menu bar. For example, to add 2 and 3, you do the following:

1. Click on the **2** button. A "2" appears in the readout.

2. Click on the **+** button.

3. Click on the **3** button. A "3" appears in the readout.

4. Click on the **=** button. A "5" appears in the readout.

You can even use your keyboard if you want. Simply use the numbers and operators from the numeric keypad (make sure you have Num Lock on, though). To see the results of a calculation, you can either press the equals sign (=) or the **Enter** key.

## The Scary-Looking Scientific Calculator

Calculator also includes a Scientific calculator that you display by pulling down the **View** menu and selecting the **Scientific** command. This scary-looking thing is sure to warm the hearts of the tall forehead types who actually *enjoy* using things like hexadecimal numbers. The rest of us can simply shudder once or twice and then scurry back to the safety of the Standard calculator (by selecting the **View** menu's **Standard** command).

## Doing Time with Date/Time

As you know, Windows 95 displays the time on the right-hand side of the taskbar. But here are a couple of things you may not know:

➤ You can also use the taskbar to display the current date.

➤ You can adjust both the time and the date.

Displaying the date is a piece of cake: just point your mouse at the time on the taskbar, and a second or two later, Windows 95 pops up a banner that contains the date (see the figure below).

*Point your mouse at the time to display the date.*

Adjusting the time and/or date requires a bit more effort. For openers, display the **Start** menu, open the **Settings** folder, and select **Control Panel**. When the Control Panel window appears, double-click on the **Date/Time** icon (or use the arrow keys to highlight the icon, and then press **Enter**). Windows 95 displays the Date/Time Properties dialog box shown in the figure below.

Use the controls in the **Date** and **Time** boxes to adjust the date and time, and then select **OK** to put the new settings into effect.

**A Faster Way to Get There**
To bypass the Control Panel middleman and get to the Date/Time Properties dialog box directly, double-click on the time in the taskbar.

*Use the Date/Time Properties dialog box to adjust the current date and time.*

# Taking Files on the Road with Briefcase

Windows 95, unlike any of its predecessors, recognizes an important fact of notebook computing life: your notebook often has to use documents from your desktop machine. Windows 95's Briefcase feature makes it a breeze to swap documents between a desktop and a notebook (provided, of course, that both machines are running Windows 95) because it keeps track of which files are changed. Updating one system or the other takes only a couple of mouse clicks or keystrokes. This section introduces you to Briefcase and shows you how to use it to keep your desktop and notebook in perfect harmony.

## Briefcase: From Road Worrier to Road Warrior

Briefcase is a special folder on your computer that you can use to hold the documents you transfer between your desktop and notebook computers. Instead of always copying individual documents back and forth, you usually just work with the Briefcase folder. The real advantage of using Briefcase, however, is that it synchronizes the documents on both machines automatically. If you work on a few documents on your notebook, for example, Windows 95 can figure out which ones are different and then lets you update the desktop machine by running a simple command. There's no guesswork and no chance of copying a file to the wrong folder; no muss, no fuss.

Okay, let's put Briefcase to work. The next few sections take you through the whole Briefcase show, from go to whoa.

## Step 1: Load Up the Briefcase

Once you've decided which documents you want to work with on your notebook, use Explorer or My Computer to copy the documents into the Briefcase folder.

When you copy a file to the Briefcase for the first time, the Welcome to Windows Briefcase dialog box appears. After you've read the brief overview of Briefcase, select **Finish** to get rid of it.

Once you've copied all your documents to the Briefcase, insert a disk into one of your desktop computer's floppy disk drives and then use the **Copy** command to copy the Briefcase folder to the floppy disk. (I told you how to copy folders back in Chapter 13, in the "Copying and Moving Folders" section.)

## Step 2: Copy the Files to the Notebook's Briefcase

Your next task is to get the files onto the notebook computer. To make life easier, we'll copy them into the notebook's Briefcase. Begin by inserting the disk containing the desktop Briefcase into the notebook's floppy disk drive. Using Explorer or My Computer, display the notebook floppy drive and open the My Briefcase folder. You'll see a window similar to the one shown below.

*The floppy copy of the desktop Briefcase.*

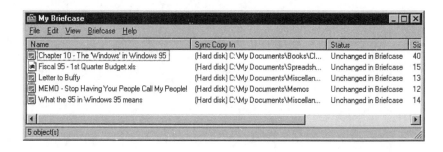

In the My Briefcase window, select the files you want to work with. (You'll usually want to work with all the documents in the Briefcase; if so, press **Ctrl+A** to easily select everything.) Finally, copy the files to the notebook's My Briefcase folder.

## Step 3: Work with the Files on the Notebook

With the documents now safely stowed in the notebook's Briefcase, you can go ahead and work on the files. The easiest thing to do is just work on the files directly from the notebook's My Briefcase folder.

## Step 4: Update the Briefcase on the Floppy Disk

When you've completed your notebook labors, the documents you worked with are out of sync with the documents in the floppy disk Briefcase. So your next chore is to update the Briefcase on the floppy disk.

Since the modified documents are in the notebook's Briefcase, you first have to display the notebook's My Briefcase folder. Then pull down the **Briefcase** menu and select the **Update All** command. Windows 95 examines the documents, compares them with the ones in the floppy disk Briefcase, and displays the Update My Briefcase dialog box to show you which documents need updating (see the following figure). Select the **Update** button, and Windows 95 updates the floppy disk Briefcase with the modified documents.

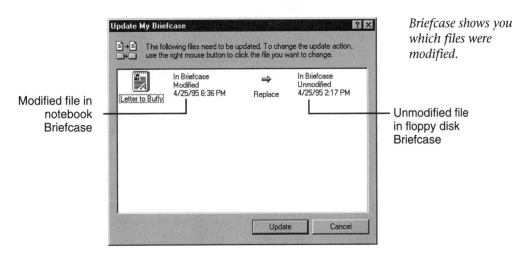

Modified file in
notebook
Briefcase

*Briefcase shows you which files were modified.*

Unmodified file
in floppy disk
Briefcase

## Step 5: Update the Briefcase on the Desktop

When you get back to the office, slip the floppy disk into your desktop and open the disk's My Briefcase folder. As you can see in the following figure, Briefcase shows you which documents were modified by displaying **Needs updating** in the Status column.

*Files that have been changed display a "Needs updating" message in the Status column.*

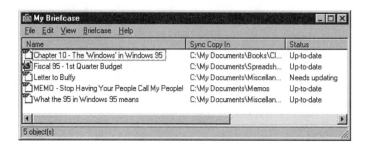

Pull down the **Briefcase** menu and select **Update All**. This time, Windows 95 compares the contents of the floppy disk Briefcase with the original files on your desktop computer. If it finds any discrepancies, it displays the Update My Briefcase dialog box again. Select **Update**, and Windows 95 perfectly synchronizes your desktop and notebook files.

# Making a Date with Calendar

It's almost redundant to say that modern life is "busy." People are working more than ever and they're cramming more and more activities into their so-called "leisure" hours. So the question is, how do those of us who are organizationally challenged stay on top of our things-to-do-places-to-go-have-your-people-call-my-people lives?

With Windows' Calendar accessory! It's a sort of electronic secretary that, while it won't get coffee for you, will at least help you keep your affairs in order. Calendar is a simple electronic day-planner you can use to keep track of appointments, meetings, and other commitments. So, whether you have a date and you can't be late, or you have a rendezvous you need to remember, Calendar can handle it.

To start Calendar, you need to display the Start menu, open the **Programs** folder, open the **Accessories** folder, and then select **Calendar**. You'll see the window shown in the following figure.

**3.1**

**A Calendar Caveat**

Calendar is a holdover from the previous version of Windows, so if you're not upgrading, you won't find Calendar no matter how hard you look. Sorry about that. Also, because Calendar wasn't designed specifically for Windows 95, you can't assign long file names to Calendar documents, and the Open and Save As dialog boxes are the boring, old-style versions from Windows 3.1.

# Checking Out the Calendar Window

As you can see, the Calendar window sports the standard window features that you've come to know and love: a menu bar, a title bar, Minimize, Maximize, and Close buttons, and so on. The rest of the window is taken up by a work area that can display two different views: the Day view or the Month view.

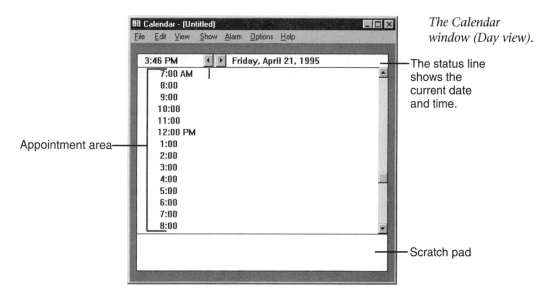

*The Calendar window (Day view).*

## The Day View

The Day view is the window you see when you first start Calendar. It's set up to look like a typical appointment book displaying a daily schedule in hourly intervals, called the *Appointment area* (see the previous figure). Calendar opens with the current date, showing times from 7:00 AM to 8:00 PM. As you navigate the appointment area, an insertion point cursor moves with you to show you where you are. This insertion point also marks the spot where any text you enter will appear.

## The Month View

If you like to plan ahead, try working in Calendar's Month view. You can get there from here (i.e., from the Day view) by pulling down the **View** menu and selecting the **Month** command. (You can also display the Month view either by double-clicking on the date in the status line or by pressing **F9**.)

For the Month view, Calendar replaces the appointment area with a bird's-eye view of the entire month. The current date is highlighted. To return to Day view, you can either open the **View** menu and select the **Day** command, double-click on a date, or press **F8**.

## Navigating Calendar

The following table summarizes the techniques you can use when working in either Day or Month view.

**Navigation Techniques for Calendar's Day and Month Views**

| To Move To... | Do This... |
| --- | --- |
| Another time/date | Click on the time or date or use the arrow keys. |
| The next day/month | Select the **Show** menu's **Next** command, or click on the right arrow in the Status line, or press **Ctrl+Page Down**. |
| The previous day/month | Select the **Show** menu's **Previous** command, or click on the left arrow in the Status line, or press **Ctrl+Page Up**. |
| Today's date | Select the **Show** menu's **Today** command. |
| Any date | Select the **Show** menu's **Date** command or press **F4**, enter the date in MM/DD/YY format, and then select **OK**. |
| The scratch pad | Click inside the scratch pad or press **Tab**. |

## Setting Your Social Schedule: Entering Appointments

Got a party to plan, a meeting to make, or a lunch to linger over? The gadabouts, hobnobbers, and other social butterflies in the crowd will like how easy Calendar makes it to schedule these and other appointments.

To enter appointments, first select the day you want to work with using either the Day view or the Month view. (If you use the Month view, be sure to return to the Day view for entering the appointments.) Next, move the insertion point to the time you want to schedule the appointment. Then simply type a brief description of the appointment. The following figure shows a Calendar file with a few appointments added.

*A Calendar file
with some example
appointments.*

## Adding Notes in the Scratch Pad

The scratch pad is handy for leaving daily notes or reminders to yourself. Just click inside
the scratch pad area (or press **Tab**) to move the insertion point into the scratch pad, and
start typing. Calendar lets you add up to three lines of text, and automatically wraps your
text from one line to the next. When you're done, click inside the appointment area (or
press **Tab** again).

## Keeping Track of Cardfile

Organized people do such things as keep their recipes in a recipe box on those 3x5 cards
and their business cards in alphabetical order in a business card file. If you'd like to be
more organized but you don't know if you've got it in you, don't worry; you can get
Windows 95's Cardfile accessory to do it for you. This section will show you how. (Like
Calendar, Cardfile is an older Windows 3.1 program, so you won't have it on your system
if you're not upgrading to Windows 95 from a previous version.)

To start Cardfile, select the **Start** button, open the **Programs** folder, open the **Accessories**
folder, and select **Cardfile**. Windows 95 displays the Cardfile window with a blank card.
(In the figure shown below, I've jumped the gun a little and added a few cards to give you
a better idea of what to expect.)

*The Cardfile window with a few cards already added.*

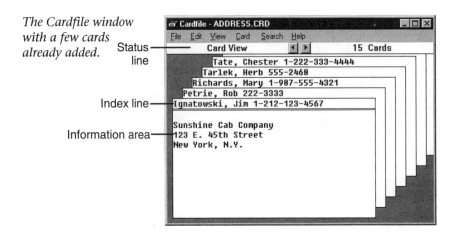

Status line

Index line

Information area

# Getting Comfy with the Cardfile Window

Besides its own menu bar, the Cardfile window contains two unique features: the status line and a blank card. These features are covered in the next couple of sections.

## The Status Line

The *status line* below the menu bar tells you two things:

➤ The right side of the line tells you how many cards are in the current file.

➤ The left side of the line tells you the current *view*. (As you'll see later, Cardfile has two views: the *card view* and the *list view*.)

The status line also includes two scroll arrows that you can use to navigate your cards (which I'll talk about shortly).

## The Cardfile Cards

When you first start Cardfile, you see a blank card in the area below the status line. It's no coincidence that this card looks just like one of those darn 3x5 cards. The idea is that you use the card to fill in whatever information you want to save (someone's name and address, information on your baseball card or CD collection, your favorite haggis recipe, or whatever). You then add a new card, fill in more info, and so on. The cards themselves are divided into two sections: the index line and the information area.

The *index line* is the bar along the top of the card. As you can probably guess, Cardfile uses the information you enter in this area to determine the sort order for the cards (i.e., to *index* them). So, for example, if you're using Cardfile as an address book, you enter each person's last name at the beginning of the index line so Cardfile will sort the cards in alphabetical order by last name. (Or, what the heck, you can sort by first name if you really want to. Hey, it's your life.)

The *information area* holds the card information, such as the actual address or the recipe instructions. You usually just type in the information, but you can also paste in stuff you've cut or copied from another application. (I'll talk more about sharing data between programs in Chapter 19.)

# Filling Out the First Card

When you first start the program (or when you start a new Cardfile document by selecting the File menu's New command), Cardfile displays a blank card ready to receive your information. To fill out this card, pull down the **Edit** menu and select the **Index** command to display the Index dialog box shown below. (Keyboard fans can press **F6**.)

*Use the Index dialog box to fill in (or edit) a card's index line.*

In the **Index Line** text box, enter the information you want to appear in the card's index line. Remember that Cardfile uses the index line data to sort the cards in alphabetical order. This means you need to plan your index lines to make it as easy as possible to find the card you need. For example, if you're entering addresses, begin the index line with each person's last name. For recipes, you might want to sort them by category (Appetizers, Desserts, Chicken and Anything That Tastes Like Chicken, etc.), in which case, you'd begin the index line with the appropriate category and then add the name of the recipe. When you're done, select **OK**. Cardfile returns you to the card and places the insertion point cursor at the top of the card's information area.

The information area is essentially just a large text box. You can enter up to 40 characters on each line, and you have a total of 11 lines per card. You can either type the information yourself, or you can copy it from another application.

**Index Line Editing**

If you need to make changes to an existing card's index line, bring the card to the front (as explained in the "Getting Around in Cardfile" section, below) and then double-click on the index line, or select the **Edit** menu's **Index** command, or press **F6**. Make your changes in the Index dialog box that appears, and then select **OK**.

# Adding New Cards

Once you've completed your first card, you can add more cards by selecting the **Card** menu's **Add** command (or by pressing **F7**). In the Add dialog box that appears, enter the index line information in the **Add** text box, and then select **OK**. As before, enter the rest of the data in the information area.

# Getting Around in Cardfile

Once you have two or more cards in a file, you need some way of navigating among them. You can use either of the following techniques to navigate your cards:

➤ Click on a visible card to bring it to the front of the pile.

➤ Click on the arrows in the status line to scroll through the cards one at a time. Click on the left-pointing arrow to move backward (from Z to A); click on the right-pointing arrow to move forward (from A to Z). If you prefer the keyboard, press **Page Up** to display the next card, or **Page Down** to display the previous card.

# Let the Good Times Roll: Windows 95 Games

You (or your company) didn't shell out the bucks for Windows 95 just so you could keep your nose grindstone-bound all day. Hey, you work hard, so why not play hard, too? Fortunately, playing is easier than ever because you get not one, but *two* games in the Windows 95 package: FreeCell and Minesweeper. The next two sections get your recreation off to a rousing start by introducing you to both games.

## Filling Your Free Time with FreeCell

FreeCell is a variation on the solitaire theme. You get several rows of cards, and the object is to arrange them in piles, where each pile represents one of the card suits arranged in order of rank. FreeCell differs from straight solitaire in that you get four slots—called *free cells*—that you can use as temporary placeholders for your cards.

To start FreeCell, first select the **Start** button to display the Start menu. Then open the **Programs** folder, the **Accessories** folder, and the **Games** folder, and select **FreeCell**. When the FreeCell window appears, pull down the **Game** menu and select **New Game** (or you can bypass the menu by pressing **F2**). FreeCell deals out eight stacks of cards onto the desktop, as shown in the figure below.

Free cells

Home cells

*Your goal in FreeCell is to move the cards from the card stacks into the home cells.*

Card stacks

Your mission (should you decide to accept it) is to move these cards from the stacks into the home cells (the four boxes in the top-right corner of the window) while satisfying the following criteria:

➤ One card suit per home cell.

➤ The home cell stacks are arranged in order by rank, with the smallest card (the Ace) at the bottom and the highest card (the King) at the top.

You can use the free cells (the four boxes in the upper-left corner of the window) as temporary holding areas while you move the cards around. You move cards by dragging them with your mouse. There are three basic moves:

➤ You can move a card from the top of a card stack into the free cells only if there's at least one empty free cell.

**Free Cell Tip**
You can fire a card into the free cells quickly by double-clicking on it.

➤ You can move a card from the top of a card stack or from a free cell to the top of another card stack only if the card that's currently at the top of the other stack is a notch higher in rank and of the opposite color. For example, you can move the six of Hearts (red) to another stack only if the card at the top of that stack is the seven of Spades or Clubs (black).

➤ You can move a card from the top of a card stack or from a free cell to the home cells only if the home cell for the card's suit contains a card that is one lower in rank than the card you want to move. For example, if the card is the Queen of Diamonds, you can only move it onto the Diamonds home cell stack if the card currently on top of the stack is the Jack of Diamonds.

The overall strategy is to rearrange the card stacks to expose, at first, the lower ranked cards so you can get them into the home cells. Remember that Aces are low, so they're the first cards you want to expose. Once you've got an Ace in a home cell, you can look for that suit's two and move it into the home cell, then the three, and so on. While you're rearranging, you can move cards into the free cells if you need to get them out of the way temporarily.

## The Game of Living Dangerously: Minesweeper

Minesweeper is an extremely simple game to play, but it really gives your logic circuits a workout. To see what I mean, select the **Start** button to display the Start menu, open the **Programs** folder, the **Accessories** folder, and the **Games** folder, and select **Minesweeper**. Windows 95 displays the Minesweeper window.

To play Minesweeper, click on the various squares you see to uncover what's underneath. Each square will either turn up nothing (which is good) or one of the following:

➤ A mine. When you click on a mine, the game ends in disgrace.

➤ A number. The number tells you how many adjacent squares have mines under them. For example, if you click on a square and the number 2 shows up, it means that two of the adjacent squares (left, right, top, bottom, or diagonal) have a mine lying in wait for a careless click.

In theory, by looking at the squares already uncovered and the numbers, you should be able to deduce which squares have mines. When you think you know, you can mark a square as mined by right-clicking on it. Minesweeper places a flag on the square to remind you the square is (possibly) mined. (If you're not too sure about a square, you can right-click on it again to change the flag to a question mark.) The figure below shows a game in progress. You win Minesweeper by successfully marking all the mined squares and uncovering all the unmined squares.

Elapsed time

Remaining mines

Mine markers

*Mark a square that you think may be mined by right-clicking on it.*

# The Least You Need to Know

This chapter added a few more courses to the free lunch of Windows 95 accessories. We looked at the Notepad text editor, the Calculator, Date/Time, Briefcase, Calendar, Cardfile, and the games FreeCell and Minesweeper.

Our next stop (assuming, that is, that you can drag yourself away from FreeCell or Minesweeper) is to check out some techniques for sharing info between Windows (and even DOS) programs.

# Chapter 19

# Sharing Info Between Programs

### In This Chapter

➤ Copying information from DOS and Windows applications

➤ What OLE is, and how it can change your life

➤ Setting up links between the data in your Windows applications

➤ A treasure trove of techniques that'll help you get your programs to share and share alike

The mind is a strange thing. Take my mind, for example (please). I'm constantly forgetting important things like friends' birthdays, paying the mortgage, and doing the dishes. On the other hand, I vividly remember a commercial that was on TV, oh, about 20 years ago. It showed a father eating a chocolate bar and asking his daughter what she learned in school today. She replied, gazing longingly at the chocolate bar, "Shaaaring."

This chapter shows you what to do if one of your applications has the computer equivalent of a chocolate bar that you want to share with another program.

## Dividing the Spoils: Data Sharing Basics

A friend of mine in the business world once told me a hilarious story about trying to work out a deal between two people who, for various reasons, refused to talk to one another. (And were stubborn as mules, to boot.) On one occasion, each person was hunkered down in a hotel suite (on different floors, of course), and both refused to meet on neutral ground. To get anything done, my friend was forced to shuttle back and forth between rooms, relaying curt messages and massaging obstinate egos.

This pigheaded behavior reminds me of DOS programs: trying to get them to share information with one another is at best painful and is usually impossible. Windows changes all that by acting, as my friend did, as a go-between for all your applications (Windows *and* DOS). Windows has a number of tricks up its electronic sleeve to accomplish this, but the two most common are the *Clipboard* and *object linking and embedding* (OLE). We'll examine the Clipboard in this section, and then the rest of the chapter will focus on the hocus pocus of OLE.

# The Clipboard: A Halfway House for Your Data

Any time you cut or copy something in an application, Windows stores the data in a special place called the *Clipboard*. The data then sits there, waiting patiently, maybe reading a magazine or two, until you issue a Paste command, at which time Windows then copies the info from the Clipboard to the current cursor position in the application. The important thing to note here is that, for the most part, Windows couldn't care less which application it's pasting into. In other words, you can cut or copy data from one application, and then paste into something completely different.

### The Clipboard's Inconstant Contents

Keep in mind that the Clipboard is a bit fickle, so it'll jettison its contents as soon as something new comes along. If you copy some text and then, say, cut a piece of a Paint drawing a few minutes later, the Clipboard heartlessly discards the text and replaces it with the graphic. In other words, the Clipboard is only capable of storing the last thing you cut or copied. Not only that, but the Clipboard is emptied each time you turn off or restart your computer. (The Clipboard, apparently, has trouble handling commitment!)

For the sake of spelling all this out, let's go through the specific steps required to exchange data via the Clipboard:

1. Activate the application containing the data you want to share.

2. Select the data (by clicking and dragging with your mouse until it is all highlighted, or by using any of the other selection techniques described in Chapter 8, in the "Highlighting Text" section).

3. Pull down the **Edit** menu and select either **Cut** or **Copy**, as appropriate. (Remember, if you cut, the data is deleted from its original location and moved to the Clipboard; if you copy, the data is left intact in its original position, and a copy of it is placed in the Clipboard.) Windows transfers the data to the Clipboard.

4. Switch to the application into which you want to place the data.

5. Move to where you want the data to appear, pull down the **Edit** menu, and select the **Paste** command. The data is pulled from the Clipboard and pasted into the application. A copy of the data remains on the Clipboard, however, so you can paste it as many times as you need to.

The Clipboard sounds like some mysterious place, but it's actually just a special chunk of your computer's memory that Windows sets aside for all this cut-and-paste malarkey.

## Copying Text in a DOS Application

Copying stuff from a DOS program is another kettle of fish entirely. This section shows you how to copy text from a DOS application, and we'll focus on copying graphics in the next section.

The best way to copy text from a DOS application is to place the program in a window and highlight the text you want. Here are the steps you need to plow through:

> **A New Look for DOS** Windows 3.1 users will notice right off the bat that DOS windows have a whole new look in Windows 95. For one thing, you've got a toolbar that gives you mouse access to all the commands on the Control menu. For another, you can size the window just like any regular Windows window.

1. Open the DOS application in Windows, and place it in a window (if it's not already) by pressing **Alt+Enter**. (The program is in a window if you can see the Minimize, Maximize, and Close buttons in the upper-right corner.)

2. Click on the **Mark** button in the toolbar, or pull down the window's Control menu (by pressing **Alt+Spacebar**), select the **Edit** command, and then select **Mark**. A blinking cursor appears on the left, just below the toolbar. (If you don't see the toolbar across the top of the DOS window, pull down the window's **Control** menu and activate the **Toolbar** command.) The Mark command tells Windows 95 that you want to select some text in a DOS program.

3. Select the information you want to copy. (You can use the normal text selection techniques that you'd use in a Windows application.) Your screen should look something like the one shown in the following figure.

*Selected text in a windowed DOS application.*

Selected text ——

 **4.** Click on the toolbar's **Copy** button, or open the Control menu, select the **Edit** command, and then select **Copy** (you can also just press **Enter**). This copies the selection to the Clipboard.

## Copying Graphics in a DOS Application

If the DOS program has a picture that you want to copy, you first need to display the application in a window. Set up your window so you can see the image, and then press **Alt+Print Screen**.

### Alt+Print Screen Gives You More Than You Bargained For

This method makes a copy of the *entire* window—the title bar, scroll bars, the whole shootin' match. If you don't want these things included in your image, you should first paste the picture into Paint and remove the extraneous matter from there. See Chapter 15 for the ins and outs of working with Paint.

## Pasting Info to a DOS Application

When you copy data from a DOS program, it sits quietly in the Clipboard until you issue a Paste command from a Windows application. Pasting text *into* a DOS application takes a bit more effort, as the following steps demonstrate:

**1.** Open the DOS application in Windows and place it in a window (if it's not already) by pressing **Alt+Enter**.

2. Position the cursor where you want to insert the text.

3. Click on the toolbar's **Paste** button, or open the Control menu, select the **Edit** command, and select **Paste**. The Clipboard copies your text before your very eyes!

# OLE: Can You See?

We'll now turn our attention to OLE—object linking and embedding. (In case you're wondering, you pronounce OLE as *oh-LAY*, like the bullfight chant.) This section attempts to knock some sense into this OLE business by explaining everything in terms we mere mortals can understand, and by placing OLE in its most practical, hands-on light.

The Clipboard method's greatest virtue is its simplicity, but it suffers from two major drawbacks. First, if the data is changed in the original application, the document containing the copy becomes out of date. This has two consequences:

➤ If you know the data needs to be updated, you have to repeat the whole copy-and-paste procedure to get the latest version of the data. And if you pasted it into several different files...we're talking major pain.

➤ If you don't know the data needs to be updated (for example, if someone else changes the original data without telling you), you're out of luck because you're stuck with an old version of the info.

Consider the following scenario: you've got some spare time (hey, it could happen), and you decide to write a long-overdue letter to your mom. In fact, to show off your new skills, you decide to do it in WordPad and include some Paint drawings that the kids have done. So you write your letter, copy and paste the drawings, and then print everything out a few days later. When your kids see the letter, though, they're upset because they changed the drawings last night and the drawings in the letter don't show their updated artwork (as a parent, of course, you're *supposed* to know these things). You don't see what the big deal is, so they show you. As you can see in the following figure, the kids went to a lot of effort to finesse this masterpiece. How could you even *consider* sending that rudimentary attempt on the left?

*The Paint drawing you pasted into WordPad doesn't change when the kids edit the original.*

The original Paint picture pasted into WordPad

The edited Paint picture

As you can see, the Paint picture has been changed, but the older version you pasted into WordPad via the Clipboard just sits there, blissfully ignorant of the kids' careful coloring job.

The second drawback of the Clipboard becomes apparent when you want to make changes to the copied data. You may be able to edit the data directly (if it's just text, for example), but more often than not you need to crank up the original application, change the data there, and then do the Clipboard thing again. However, problems can arise if you're not sure which application to use or if you're not sure which file contains the original data.

These two drawbacks can create major roadblocks that slow you down when you try to share data between programs. Wouldn't it be great if you didn't have to worry about the updating of shared data? I know if I put together a wish list, it would probably contain two items:

➤ If the data changes in the original application, update the copied data automatically.

➤ If I want to make changes to the copied data, make it easy to find both the original application and the original data file.

Well, my friends, I'm here today to tell you that wishes *can* come true, because OLE addresses both of these issues. To see how, let's examine the three parts of OLE—objects, linking, and embedding.

**Object**    This is the data that's inserted into the receiving application (it could be text, graphics, sounds, or whatever). The basic Clipboard method sends raw data, but OLE is more sophisticated: it also sends information that enables you to update and work with the data easily.

**Linking**    This is one of the OLE methods you can use to insert an object into a destination document. When you link an object, OLE sets up and maintains a link between the source application and the object, which means that if the original data is changed, OLE updates the copy automatically. (I always picture the source program and the object with walkie-talkies so they can keep each other updated. Yeah, I know: I definitely need to get out more.) In the example I described earlier, suppose the copy of the picture in the WordPad document was linked to the original Paint file. When the kids made their changes to the Paint file, the WordPad document would have been updated right away, with no questions asked.

**OLE Lingo**    To get through the rest of this chapter, you'll need some terminology for the application that creates the original data, and for the application that receives the copy. The official terms are *server* and *client*, respectively, but most people can never remember which is which. Instead, I'll use the terms *source* and *destination*.

**Embedding**    This is the other OLE technique you can use to insert an object into a destination file. When you embed an object, OLE copies not only the source data, but also all kinds of info about the source application. It's easy to make changes to the object because OLE knows where it came from and can start the source application for you automatically. For example, you could make changes to a picture embedded in a WordPad document simply by selecting it (I'll show how to do this later on). OLE starts up Paint (the source application) and automatically loads the picture so you can make your changes.

# Should I Link or Embed?

This question, while not quite up there with the major philosophical conundrums of our times, illustrates what is perhaps the most confusing aspect of OLE: under what circumstances should you link your objects or embed them? The answer lies in how OLE treats the source data. When you link an object, OLE doesn't even bother sending the data to the destination. Instead, it sends a "reference" that tells the destination application which file contains the source data. This is enough to maintain the link between the two applications. When you embed an object, however, the actual data is crammed holus-bolus into the destination document.

So you should link your objects if:

➤ You want to keep your destination documents small. The destination just gets the link info, and not the data itself, so there's much less overhead associated with linking.

➤ You're sure the source file won't be moved or deleted. To maintain the link, OLE requires that the source file remain in the same place. If it's moved or deleted, the link is broken.

➤ You need to keep the source file as a separate document in case you want to make changes to it later, or in case you need it for more OLE fun. You're free to link an object to as many destination files as you like. If you think you'll be using the source data in multiple places, you should link it so you can maintain a separate file.

➤ You won't be sending the destination file via e-mail or floppy disk. Again, OLE expects the linked source data to appear in a specific place. If you send the destination file to someone else, they might not have the proper source file to maintain the link.

On the other hand, you should embed your objects if:

➤ You don't care how big your destination files get. Embedding works best in situations where you have lots of hard disk space and lots of memory.

➤ You don't need to keep the source file as a separate document. If you only need to use the source data once, embedding it means you can get rid of the source file and reduce the clutter on your hard disk.

➤ You'll be sending the destination file and you want to make sure the object arrives intact. If you send a file containing an embedded object, the other person sees the data, complete and unaltered.

# Doing the Linking and Embedding Dance

If all this seems a bit confusing, don't worry; that's a normal reaction to all this High Geek techno stuff. If it's any consolation, however, deciding whether you want to link or embed is actually the hardest part of OLE. Once you know what you want to do, the rest is straightforward. However, just to keep us all on our toes, OLE gives us a few different methods to use to link or embed an object. The following two are the most common:

➤ You can copy the object from the source application and paste it in the destination application as a linked or embedded object.

➤ You can insert a new embedded object from within the destination application.

## Linking or Embedding an Object by Pasting

If the object you want to link or embed already exists, you can place it on the Clipboard and then paste it in the destination document. If you think this sounds like what we did earlier…well, you're close. The difference, as the following steps show, is that you paste not with the Paste command, but with the Paste Special command:

1. Activate the source application, and open or create the document that contains the object.

2. Select the object you want to link or embed, pull down the **Edit** menu, and select the **Copy** command to place the data on the Clipboard.

3. Switch to the destination application and move to where you want the object to appear.

4. Pull down the **Edit** menu and select the **Paste Special** command. A Paste Special dialog box appears. (The appearance of the Paste Special dialog box varies from application to application.)

   Alternatively, some applications (such as Cardfile) have a Paste Link command on their Edit menus. If you want to link the object, you can use this command to bypass the Paste Special dialog box.

**No Paste Special, No OLE** If the destination application doesn't have a Paste Special command, it's bad news: it means the program doesn't support object linking and embedding.

5. In the list of data types, select the one with "Object" in the name (such as Paintbrush Picture Object).

6. Select either **Paste Link** (to paste the data as a linked object) or **Paste** (to paste the data as an embedded object). In some Paste Special dialog boxes, you select either the Paste Link or the Paste option button, and then select OK.

## Inserting a New Embedded Object

If the object you want to embed doesn't exist, and you don't need to create a separate file, OLE lets you insert (i.e., embed) the new object directly into the destination application. For example, suppose you want to embed a Paint drawing into a WordPad document, but the drawing doesn't exist (and you don't really need a separate Paint file for the drawing). In this case, OLE lets you embed a new Paint object in the WordPad document and create the drawing right from WordPad. Here's how it works:

1. In the destination application, move to where you want the new object to appear.

2. Either pull down the **Edit** menu and select **Insert Object**, or pull down the **Insert** menu and select **Object**. In either case, a dialog box appears.

**Updating Your Work**
In most source applications, you can embed the object without leaving the application by selecting the **File** menu's **Update** command. Since you won't be creating a separate file for the object, this is sort of like saving your work.

3. Make sure the **Create New** option is activated.

4. In the **Object Type** list, select the type of object you want to create. If you want to create a Paint drawing, for example, select the **Bitmap Image** object type.

5. Select **OK**. Windows 95 starts the source application for the object type you selected.

6. Create the object you want to embed.

7. Exit the source application. In most cases, you'll do this by pulling down the **File** menu and selecting the **Exit & Return to *document*** command, where *document* is the name of the active document in the destination application. The source application asks if you want to update the embedded object.

8. Select **Yes**, and Windows 95 embeds the object.

## Editing a Linked or Embedded Object

If you need to make changes to a linked or embedded object, you can start the source application and load the object automatically by using either of the following methods:

➤ Double-click on the object in your document.

➤ Select the object, pull down the **Edit** menu, and select the **Edit** *Type* **Object** command, where *Type* is the type of object you selected (e.g., Bitmap Image or Document).

## Working with OLE 2 Applications

The latest version of object linking and embedding—version 2—includes a fistful of new features that make creating and maintaining embedded objects even easier. Here's a summary of just a few of these features:

**Drag and Drop Objects Between Applications**   You can move information from one open OLE 2 application to another simply by dragging selected data from one and dropping it in the other. If you want to copy the data, you need to hold down **Ctrl** while dragging.

**In-Place Inserting**   If you insert a new OLE 2 object, Windows 95 activates *in-place* inserting. This means that instead of displaying the source application in a separate window, certain features of the destination application's window are temporarily hidden in favor of the source application's features:

➤ The title bar changes to tell you what kind of object you're now working with.

➤ The menu bar (with the exception of the File and Window menus) is replaced by the source application's menu bar.

➤ The toolbars are replaced by the source application's toolbars.

To exit in-place inserting and embed the object, click outside the object.

**In-Place Editing**   When you edit an OLE 2 object, the object remains where it is, and the destination application's window changes as it does with in-place inserting. Make your changes, and then click outside the object to complete the edit.

Let's look at an example to see OLE 2 in action. First off, the following picture shows the normal Microsoft Excel window.

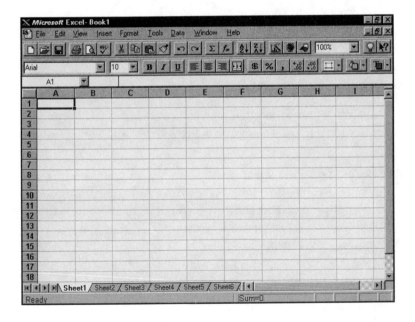

*Your basic Microsoft Excel window.*

Now I'll insert a Microsoft Word for Windows document into Excel. Word (versions 6.0 and later) is an OLE 2 application, so it supports in-place inserting. As the following picture shows, OLE 2 changes the menu bar and toolbars from Excel's to Word's.

*With in-place inserting, the destination window (Excel) assumes many features of the source window (Word for Windows).*

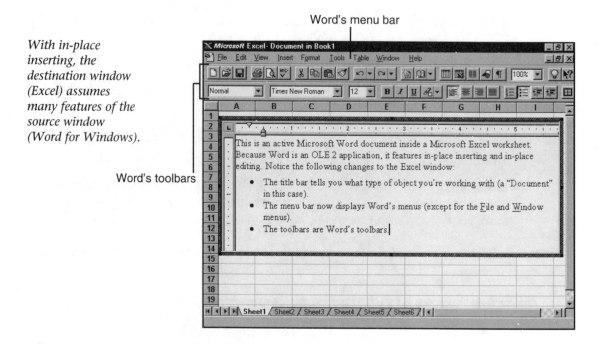

Word's menu bar

Word's toolbars

## The Least You Need to Know

This chapter covered all kinds of fun stuff about exchanging information between Windows and DOS applications. It also took you on a tour of the strange and wonderful world of OLE.

You might think that text and graphics are about the only things you'd want to share between programs. But Windows 95 also enables you to link and embed sound recordings and even videos in some applications. First, however, you need to know how to work with these kinds of objects, which is just what I'll teach you in the next chapter as we explore Windows 95's multimedia capabilities.

# Chapter 20

# The Sights and Sounds of Multimedia

## In This Chapter

➤ Using a CD-ROM drive with Windows 95

➤ Playing with sounds

➤ Jammin' to audio CDs

➤ Trying out the Media Player

➤ Learn what this multimedia mania is all about

There was a time when our computers—big, dim-witted brutes that they are—would just sit there quietly and passively, letting out only an occasional beep to let us know someone was home. Now, however, they've turned into full-fledged entertainment centers capable of showing videos, making realistic burping noises, and even playing the latest audio CD from The Tragically Hip.

If you've heard about this multimedia hoopla, but you didn't know how to become part of the show yourself, step right up. This chapter gives you the basics of Windows 95's multimedia capabilities.

I'll talk about various Windows 95 accessories in this chapter, and you may find that one or more of them don't show up in the Start menu. If they don't, you need to install the missing components from your Windows 95 installation disks or CD-ROM. To find out how to install specific chunks of Windows 95, head for Chapter 25 and check out the section titled "Adding and Removing Windows 95 Components."

# Windows 95 and CD-ROM Drives

You'll be happy to know that Windows 95 and CD-ROM drives get along just fine, thank you. If you had a CD-ROM drive attached to your machine when you installed Windows 95, the Setup program almost certainly will have recognized the drive and automatically set it up for use with Windows 95.

If you're adding a new CD-ROM drive to your machine, how Windows 95 handles it depends on the type of drive you're installing:

➤ If the CD-ROM drive is "Plug and Play-enabled," Windows 95 recognizes it as soon as you plug it in.

➤ For all other CD-ROM drives, you need to tell Windows 95 to set it up for use. To find out how to install new hardware in Windows 95, make a beeline for Chapter 25's "Adding a New Piece of Hardware" section.

Techno Talk

### What's All This About Plug and Play?

Plug and Play is a new standard that should make life easier for anyone who adds new hardware to his or her computer or upgrades existing hardware.

In a system that doesn't support Plug and Play, installing hardware is often a hair-pulling exercise in frustration. Unless, of course, you actually *like* grappling with arcana such as DIP switches, IRQ settings, DMA channels, and other TLA (three-letter acronym) gobbledygook.

With Windows 95's Plug and Play, however, such primitive rituals become a thing of the past. You can, literally, just plug in a Plug-and-Play-enabled device, such as a sound card or CD-ROM drive, and Windows recognizes it immediately. How do you know if a device supports Plug and Play? Well, the box or manual will certainly tell you, or you can just install it, cross your fingers, and see what happens.

So how do you access a CD-ROM's contents from Windows 95? Easy: just open Explorer or My Computer and select the CD-ROM drive icon. In the Explorer window shown in the following figure, the CD-ROM is shown as drive E.

*Explorer shows CD-ROM drives just like any other disk drive.*

└─The drive icon for a CD-ROM

A CD-ROM drive looks and acts just like any other drive on your computer. Well, okay, I lied: it doesn't act *quite* like a regular drive. For example, you can't move or copy files to a CD-ROM, and you can't delete files from a CD-ROM. That's what the "ROM" in CD-ROM is all about: it stands for "Read-Only Memory," which, translated from its native geekspeak, means you can only *read* the contents of a CD-ROM, you can't change them in any way. (Here, "reading" the contents means displaying text, viewing graphics, and running programs.)

Many CD-ROMs have setup programs that automatically install icons on the Start menu for easier access. Look for files named **Setup** or **Install** on the CD-ROM. Windows 95 also supports a CD-ROM feature called AutoPlay that promises to make CD-ROMs insanely easy to use. In a nutshell, a CD-ROM that supports AutoPlay automatically cranks up its setup program (if you haven't yet installed the disc) or the CD-ROM's program (if it is installed) as soon as you insert the disc! If you have the

**Don't Forget the Disc!** Once you've installed a CD-ROM, you can avoid a stern warning from the Windows 95 police by making sure the disc is in the CD-ROM drive each time you try to run the program.

Windows 95 CD-ROM, you can give this AutoPlay thing a whirl. Just plug in the disk and, a few seconds later, you'll see the Windows 95 CD-ROM window appear, as big as life. You want goodies? This baby's got goodies to beat the band. Just click on any of the following icons to get in on the fun:

**Windows 95 Tour**   Click on this icon to get the 50-cent Windows tour.

**Microsoft Exposition**   Clicking here starts the Microsoft Exposition program. This is a shameless Microsoft marketing ploy that tells you about other Microsoft products available for Windows 95.

**Hover!**   Click on this icon to start Hover!, a game that makes FreeCell and Mine-sweeper look about as exciting as watching paint peel. With Hover!, you drive a combination bumber car and hovercraft through a 3-D maze, trying to outrace and outbump your computer opponent. A major timewaster.

**Cool Video Clips**   This icon displays the Videos folder, which contains a few short digital video clips. Some of them are way cool and you'll find yourself watching them over and over. (Deadlines, shmeadlines!)

**Browse This CD**   Click on this icon to use Explorer to view the contents of the disk.

**Add/Remove Software**   Clicking on this icon displays the Add/Remove Programs Properties dialog box. I talk about this dialog box in depth in Chapter 25 (see the "Adding and Removing Windows 95 Components" section).

# Sound Advice: Working with Sounds in Windows 95

Take a stroll through any office these days and you're bound to hear all manner of boops, bips, and beeps emanating from cubicles and work areas. You might be excused for thinking the bodysnatchers have replaced your colleagues with R2D2 clones; what you're actually hearing is evidence that today's modern Windows 95 user is truly wired for sound.

If you're sick of carrying on a one-way conversation with your computer (if the yelling, cursing, and threatening that most of us direct at our digital domestics can be considered conversation), you can get into the sound thing by getting yourself a sound card. This is a circuit board that you (or a nearby, easily-cajoled-with-flattering-comments-about-his-pocket-protector computer guru) attach to your computer's innards. Popular examples include the Windows Sound System and the Sound Blaster. Many sound cards not only play sounds, but also let you record your own. (I'll show you how to record sounds later on.) If you're shopping around for a sound card, make sure the card you get is "MPC-compatible." (MPC sort of stands for Multimedia PC Marketing Council; look for an MPC logo on the sound card's box.) For the best sound, you should also spring for a pair of external computer speakers.

The next few sections assume you have some sort of sound set up on your system and show you how to play sounds, adjust the volume, and record your own sounds.

## Sounding Off: Playing Sounds

Sounds you play in Windows 95 come packaged as sound files (sometimes called *Wave* files). Windows 95 comes with a small collection of sound files that are stored in your Windows folder (look inside the Media subfolder). However, there's no shortage of sound libraries on the market that contain dozens of sound effects (I call them "CBS" collections: chirpin', burpin', and slurpin') and clips from old movies and cartoons (so you can listen to Fred Flintstone say "Yabba dabba do" all day long).

Windows 95 gives you several different ways to play sounds, but the two most common are the Sound Recorder and the Media Player. I talk about the Media Player later in this chapter, so let's check out the Sound Recorder method now. Here are the steps to follow:

1. Select the **Start** button to display the Start menu, open the **Programs** folder, open the **Accessories** folder, open the **Multimedia** folder, wipe the sweat from your brow, and then select **Sound Recorder**. The Sound Recorder window appears, as shown in the following figure.

*The Sound Recorder window, ready for action.*

2. Pull down the **File** menu and select **Open**. Sound Recorder displays the Open dialog box.

3. Highlight the sound file you want to hear, and then select **OK**. (No sound files in sight? Try heading for your Windows folder and opening the Media subfolder to see the sound files that come with Windows 95.)

4. Select the **Play** button to play the sound from the beginning. For long files, you can drag the slider bar to any position in the sound file, and then select **Play**. (The Seek to Start and Seek to End buttons move the sound to the beginning and end of the file, respectively.)

## Keeping It Down to a Dull Roar: Adjusting the Volume

If your colleagues or family start complaining about the noise pollution drifting from your computer, you'll want to turn down the volume of your sound files to keep the peace. On the other hand, if you can hardly hear what Sound Recorder is playing, you may need to pump up the volume a bit.

For either situation, Windows 95 comes with a Volume Control program that you can use to adjust the decibel level of the sounds you play. First, use either of the following methods to display the Volume Control on the desktop:

➤ Display the Start menu, open the **Programs** folder, open the **Accessories** folder, open the **Multimedia** folder, and select **Volume Control**.

➤ Double-click on the **Volume** icon in the taskbar.

Whichever method you choose, the Volume Control window appears (see the following figure). This window is divided into three sections:

**Volume Control**   This section controls the output of all the sounds you play.

**Wave**   This section controls the output of normal sound files (Wave files) only.

**MIDI**   This section controls the output of MIDI (Musical Instrument Digital Interface) files only. (See "Checking Out the Magical Media Player" later in this chapter to learn how to play MIDI files.)

Each section has two sliders: **Balance** adjusts the balance between the left and right speakers, and **Volume** adjusts the volume level (higher is louder). Use your mouse to drag the slider bars to the settings you want. When your settings are just right, pull down the **Options** menu and select **Exit** to shut down the volume control.

*Use the Volume Control program to adjust the volume for the sounds you play.*

# Rolling Your Own: How to Record Sounds

If you have a sound card capable of recording sounds (and you have a microphone attached to the sound card), you can have hours of mindless fun creating your own sound files. Preserving silly sounds for posterity is the most fun, of course, but you can also create serious messages and embed them in business documents. (Chapter 19's

"Doing the Linking and Embedding Dance" section told you how to embed items in documents.)

To record a sound file, follow these steps:

1. Start the Sound Recorder, as described earlier.

2. If Sound Recorder already has a sound file opened and you want to start a new file, select the **File** menu's **New** command. If you'd prefer to add sounds to an existing file, open it, and find the position in the sound file where you want your recording to start.

3. If you're starting a new recording, Sound Recorder displays the New Sound dialog box. Use the **Name** drop-down list to select the quality level of your recording, and then select **OK**. There are three levels to choose from:

> **CD Quality**   This level produces high-quality stereo sound, but it eats up disk space like nobody's business (a whopping 172 kilobytes per *second*!). Use this level only if you absolutely need the best sound possible and have a few acres of hard disk real estate to play around with.

> **Radio Quality**   This level gives you a lower-quality mono sound. As you might expect, though, its appetite for disk space is a lot less, clocking in at "only" 21 kilobytes per second. This is a good level for presentations and notes to colleagues.

> **Telephone Quality**   This level gives you the lowest-quality mono sound, but it usurps a mere 10 kilobytes for every recording second. Use this level for experimenting or creating "for-your-ears-only" sound files.

4. Grab your microphone, clear your throat, get your script, and do whatever else you need to do to get ready for the recording.

5. Select the **Record** button.

6. Speak (yell, groan, belch, whatever) into the microphone. Sound Recorder shows you the length of the file as you record. Note that you have a maximum of 60 seconds to do your thing.

7. When you're done, select the **Stop** button.

8. Select the **Seek to Start** button and then the **Play** button to hear how it sounds. If you're happy with your recording, select the **File** menu's **Save** command, enter a name for the file in the Save As dialog box, and select **Save**.

**Check This Out...**

**A Mini Look at MIDI**   What's this MIDI stuff all about? Well, MIDI enables computers and musical instruments (especially synthesizers) to talk to each other. With MIDI, a musician can crank out a tune on his instrument, and the notes are transcribed automatically on the computer. You can edit the resulting MIDI file note-by-note, or you can alter the pitch and tempo of certain sections to get the jingle just so.

As if letting you record your own sounds isn't enough, Sound Recorder also comes with a host of cool options for creating some really wild effects. Here's a summary:

**Mixing sound files**   You can mix two or more sound files so they play at the same time. So, for example, you could combine one sound file that contains narration with another that has some soothing music. To try this out, open one of the sound files and move to where you want the second file to start. Pull down the **Edit** menu, select **Mix with File**, highlight the other sound file in the Mix With File dialog box, and then select **Open**.

**Changing the volume**   If you recorded your sound file too loudly or too softly, pull down the **Effects** menu and select either **Increase Volume** (to make the sound louder by 25%) or **Decrease Volume** (to make the sound quieter by 25%).

**Altering the playback speed**   You can make your voice recordings sound like Alvin and the Chipmunks or Darth Vader by adjusting the speed of the playback. Pull down the **Effects** menu and choose either **Increase Speed** (to double the speed) or **Decrease Speed** (to halve the speed).

**Adding an echo...echo...echo**   The **Effects** menu's **Add Echo** command creates a neat echo effect that makes your sound files sound like they're being played in some cavernous location.

**Reversing a sound**   Playing a sound file backwards can produce some real mind-blowing effects. To check it out, pull down the **Effects** menu and select the **Reverse** command.

# Playing Audio CDs in Your CD-ROM Drive

Another advantage of having a sound card lurking inside your system is that you can use it to play audio CDs through your CD-ROM drive. That's right, whether you're into opera or alternative, classical or country, rock or rap, your favorite tunes are now only a few mouse clicks away.

The Windows 95 program that makes this possible is called CD Player. Before we look at it, take a second to pop an audio CD into your CD-ROM drive. When you're done, poke the **Start** button to get the Start menu on-screen, open the **Programs** folder, the **Accessories** folder, and the **Multimedia** folder, and select **CD Player**. You'll soon see the CD Player window, which is shown in the following figure. (If you don't see the toolbar in your window, pull down the **View** menu and activate the **Toolbar** command.)

Toolbar   Track  Elapsed
number  time

*Use the CD Player window to crank out your favorite tunes through your CD-ROM drive.*

Controls

## Operating the CD Player

The CD Player is set up to look more or less like a real CD player. The large black box shows the current track number in square brackets and (once the disc starts playing) the elapsed time for the track. Beside the box are the controls you use to operate the CD. The following figure shows the controls you have at your disposal.

Pause  Stop     Rewind  Fast forward

Start

Eject the disc (doesn't work for all CD-ROM drives)

Skip to the previous track (or the beginning of the current track)

Skip to the next track

CD Player also gives you a few more playing options, some of which you normally find only on mid- to high-end CD players:

If you want to play a specific track, select it from the Track drop-down list.

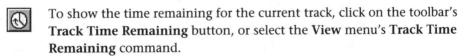

To show the time remaining for the current track, click on the toolbar's **Track Time Remaining** button, or select the **View** menu's **Track Time Remaining** command.

To show the time remaining for the entire disc, click on the **Disc Time Remaining** button, or pull down the **View** menu and select the **Disc Time Remaining** command.

To play the tracks in random order, click on the toolbar's **Random Track Order** button, or pull down the **Options** menu and select the **Random Order** command.

The play the disc continuously (i.e., to start the disc over when the last rack is done), click on the **Continuous Play** button, or select the **Options** menu's **Continuous Play** command.

 To hear just the first 10 seconds of each track, click on the **Intro Play** button in the toolbar, or pull down the **Options** menu and select the **Intro Play** command.

## Becoming a Music Director: How to Create a Play List

When you first slip in an audio CD, the CD Player displays "New Artist" in the Artist box and "New Title" in the Title box. Because it's unlikely that these are the actual names of the artist and disc, you may want to fill in the correct info yourself. Not only that, you can also enter a title for each track on the CD, and you can create a *play list*. A play list is a list of the tracks you want to hear, in the order you want to hear them. Amazingly, CD Player "remembers" this info and loads it automatically the next time you plop that particular CD into your CD-ROM!

To try this out, click on the **Edit Play List** toolbar button, or pull down the **Disc** menu and select **Edit Play List**. CD Player displays the Disc Settings dialog box, shown in the following figure.

In the **Artist** text box, fill in the name of the group or singer, and in the **Title** text box, enter the disc's title. To enter the track titles, follow these steps:

1. Select a track in the **Available Tracks** list.

2. In the **Track** text box, enter the title.

3. Select the **Set Name** button.

4. Repeat steps 1–3 for the other tracks.

The Play List list box shows the current tracks in the disc's play list (which is every track, at first). To modify the play list, use the following techniques:

➤ To remove a track from the play list, select it in the **Play List** and click on **Remove**.

➤ To add a track to the play list, select it in the **Available Tracks** list and click on **Add**. (Yes, you can add your favorite tunes more than once.)

➤ To clear everything from the Play List, click on **Clear All**.

➤ To revert to the original play list (all tracks, in disc order), click on **Reset**.

When you're done, select **OK** to put your play list into effect. The following figure shows an example of a completed dialog box.

*A sample CD Player play list.*

# Checking Out the Magical Media Player

One of Windows 95's best-kept secrets is the Media Player application. Depending on the hardware you've crammed into your system and the devices you've installed, this little gem can play sounds, MIDI (Musical Instrument Digital Interface) files, audio CDs, video files, and more.

To see what's what, follow these steps to use Media Player:

1. Select the **Start** button to display the Start menu, open the **Programs**, **Accessories**, and **Multimedia** folders, and then select **Media Player**. The Media Player window appears, as shown below.

*The Media Player window.*

2. Pull down the **Device** menu and select the type of device you'll be using, such as **Video for Windows**. (If you're going to select **CD Audio**, first make sure an audio compact disc is in your CD-ROM drive.) In most cases, Media Player displays the Open dialog box so you can select the file to play.

3. Select the file, and then select **Open**.

4. Select the **Play** button to start playing. The following figure shows Media Player's buttons and their uses. (As with the Sound Recorder, you can also use the slider to move to any position in the media.)

## The Least You Need to Know

This chapter took you on a magical multimedia mystery tour. We looked at CD-ROMs, playing and recording sounds with Sound Recorder, adjusting the volume with Volume Control, playing audio CDs with CD Player, and playing MIDI files, videos, and more with Media Player.

# Chapter 21

# The Typology of Type: Working with Fonts

## In This Chapter

➤ Font basics, including the lowdown on those newfangled TrueType fonts

➤ Selecting different fonts, and tips for using fonts like a pro

➤ Using the Character Map program to add cool symbols to your documents

➤ Adding new fonts to your system

➤ Some good maternal advice and fascinating tales of flying buttresses and cars as clothes

"The least you can do is *look* respectable." That's what my mother always used to tell me when I was a kid. My innate messiness meant I couldn't always follow that advice, but it's still something I keep in mind in these image-conscious times. If you don't look good up front (or if your work doesn't look good), you'll often be written off (and your work sent to the nearest round file) without a second thought.

When it comes to looking good—whether you're writing up a memo, slicking up a spreadsheet, or polishing up your résumé—fonts are a great place to start. This chapter gives you the skinny on what fonts are, how to use them, and how to add new ones to your system.

# Just What the Heck Is a Font, Anyway?

Before I started using Windows, I didn't think too much about the individual characters that made up my writings. To me, an *a* was an *a*. End of story. Windows changed all that. Suddenly, it was easy to produce an *a* that looked, well, different. Suddenly, it was easy to make a really BIG *a*, if that was what I wanted, or an italic *a*, or a bold **a**. In other words, I discovered *fonts*.

I've become the Prince Charles of fonts: fonts are to characters what architecture is to buildings. In architecture, you look at certain features and patterns, and if you can tell a Doric column from a flying buttress, you can tell if the building is Classical or Gothic or whatever. Fonts, too, are distinguished by a unique set of features and patterns. You won't see any buttresses flying around, but there are four things to look for: the typeface, the type size, the type style, and the character spacing.

## The Typeface

Any related set of letters, numbers, and other symbols has its own distinctive design called the *typeface*. Typefaces, as you can see in the following figure, can be wildly different depending on the shape and thickness of the characters, the spacing, and the mood of the designer at the time.

*Some example typefaces.*

Typefaces come in three flavors: *serif*, *sans serif*, and *decorative*. A serif (it rhymes with *sheriff* ) typeface contains fine cross strokes (typographic technoids call them *feet*) at the extremities of each character. These subtle appendages give the typeface a traditional, classy look. Times New Roman is a common example of a serif typeface.

A sans serif typeface doesn't contain these cross strokes. As a result, sans serif typefaces usually have a cleaner, more modern look (check out Arial in the previous figure).

Decorative typefaces are usually special designs used to convey a particular effect. So, for example, if your document really needs a classy, handwritten effect, something like Brush Script (shown above) would be perfect. Unfortunately, the Brush Script typeface doesn't come with Windows 95. However, lots of companies are selling font collections that include all kinds of strange and useful fonts. Expect to pay about a buck per font.

## Type Size and Style

The *type size* measures how tall a font is. The standard unit of measurement, just so you know, is the *point*; there are 72 points in an inch. So, for example, the individual letters in a 24-point font would be twice as tall as those in a 12-point font.

The *type style* of a font refers to its attributes, such as **bold** and *italic*. Other type styles (often called type *effects*) are <u>underlining</u> and ~~overstrike~~ (sometimes called "strikethru") characters. These styles are normally used to highlight or add emphasis to sections of your documents.

**The True Measure of a Font**
Technically, type size is measured from the highest point of a tall letter, such as "f," to the lowest point of an underhanging letter, such as "g."

## The Character Spacing

The *character spacing* of a font can take two forms: *monospaced* or *proportional*. Monospaced fonts reserve the same amount of space for each character. For example, take a look at the Courier New font shown earlier. Notice that skinny letters such as "i" and "l" take up the same amount of space as wider letters such as "y" and "w." While this is admirably egalitarian, these fonts tend to look like they were produced with a typewriter (in other words, they're *ugly*). By contrast, in a proportional font, such as Arial or Times New Roman, the space allotted to each letter varies according to the width of the letter.

# Okay, So How Does TrueType Fit In?

Imagine a world where individual cars, like clothes, could only fit people of a certain size. If you were 5'10", you'd be too big to fit into a car designed for a person who was 5'6" and too small for a car designed with someone 6'2" in mind. Dealers would need huge tracts of land to park all the models they'd need to keep in stock. If the land wasn't available, you'd only see a minimal selection to cover the normal size ranges of society.

This bizarre scenario is actually a good description of font technology before the advent of TrueType and other font management programs. For any combination of typeface and type style, you had to have a separate file on your system for each type size. If you wanted to use, say, 8-point Courier italic, you'd have to have the appropriate file. Changing to 12-point Courier italic would require that your application load another file. Switching to Courier bold meant a whole new set of files. And these were just the fonts that you displayed on your screen. If you wanted to print anything, you had to have a completely separate collection of files. Ay caramba!

All these files, of course, took up acres of precious hard disk real estate. If you didn't have the room, you had to go without some fonts.

## Scalable Fonts to the Rescue

But just as some genius came up with the idea of adjustable car seats, so, too, do we now have *scalable* fonts. Put simply, a scalable font is one that contains only one representation of each character. If you want a different size or style, a font management program kicks in and automatically *scales* the characters to the new size. It does this for both screen and printer fonts, so when the dust clears, you need only one file for each font family. Whew!

## TrueType Is Scalable

TrueType, to get to the point, is a scalable font technology that's built right into Windows 95. You get not only a font manager program, but also a collection of TrueType fonts for the program to play with (the TrueType program has no effect on non-TrueType fonts). Here are a few other benefits of TrueType:

➤ It doesn't cost anything. Instead of spending your hard-earned money on a third-party type manager (such as Adobe Type Manager), you get TrueType free with Windows 95.

➤ Because they're scalable, TrueType fonts look good at large type sizes. Other fonts, while they may print okay, display ugly, jagged lines on your screen.

➤ You can exchange files with other Windows users without hassle. With other types of fonts, you never know if someone else will be able to view or print your documents properly.

➤ TrueType fonts will print on any printer that Windows 95 supports. Other fonts are often printer-specific, so if you switch printers you have to switch fonts.

# Selecting Different Fonts in Applications

My mother also used to say that you'll never plow a field by turning it over in your mind, so that's enough theory. Let's get down to business and see how you go about selecting different fonts in your programs.

How you select a font depends on the application you're using. Most programs that use fonts have a Format menu with a Font command. If you don't see a Format menu, look for Layout or something similar; if you don't see a Font command, look for a Text command or a Character command instead. (So much for Windows' consistent interface!) In any case, once you've found the appropriate command, you'll see a dialog box that looks something like WordPad's Font dialog box shown below. (To display this dialog box, pull down WordPad's **Format** menu and select the **Font** command.

*The Font dialog box from WordPad.*

From here, selecting the font you want is easy. First, use the **Font** list box to select the typeface. (Yeah, I know, it should be called the "Typeface" list. Ah, well....) Just so you know, the ones with the "double-T" symbol beside them are the TrueType fonts (which we talked about in the previous section).

Once you've settled on a typeface, you need to select a type style (in WordPad, you use the **Font** style list), the type size (the **Size** list), and any extra effects (WordPad has two: **Strikeout** and **Underline**).

**Watch the Sample Box**
As you're selecting your font options, keep an eye peeled on the Sample box. It'll give you an idea of what your font will look like.

(Note, too, that WordPad's Font dialog box gives you two other options. Use the Color drop-down list to change the color of your text; use the Script drop-down list to work with different languages, if your system supports them.) Once you're done, select OK to return to the application.

If you highlighted some text before starting, the application converts the text to the new font. If you didn't select any text, the application displays anything you type from the current cursor position in that font. In the latter case, when you're done with the font, you can return to your regularly scheduled font by redisplaying the Font dialog box and turning off the options you selected earlier.

## Getting Silly with the Character Map

A given typeface covers not only the letters, numbers, and symbols you can eyeball on your keyboard, but dozens of others besides. For example, were you stumped the last time you wanted to write "Dag Hammarskjöld" because you didn't know how to get one of those ö thingamajigs? I thought so. Well, hang on to your hats because I'm going to show you an easy way to get not only an ö, but a whole universe of strange and wondrous symbols.

It all begins with one of the accessories that comes with Windows 95: the Character Map. To check it out for yourself, select the **Start** button, open the Start menu's **Programs** folder and **Accessories** folder, and select **Character Map**. (Is Character Map missing in action? Then head for Chapter 25 and read the section titled "Adding and Removing Windows 95 Components" to learn how to install it.) The figure below shows the Character Map window that appears.

The layout is pretty simple: the squares show you all the symbols available for whatever typeface is displayed in the Font drop-down list box. If you select a different typeface, a whole new set of symbols appears.

*The Character Map window gives you access to the full spectrum of Windows 95 characters.*

To use a symbol from Character Map in an application, first select the symbol you want by double-clicking on it with your mouse or by using your keyboard's arrow keys to highlight it and then pressing **Enter**. The symbol appears in the Characters to copy box. When you're ready, select the **Copy** button to copy the character to the Clipboard. (The Clipboard is Windows 95's temporary storage area for copied objects. I talk more about it in Chapter 19.) Finally, return to your application, position the cursor where you want the character to appear, and select the **Edit** menu's **Paste** command.

### A Cornucopia of Characters

Foreign characters are only the beginning of what you can get from Character Map. In the program's Font list, you should also check out typefaces such as Wingdings or Symbol for such exotica as astrological signs, currency symbols, and even clock faces! Note, as well, that some programs (such as Word for Windows and WordPerfect for Windows) have built-in commands for accessing these symbols.

## Avoiding the "Ransom Note" Look

The downside to Windows 95' easy-to-use fonts is that they can sometimes be *too* easy to use. Flushed with your newfound knowledge, you start throwing every font in sight at your documents. The result, as you can see in this example, is usually a mess.

*Overdone fonts can give even the most solemn text the dreaded "ransom note" look.*

The problem, of course, is that there are just too many different fonts in one document. It turns even the most profound and well-written documents into a dog's breakfast. (It's known in the trade as the "ransom note" look.) Here are some tips you can use to avoid overdoing your fonts:

➤ Never use more than a couple of typefaces in a single document. Anything more looks amateurish and will only confuse the reader.

➤ If you need to emphasize something, bold or italicize it in the *same* typeface as the surrounding text. Avoid using underlining for emphasis because it's sophomoric, and some monitors don't display underlines very well.

➤ Use larger sizes only for titles and headings.

➤ Avoid bizarre decorative fonts for large sections of text. Most of those suckers are hard on the eyes after a half dozen words or so. Serif fonts are usually very readable, so they're a good choice for long passages. The clean look of sans serif fonts makes them a good choice for headlines and titles.

# Adding New Fonts

Windows 95 comes with various fonts, including five TrueType font collections (Arial, Courier New, Symbol, Times New Roman, and Wingdings). This is usually fine for most people, but there are lots of inexpensive font collections on the market these days. If you buy one of these collections, here's how to add the fonts to your system:

1. Select the **Start** button to display the Start menu, open the **Settings** folder, and then select the **Control Panel** icon. Windows 95 displays the Control Panel window.

2. Select the **Fonts** icon. Control Panel opens the Fonts folder.

3. Pull down the **File** menu and select the **Install New Font** command. The Add Fonts dialog box appears.

4. Insert the disk containing the font files, and then select the appropriate disk drive from the **Drives** list. (You may also need to select a different folder using the **Folders** list.) Windows 95 reads the font names from the disk and displays them in the List of fonts box, as shown in the following figure.

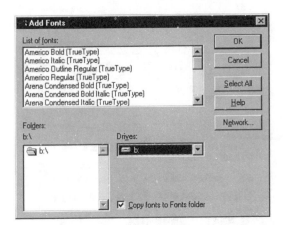

*Use the Add Fonts dialog box to add new fonts to your system.*

5. To install all the fonts on the disk, choose the **Select All** button. Otherwise, in the **List of fonts** box, use either of these techniques to highlight the fonts you want to install:

   Mouse users: hold down the **Ctrl** key and click each font.

   or

   Keyboard users: press **Tab** to move to the list of fonts. Then press **Shift+F8** and, for each font, move to it using the up and down arrow keys and press the **Spacebar**. When you're done, press **Shift+F8** again.

6. When you're ready to roll, select **OK** to return to the Fonts dialog box.

If you'd like to take a peek at some of your new fonts, you can do it right from the Fonts folder. Highlight the font you want to see and then select the **File** menu's **Open** command. (Or you can right-click on the font and select **Open** from the shortcut menu.) Windows 95 displays some info and some samples for the font in a window like the one in the following figure. When you're done, select **Done**.

*When you "open" a font, Windows 95 displays a window like this one.*

## The Least You Need to Know

This chapter introduced you to fonts in Windows 95. After a long-winded introduction on font nuts and bolts, we covered how to use fonts, how to extract symbols from the Character Map, and how to add fonts to your system.

# Chapter 22

# An Introduction to Windows 95 Networking

## In This Chapter

➤ Setting up your computer for networking

➤ Accessing folders and printers on other computers

➤ Sharing your folders and printers with others

➤ A brief networking primer that'll have you surfing your "net" in no time flat

Back in the high-flying '80s, *networking* was the buzzword du jour. Although to the innocent observer networking appeared to be a social skill designed to augment business contacts, it was really just a high-falutin' euphemism for unabashed *schmoozing*.

Nowadays, though, the meaning of networking has changed from cocktail party conversations to computer system connections. Everywhere you turn, people are hooking computers together to see what happens. If you're a budding network administrator and you've connected a couple of machines at home or at the office, this chapter looks at some simple network stuff: setting up your computer, sharing files, sharing printers, accessing other computers, and other networking know-how.

# Networking for Novices

If you'd like to take the networking plunge and connect a couple of computers for sharing files and printers (which is the simple definition of a network), Windows 95 is probably your best way to go. Why? Well, it takes most of the pain out of connecting computers, and you can share stuff with others in your network using the familiar Explorer tools we looked at back in Part 3.

When most people think of networks (if, in fact, they ever think of them at all), the image that springs to mind is one of a central, monolithic computer that contains all the data and applications and has dozens or even hundreds of "terminals" attached to it. *Workgroups*, however, are different. A workgroup is a small group of computers connected by some kind of network cable. Each computer has its own applications and data, but the other computers in the workgroup can share these resources. In this egalitarian setup, all the computers in the workgroup are treated equally; no one machine is "better" or more important than any other. In most workgroups, the computers are related to each other somehow. For example, all the computers in a company's accounting department could form one workgroup, while the marketing department might have its own workgroup.

**Check This Out...**

## Some Net-Words

Networks in which all the machines have their own programs and data and can share these with the other computers are called *peer-to-peer* networks.

A networked computer's *resources* include the disk drives, folders, programs, documents, and printers associated with that computer. The *raison d'être* for networks is to share these resources among several computers.

Each workgroup has a name (Accounting, for example), and each computer in the workgroup has its own name (this is usually the name of the person using the computer, but it can be just about anything you like). You specify the workgroup name and computer name when you set up Windows 95. In my case, I have three computers set up as a workgroup. My group name is *Lonewolf* (the name of my company), and the three computer names are *Hermes*, *Apollo*, and *Dionysus* (don't ask).

The whole point of setting up a workgroup is so the members of the group can share their resources. For example, if you have three computers in the group but only one printer (as I do), you can set things up so that each machine can print from that one printer. Cool.

Similarly, you can share files, applications, and even CD-ROM drives. Does this mean that other people in the group can just play with your machine willy-nilly? Heck no, not if you don't want them to. *You* decide which resources on your computer are shared, and for extra safety, you can set up passwords to prevent undesirables and other members of your family from accessing sensitive areas.

# Getting Your System Network-Ready

A single chapter is, of course, a pitifully small amount of space to devote to a large topic like networking. Because I can't cover everything, I'm going to assume that you have (or some cajolable networking sage has) installed the necessary network hardware on your computers.

With that disclaimer out of the way, I can show you how to set up Windows 95 for network use. The next two sections take you through the two main steps: installing the network software and identifying your computer for network purposes. (If you see the Network Neighborhood icon on your Windows 95 desktop, you can skip both steps because—lucky you—it means networking is already installed on your computer.)

## Setting Up the Network Software

Most network noodling is done via a *network adapter*, which is a component that sits inside your computer. You plug the network cables into the adapter, and the adapter takes care of the dirty work of sending data out to the network and receiving data coming in from the network. For all this to run smoothly, you have to tell Windows 95 what kind of adapter you're using. Here are the steps to follow:

1. Select the **Start** button, open the **Settings** folder, and select **Control Panel**. Windows 95 displays the Control Panel window.

2. Select the **Network** icon, and the Network dialog box appears.

3. Select the **Add** button. Control Panel displays the Select Network Component Type dialog box.

4. Select **Adapter** and then select **Add**. The Select Network adapters dialog box appears.

5. Use the **Manufacturers** list to highlight the manufacturer of your network adapter; use the **Network Adapters** list to highlight the adapter (you should find both things either on the box the adapter came in or in the adapter's manual); and then select **OK**. Control Panel returns you to the Network dialog box.

## Setting Up Sharing

If you want to be a good network citizen and share stuff on your computer with your net friends (which I'll show you how to do later in this chapter), follow these steps to activate sharing:

1. In the Network dialog box select the Configuration tab, and then select the **File and Print Sharing** button. The File and Print Sharing dialog box appears.

2. Activate the two check boxes.

3. Select **OK**.

## Establishing Your Computer's Network Identity

Your next task is to give your computer a name and address on the network. The name is what appears in Explorer when you hang out in the Network Neighborhood (which I'll talk about later on). The "address" is actually the name of the workgroup that your computer is a member of.

To do this, select the **Identification** tab in the Network dialog box (see the figure below). Then fill in the fields as explained on the following page.

*Use the Identification tab to establish a network name for your machine.*

**Computer name**   Enter a network name for your computer (15 characters maximum). Ideally, you should enter a name that'll make it easy for others on the network to figure out which computer they're working with.

**Workgroup**   Enter the name of your network workgroup. If you're setting up your own network at home or in the office, you can enter any name you like (again, use a maximum of 15 characters). Just be sure to use the same name for each computer you're including in your network. If you're hooking into a larger network at the office, the network system administrator assigns you a workgroup name.

**Computer Description**   Use this text box to enter a description for your computer (up to 48 characters). Windows 95 shows this description in some networks lists to help others figure out which computer they're working with. This doesn't have to be anything fancy; a simple "Biff's Computer" or "Buffy's Honkin' Pentium Beast" will do.

When all that's done, select **OK** to put your changes into effect. When Windows 95 asks if you want to restart your computer, select **Yes**.

# Logging In to Your Network

After you've set up your network and restarted Windows 95, eventually you'll be pestered to enter a "user name" and a password. Here are the steps to follow to get through this:

1. The default name shown in the **User name** text box is the computer name you entered during setup. If you want, you can change the logon name to something different (such as, say, your first name).

2. Use the **Password** text box to enter a password if you want to prevent others from getting into your copy of Windows 95. If your network is at home, you may not want to bother with a password (you *do* trust those kids of yours, don't you?), in which case you can leave the Password text box blank.

   If you do use a password, make sure you enter one that's easy for you to remember but hard for others to figure out. When you enter the password, the letters appear as asterisks (*) for security reasons (you never know who might be peeking over your shoulder!).

3. Select **OK**. The Set Windows Password dialog box appears.

4. Reenter your password in the **Confirm new password** text box, and then select **OK**. Windows 95 finishes loading.

When you start Windows 95 in the future, all you'll have to do is enter your password. If, however, you change your user name, you'll have to repeat the whole process.

# A Tour Around the Network Neighborhood

Okay, you're ready to do some networking! Windows 95 calls your workgroup and network the "Network Neighborhood," which certainly sounds friendly enough. Here's how to see what's in your Network Neighborhood:

➤ Double-click on the desktop's **Network Neighborhood** icon.

➤ Open Explorer and select **Network Neighborhood** in the All Folders list.

The figure below shows Explorer with the Network Neighborhood folder selected. The Contents list shows two things:

**Entire Network**  Open this folder to see all the workgroups that are part of the full network to which your computer is attached. (If you're just hooked up to your own workgroup, Entire Network shows only that workgroup.) Opening these workgroup folders displays the names of all the computers that comprise each workgroup.

**Some computer names**  The computer names shown below Entire Network are the names of the computers in your workgroup (including your own). Note that the Comment column contains the computer descriptions you entered earlier. (If you don't see this column, pull down the **View** menu and select the **Details** command.)

*The Network Neighborhood: your computer's community.*

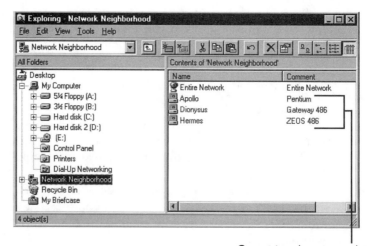

Computers in your workgroup

Because each Network Neighborhood computer is really just a folder, you can use the usual Explorer techniques to check out what's on each computer. For each computer, you'll see those resources that the owner of the computer has chosen to share with the network. (I'll tell you how to share your resources later in this chapter.) For example, in the following figure, Explorer displays the computer named "Apollo." Notice that this computer is sharing two hard disks (drives C and D), a CD-ROM drive (drive E), and a couple of printers. The other computers in the workgroup can access these resources as though the hardware is part of their own systems.

*If you select a Network Neighborhood computer, Windows shows its shared resources in the Contents list.*

Actually, the level of access available for a shared resource depends on the *access rights* the sharer has granted the sharees. As you'll see later on, you can prevent others from messing with your resources by giving them "read-only" access. If you run into, say, a shared folder that's read-only, you won't be able to change any of the folder's files. If you try, you'll see a curt error message telling you that "Network Access is denied." Bummer.

It's also possible to tailor access to a shared resource by using passwords. For example, if you try to view a shared disk drive that's been password-protected, Windows 95 displays the Enter Network Password dialog box, shown in the following figure. You won't be able to access the drive until you enter the correct password in the **Password** text box. (Note, too, that unless you want to reenter the password every time you access this resource, you should leave the **Save this password in your password list** check box activated.)

*Windows 95 displays this dialog box if a resource is protected by a password.*

# Working with the Resources in Your Workgroup

As I've said, one way to play with the shared resources in your workgroup is to head into the Network Neighborhood and "open" the computers you see listed. Here are two other ways to work with these resources:

➤ You can "map" a network disk drive so that it appears to be a disk drive on your computer. For example, let's say your system has two floppy disk drives (drives A and B) and a hard disk drive (drive C). You could map a network drive, and it would appear as drive D on your computer. This makes it easier to copy and move files to and from the network drive, it makes it easier to open files on the drive, and it makes the drive accessible from the MS-DOS prompt.

➤ You can install a network printer and use it (more or less) just like a printer attached directly to your computer. (Why "more or less"? Well, there are some things you won't be able to do, such as purging the current print jobs.)

## Mapping a Network Drive

Mapping a network drive is easier done than said. For starters, open Explorer and try any of the following techniques:

➤ Highlight the network drive you want to work with, pull down the **Tools** menu, and select the **Map Network Drive** command.

➤ Right-click on the network drive and select **Map Network Drive** from the shortcut menu.

 ➤ Highlight the network drive and click on the **Map Network Drive** button in the toolbar.

Whichever method you choose, the Map Network Drive dialog box appears, as shown in the following figure. (Unless, that is, the drive is protected by a password, in which case you'll see the Enter Network Password dialog box so you can enter the appropriate password.) The Drive box shows you the drive letter that Windows 95 will use to map the network drive. If you'd like this drive to be mapped every time you log on to Windows 95, activate the **Reconnect at logon** check box. When you're ready, select **OK** to map the drive. After a few seconds, the new drive appears in Explorer's All Folders list as part of the My Computer folder. (For those of you who have been paying attention: yes, the mapped drive also appears in the My Computer window.)

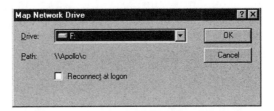

*This dialog box tells you the drive letter that Windows 95 will assign to the mapped network drive.*

To disconnect a mapped drive, use one of the following techniques:

➤ Highlight the mapped drive, pull down the **Tools** menu, and select the **Disconnect Network Drive** command.

➤ Right-click on the network drive and select **Disconnect** from the shortcut menu.

 ➤ Highlight the network drive and click on the **Disconnect Net Drive** button in the toolbar.

If you use either of the first two methods, the Disconnect Network Drive dialog box appears. (If you choose the third method, Windows just disconnects the drive without further ado.) Make sure the drive you want to disconnect is highlighted, and then select **OK**. If Windows 95 asks if you're sure you want to disconnect, select **Yes**.

# Installing a Network Printer

One of the big advantages of setting up a workgroup in your workplace or home is that you can share expensive items (such as printers) among all your computers. You don't need to get a separate printer for each machine or put up with the hassle of swapping printer cables around. Here are the steps to follow to install a network printer for use on your computer:

1. Select the **Start** button to open the Start menu, select **Settings**, and select **Printers**. Windows 95 opens the Printers folder.

 2. Select the **Add Printer** icon to display the first Add Printer Wizard dialog box.

3. Select **Next >** to move on to the next dialog box.

4. Activate the **Network printer** option and select **Next >**.

5. Use the **Network path or queue name** text box to enter the following info: two backslashes (\\), followed by the name of the computer that has the printer, followed by another backslash, followed by the name of the printer. For example, the network path for "printer 1" on the "Apollo" computer shown earlier is **\\Apollo\printer 1**.

   If you're not sure about any of this, select the **Browse** button, highlight the printer in the Browse for Printer dialog box (see the following figure), and select **OK**.

*Use the Browse for Printer dialog box to select the network printer you want to use.*

6. If you'll be printing from MS-DOS programs, activate the **Yes** option button in the Add Printer Wizard dialog box, and then select **Next >**.

7. From here, you follow the same steps that I outlined for installing a printer back in Chapter 9, in the "Telling Windows 95 About Your Printer" section.

## Playing Nicely with Others: Sharing Your Resources

Networking is, literally, a two-way street. It's fine to play around with the resources on other people's machines, but only a real greedy-guts would refuse to share his own computer's resources. To avoid being shunned by your peers, you need to designate a resource or two that can be shared. Read on to learn how.

# Part I: Sharing Disk Drives and Folders

If you have a CD-ROM drive or perhaps some data in a folder that the others in your workgroup are lusting after, you should put your coworkers out of their misery by sharing the drive or folder with them.

The first thing you need to decide is how you want to share your resources. For each drive or folder you share, Windows 95 gives you three choices (called *access rights*):

**Read-Only**   At this level, someone else accessing one of your shared drives or folders can only copy, open, and view files. They can't move files, modify them, rename them, delete them, or add new ones.

**Full**   This anything-goes level gives others complete access to the files in the shared drive or folder. They can move, copy, open, view, modify, rename, and delete files, and they can even create new files.

**Depends on Password**   This level enables you to assign separate passwords for read-only and full access. At home, for example, you might want to give the kids read-only access to certain folders, but give yourself and your spouse full access. That's no problem; you simply assign a read-only password and tell it to the kids, and you assign a separate full-access password for you and your spouse.

Here are the steps you need to follow to share a disk drive, CD-ROM drive, or folder:

1. In Explorer or My Computer, highlight the disk drive or folder you want to share.

2. Pull down the **File** menu, select the **Properties** command, and select the **Sharing** tab in the Properties dialog box that appears (see the figure below). Alternatively, you can right-click on the drive or folder and select **Sharing** from the shortcut menu.

*Use the Sharing tab to share a drive or folder with your workgroup pals.*

3. Activate the **Shared As** option button.

4. The **Share Name** text box shows either the letter of the disk drive or the name of the folder. Because this is what appears in Explorer's Name column when other people access your computer, it's probably best that you leave the name as is. You should, however, enter a brief description of the resource in the **Comment** text box. (Something like "Hard disk" or "CD-ROM drive" or "Crucial workgroup files" is sufficient.)

5. Select the type of access you want for this resource: **Read-Only**, **Full**, or **Depends on Password**.

6. If you want others to be required to enter a password in order to access the shared drive or folder, enter the appropriate password in either the **Read-Only Password** or the **Full-Access Password** text box. If you selected **Depends on Password**, you need to enter a password in both text boxes. (If you do enter a password, don't forget to let the other people in your group know what it is!)

 7. Select **OK**. If you entered a password, you're asked to confirm it. In this case, reenter the password and select **OK**. When you return to Explorer or My Computer, you see a little hand under the folder's icon. This reminds you that you've shared the folder.

## Part II: Sharing Printers

Sharing a printer among several computers in a workgroup is similar to sharing folders. First off, you need to open the Printers folder either by highlighting it in Explorer's All Folders list or by selecting **Start**, opening the **Settings** folder, and selecting **Printers**.

Highlight the printer you want to share, and then select the **File** menu's **Sharing** command (or right-click on the printer and select **Sharing** from the shortcut menu). Windows 95 displays the printer's Properties dialog box and selects the **Sharing** tab (see below). Activate the **Share As** option, enter a comment, and then enter an optional password. Select **OK** to enable sharing. (If you entered a password, the Password Confirmation dialog box appears. Reenter the password and select **OK**.)

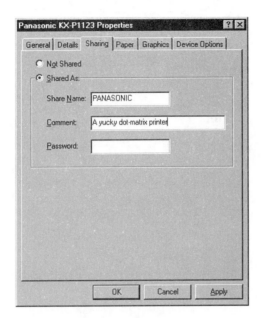

*The Sharing tab in a printer's Properties dialog box.*

# The Least You Need to Know

This chapter taught you how to set up your computer for networking, how to access the shared resources on other network machines, and how to share your own resources with your workgroup peers.

That ends our look at the Windows 95 features you use to get your work done. For our next trick, we'll tackle the many options you get for customizing Windows 95 to suit your style.

# Part 5
# A Few Windows 95 Odds and Ends

*Well, your Windows 95 education seems to be coming along quite nicely. You've got the basics down pat, you've explored Explorer, and you've managed to digest all that work-related stuff in Part 4. So far so good. We'll spend the rest of the book ringing a few more Windows bells and blowing a few more Windows whistles. In our travels, we'll sail over what I call the high Cs of Windows: customization (Chapters 23, 24, and 25), communications (Chapters 26 and 27), and complaints (Chapters 28 and 29).*

# Chapter 23

# Makeover Time: Customizing the Desktop

## In This Chapter

➤ Playing with Windows 95's colors

➤ Changing the desktop's background

➤ Setting up the Windows 95 screen saver

➤ Customizing the Start menu and taskbar

➤ Creating shortcuts for your programs and documents

➤ A veritable cornucopia of customization coolness

*Fritterware* is a nickname given to any option-ladened software program that makes you fritter away your time playing around with its bells and whistles. Windows 95, with its seemingly infinite number of customization options, is the undisputed fritterware champ. To prove it, this chapter looks at all the different ways you can spruce up the Windows 95 desktop.

# Renovating the Desktop

In its default incarnation, the Windows 95 desktop is a pleasant-looking—but wholly uninspiring—teal color; a true yawning festival. Teal, schmeal, I say. If you'd prefer something with a little more pizzazz, why not go for the gusto and use any of Windows 95's umpteen methods for remaking the desktop in your own image?

For starters, you need to get the Display Properties dialog box on-screen by using either of the following methods:

**The easy way:** Right-click on an empty area of the desktop and click on **Properties** in the shortcut menu.

 **The hard way:** Select the **Start** button to display the Start menu, open the **Settings** folder, and then select **Control Panel**. In the Control Panel window, select the **Display** icon.

Whichever method you choose, the Display Properties dialog box appears, as shown in the following figure. The next few sections take you through most of the tabs in this dialog box. (Note that while you're working in this dialog box, you can select the **Apply** button at any time to see what kind of mess the choices you've made will make of your desktop. When you're done fiddling with all of the options, select **OK**—or possibly **Close**, depending on what mood Windows is in—to put your changes into effect.)

*Use the Display Properties dialog box to customize the look and feel of the desktop.*

# Doing Windows 95's Colors

The scene outside my window on this chilly April morning is not a pretty one. I see leafless, lifeless trees that haven't yet answered the call of spring; I see rain drizzling down in one of those April showers that, allegedly, bring May flowers; and I see a sky covered with colorless, foreboding clouds that promise, for a while anyway, uninterrupted irrigation for all the would-be buds. Yuck!

Believe me, the *last* thing I want to see on my computer screen is Windows 95's usual teal-and-steel, the-bland-leading-the-bland, colors. If you, too, feel like giving Windows 95 a makeover, the screen colors are a good place to start.

The easiest way to change Windows 95's colors is to select one of the predefined color schemes. These schemes control the colors of just about everything you see in Windows, including the desktop background, the pull-down menus, and all the window nuts and bolts (the title bars, borders, scroll bars, and so on).

To choose a scheme, begin by selecting the **Appearance** tab in the Display Properties dialog box (see the following figure).

Watch these fake windows to see what effect your scheme will have.

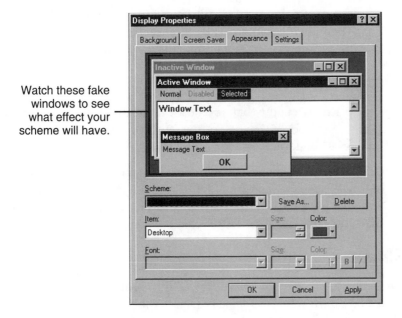

*Use the Appearance tab to select a different Windows 95 color scheme.*

The items in the Scheme drop-down list affect two things:

➤ The color of Windows 95 components.

➤ The font used in those elements that contain text (such as title bars).

**Check This Out...**

**Stop Squinting!** If your eyesight isn't what it used to be, Windows 95's title bar and dialog box text may be a strain on your peepers. If so, try out any of the Scheme items that have (large) in their names—such as Flat (large) or Windows Standard (extra large).

The box above the Scheme list contains a couple of phony windows—one active and one inactive—and a pretend dialog box. By looking at the way your color choices affect these objects, you can see what havoc each scheme will wreak on your desktop, without actually changing anything. Use the **Scheme** list to try out some other schemes until you find one that strikes your fancy. Perhaps the Stars and Stripes scheme, if you're feeling patriotic, or maybe you'd prefer something sillier, such as Eggplant or Pumpkin? (No, I did *not* make up those last two!)

## Trying Out a Desktop Pattern

Like the color schemes you saw in the previous section, Windows also comes with a selection of desktop patterns (and some of these have silly names, too). To pick out one of these patterns, first select the **Background** tab. (I showed the controls on this tab in the figure on Page 270.) Then use the **Pattern** list box to select a pattern. The sample computer screen above the list shows you what each pattern looks like.

## Wallpapering the Desktop? Why Not!

In the real world, wallpapering is a chore that, for most people, ranks right up there with grouting the bathtub and shampooing the cat. Fortunately, this isn't the real world, and wallpapering the Windows 95 desktop is actually quite entertaining.

On the **Background** tab, use the **Wallpaper** list to browse through the selection of wallpapers. When you see one that sounds like fun, highlight it and check out the sample computer screen. (Note that most of the wallpapers are just tiny squares; to get the full effect, you need to make sure the **Tile** option is selected.)

## Screen Saver Silliness

In olden times (say, five or six years ago), monitors weren't as good as they are today, and most of us struggled along using ugly DOS screens. One of the problems people faced was leaving their monitors on too long and ending up with some DOS hieroglyphics burned permanently into the screen (this is usually referred to, not surprisingly, as *burn-in*). To prevent this from happening, some genius came up with the idea of a *screen saver*: a program that automatically kicks in after the computer is idle for a few minutes.

The screen saver displays some kind of moving pattern on the screen that helps prevent burn-in. However, with a simple touch of a key or jiggle of a mouse, the normal screen returns, unharmed and none the worse for wear.

Nowadays, it's pretty tough to burn an image into your screen. Improvements in monitor quality and the graphical nature of Windows 95 have made such a fate virtually impossible. Curiously, though, screen savers are still around and are, in fact, flourishing. The reason: most of them are just plain cool. Who cares about preventing burn-in when you can watch wild, psychedelic patterns or your favorite cartoon every few minutes?

There are scads of commercial screen savers on the market, and Windows 95 comes equipped with some of its own. To try them out, select the **Screen Saver** tab in the Display Properties dialog box, drop down the **Screen Saver** list, and select a screen saver. You can also choose the following options:

**Wait**   This spinner controls the amount of time your computer must be inactive before the screen saver starts doing its thing. You can enter a number between 1 and 60 minutes.

**Preview**   Select this button to give the screen saver a trial run. To return to the dialog box, move your mouse or press any key.

**Settings**   Select this button to set various options for the screen saver. The Setup dialog box that appears depends on which screen saver you chose. For example, the figure below shows the dialog box that appears for the Flying Through Space screen saver. Make your selections, and then select **OK** to return to the Display Properties dialog box.

*An example of a dialog box that appears when you select the Settings button.*

# Customizing the Taskbar and Start Menu

As you've seen throughout most of this book, the taskbar and the Start menu are two of Windows 95's truly indispensable features. So it's nice to know that, handy as they are, there are ways to make both the taskbar and the Start menu even handier. It's all done through the Taskbar Properties dialog box, which you can plop onto the desktop using either of the following methods:

➤ Select the **Start** button, open the Start menu's **Settings** folder, and select **Taskbar**.

➤ Right-click on an empty part of the taskbar and select **Properties** from the shortcut menu.

Windows 95 displays the Taskbar Properties dialog box, shown below. The next couple of sections give you the scoop on the options available in this dialog box. When you've completed your labors in this dialog box, select **OK** to put your changes into effect.

*Use the Taskbar Properties dialog box to renovate the taskbar and Start menu.*

The sample taskbar area—

## Some Taskbar Tidbits

The Taskbar Options tab presents several check boxes that control the behavior of the taskbar. Here's a rundown:

**Always on top** As you saw back in Chapter 10, when you maximize a program's window, it enlarges to consume all of the screen *except* for the taskbar. If you're looking to eke out a little bit of extra screen acreage for your programs, deactivate the **Always on top** check box. Then, when you maximize a program, its window takes up the entire screen, taskbar and all. The taskbar is still there, but the window now sits "on top" of it, which means, of course, that you lose all the convenience of the taskbar. Pitsville. However, all is not lost: you can get the taskbar back on-screen by pressing **Ctrl+Esc** to display both the taskbar and Start menu, and then pressing **Esc** by itself to close the Start menu.

**Auto hide**   This check box gives you a better way to create more room for your programs to roam. When you activate **Auto hide**, Windows 95 reduces the taskbar to a thin, gray line at the bottom of the screen whenever you're working in a program's window. This gives you, effectively, the entire screen to work with. The trick, though, is that you can redisplay the full taskbar simply by moving your mouse pointer to the bottom of the screen. Move the mouse back up again, and the taskbar retreats to its gray line.

**Show small icons in Start menu**   Activating this check box reduces the icons used for each item in the Start menu to smaller, cuter, versions of themselves. Although this makes each icon a little harder to see, it reduces the overall size of the Start menus, which makes them a bit easier to navigate.

**Show Clock**   This check box toggles the Clock in the bottom-right corner on and off. If you're not into time, man, deactivate this check box.

## Adding Items to the Start Menu

When you install a program, it's usually decent enough to add an icon for itself to your Start menu. However, most DOS-based programs wouldn't know the Start menu from a Denny's menu, so they won't create Start menu icons for themselves. DOS programs, Windows-ignorant savages that they are, have an excuse, but you may come across a few ornery Windows-based programs that won't do it, either. That means you've got to add these programs to the Start menu (ugh) manually. To give it a go, follow these steps:

1.  Select the **Start Menu Programs** tab in the Taskbar Properties dialog box, and then select the **Add** button to display the Create Shortcut dialog box, shown on the following page.

### Why Is It Called a "Shortcut"?

Well, because the icons you select on the Start menu aren't the programs themselves. You simply use them to tell Windows 95, "Yo, I want to start this program. *You* do all the hard work of finding the file and cranking it up." So, in that sense, a Start menu icon is a shortcut because it's a faster way for you to start your programs.

*Use the Create Shortcut dialog box to fire a program onto the Start menu.*

2. If you happen to know the name of the file that starts the program, and if you know the drive and folder where it resides, type all that in the **Command line** text box. For example, suppose the file that starts your program is called WP51.EXE, and it's on drive C in the WP51 folder. Then you'd enter the following in the Command line box: **c:\wp51\wp51.exe.**

   If you're not sure about any of this, select the **Browse** button to display the Browse dialog box, hunt down the file that starts the program, highlight it, and then select **Open.**

3. Select **Next >.** Windows 95 displays the Select Program Folder dialog box, shown below.

*Use the Select Program Folder dialog box to pick out a Start menu home for your program.*

4. Highlight the folder where you want the program's icon to appear. Note that if you highlight Start Menu, the icon appears on the main Start menu (the one that

appears when you select the Start button). If you highlight Desktop, the program's icon appears right on the Windows 95 desktop. (For the latter, however, you can only start the program by double-clicking on it; for more about desktop shortcuts, see the section "Easy Program Access: Creating Shortcuts on the Desktop," later in this chapter.)

5. Select **Next >**. The Select a Title for the Program dialog box appears.

6. Use the **Select a name for the shortcut** text box to enter the name you want to appear on the Start menu.

7. Select **Finish** to, well, finish.

# Starting Programs Automatically When You Start Windows 95

Windows 95 has a slick feature that makes starting programs a breeze: the Startup folder. The icons you stuff into this folder load automatically each time you start Windows 95. This is great for applications, such as WordPad or Explorer, that you use constantly or for documents (such as a to-do list) that you start up first thing every day.

Use the same technique I outlined in the previous section to create a Start menu icon for the program or document. When you get to Step 4, highlight the Startup folder. When you're done, you can see what's in your Startup folder by selecting the **Start** button, opening the **Programs** folder, and then opening the **Startup** folder.

## Removing Items from the Start Menu

As you'll see in Chapter 25, Windows 95 has a feature that enables you to "uninstall" some programs. (See the section titled "Wiping a Program Off Your Computer.") One of the chores this feature takes care of for you is to expunge any traces of the program from the Start menu. If it misses something, however, or if you need to get rid of a Start menu shortcut that you added manually, you need to clean up the Start menu yourself.

To try it, select the **Start Menu Programs** tab in the Taskbar Properties dialog box, and then select the **Remove** button to display the Remove Shortcuts/Folders dialog box. Open the folder containing the shortcut, highlight the shortcut, and then select **Remove**. Select **Close** to head back to the Taskbar Properties dialog box.

## Making More Room to Maneuver on the Taskbar

Although you'll probably only work with, at most, a few programs at once, Windows 95's multitasking capabilities sure make it tempting to open a boatload of applications.

The problem, though, is that it doesn't take long for the taskbar to become seriously overpopulated. As you can see in the following figure, with ten programs on the go, the taskbar buttons become all but indecipherable. ("Hey, Vern! What's this here 'Ph...' program supposed to do?") If you can't figure out what a particular taskbar button represents, point your mouse at the button you're puzzling over, and after a couple of seconds a banner appears telling you the full name of the program.

*An example of taskbar overcrowding.*

If you'd prefer to take in everything at a glance and you don't mind giving up a little more screen area, you can expand the taskbar to show two or more rows of buttons. To give 'er a go, point your mouse at the top edge of the taskbar (when it's positioned properly, the pointer changes to a two-headed arrow). Then drag the edge of the taskbar up until you see the dotted line above the taskbar. When you release the mouse button, Windows 95 expands the taskbar (see the following figure). You can enlarge the taskbar to include as many as ten (!) rows.

*With two rows, the buttons have some breathing room.*

# Easy Program Access: Creating Shortcuts on the Desktop

For our final desktop customization trick, I'll show you some other methods for creating shortcuts directly on the Windows 95 desktop. Why would you want to do that? Well, anything on the desktop is accessible with a simple double-click, so there are lots of good reasons for such convenience.

➤ If you have a favorite program that's buried under interminable Start menu folders, placing a shortcut for it on the desktop lets you crank it up lickety-split.

➤ If you have a document you use regularly (such as a to-do list or, like me, a never-put-off-until-tomorrow-what-you-can-put-off-until-the-day-after-tomorrow list), you can create a shortcut for the document to keep it within easy reach.

➤ If you do a lot of work in a particular folder, you can create a shortcut for the folder. Double-clicking the folder's shortcut icon opens the folder right away. (No more wading through windows in My Computer, or tracking down the folder in Explorer.)

➤ You can also create shortcuts for disk drives. So, for example, you might want to add a shortcut for your CD-ROM drive or for a floppy disk drive.

➤ Printers are shortcut candidates, too. If you create a printer shortcut, you have quick access to your printer's folder so you can watch the progress of your print jobs. You can also drag a document from Explorer or My Computer, drop it on the printer, and Windows 95 will print it for you, no questions asked!

> **Check This Out...**
>
> **A Desktop Shortcut Bonus** As an added bonus, if you have a folder or disk drive shortcut on the desktop, you can move or copy files by dragging them from Explorer or My Computer and dropping them on the shortcut.

As you saw earlier, you can use the Taskbar Properties dialog box to add shortcuts to the desktop. But Windows 95, of course, never gives you just one way to do anything. So, as a public service (it's a tough job but, hey, somebody's gotta do it), here are three other methods you can use:

➤ Right-click on an empty part of the desktop, select **New** in the shortcut menu, and select **Shortcut**. Follow the instructions given earlier to fill out the Create Shortcut dialog box that appears.

➤ In Explorer, highlight **Desktop** at the top of the All Folders list, select the **File** menu's **New** command, and then select **Shortcut** (or right-click on **Desktop**, select **New**, and select **Shortcut**). Again, fill out the Create Shortcut dialog box.

➤ Drag the program, document, folder, drive, Control Panel item, printer, or whatever from Explorer (or My Computer) and drop it on the desktop. If Windows 95 asks if you want to create a shortcut for the item, select **Yes**.

> **Check This Out...**
>
> **Drag-and-Drop Warning!** If you drag a file or folder onto the desktop, Windows 95 *moves* it there. To create a shortcut, instead, right-drag the file or folder and then, when you drop it on the desktop, select **Create Shortcut(s) Here** from the menu.

The following figure shows my desktop with a random sampling of shortcuts. Notice that each shortcut icon has a small arrow in the lower-left corner; this is Windows 95's way of telling you that an icon is a shortcut.

*Desktop shortcuts give you easy double-click access to programs, files, folders, drives, printers, and more.*

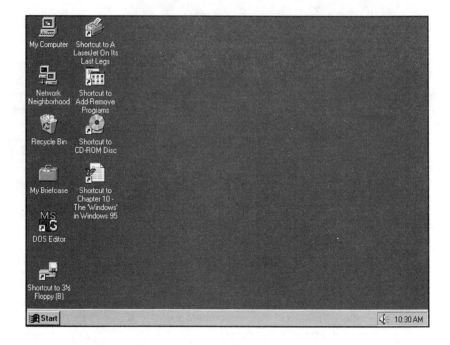

Are you wondering how I got my shortcuts to line up in apple-pie order? It's easy: just right-click on an empty part of the desktop, select **Arrange Icons** from the shortcut menu, and then select **by Name**, **by Type**, **by Size**, or **by Date**, by Jove. Neat freaks can also activate the **Auto Arrange** command to tell Windows 95 to keep the desktop spic-and-span all the time.

To delete a shortcut, either right-click on it and select **Delete** from the menu, or drag the shortcut into the **Recycle Bin**. (If you use the right-click method, a dialog box appears asking if you're sure you want to delete the shortcut. In this case, select **Yes**.) Note, however, that deleting a shortcut does *not* delete the program, file, folder, or whatever, only the shortcut icon.

## Sharing Your Computer? Here's How to Avoid Fistfights

Do you share your computer with other people either at work or at home? Then you've probably run smack dab into one undeniable fact: people are individuals with minds of their own! One person prefers Windows in a black-and-purple color scheme; another person just loves that annoying "Cars" wallpaper; yet another person prefers to have a zillion shortcuts on the Windows 95 desktop; and, of course, *everybody* uses a different mix of applications. How can you possibly satisfy all these diverse tastes and prevent people from coming to blows?

Well, it's a lot easier than you might think. Windows 95 enables you to set up a different *user profile* for each person who uses the computer. Each profile includes all the customization stuff we've covered in this chapter, such as colors, patterns or wallpapers, shortcut icons, the screen saver, and the programs that appear on the Start menu.

This means that each person can customize Windows 95 to her heart's content without foisting her tastes on anyone else. To set up a user profile, follow these steps:

1. Select the **Start** button, open the **Settings** folder, and select the **Control Panel** icon. Windows 95 throws the Control Panel window on the screen.

2. Select the **Passwords** icon and, in the Passwords Properties dialog box that appears, select the **User Profiles** tab.

3. Activate the **Users can customize their preferences and desktop settings** option button, activate the two check boxes in the **User Profile Settings** box, and then select **OK**. Windows 95 asks if you want to restart your computer.

4. Select **Yes**.

When Windows 95 reloads (and each subsequent time you crank up Windows 95), you'll see the Welcome to Windows dialog box. The idea here is that each person who uses the computer will have his or her own user name, which Windows will use to save his or her settings. So when you log on, you type your user name in the **User name** field, type an optional password in the **Password** field, and then select **OK**. If this is the first time you've entered your password (even if you leave it blank), the Set Windows Password dialog box appears. In the **Confirm new password** text box, reenter the password and select **OK**.

**A Faster Way to Log On** If someone else is logged on to Windows 95 and you prefer to use your settings, you don't have to restart Windows. Instead, select the **Start** button and select the **Shut Down** command. In the Shut Down Windows dialog box that appears, activate the **Close all programs and log on as a different user?** option and then select **Yes**.

If this is the first time you've logged on, the Windows Networking dialog box appears to ask if you want Windows 95 to save your settings. Select **Yes**. Windows 95 loads normally, and you can start customizing willy-nilly.

# The Least You Need to Know

This chapter showed you how to give the Windows 95 desktop a makeover to make it look its best. I showed you how to change colors, cover the desktop with a pattern or wallpaper, set up a screen saver, customize the taskbar and Start menu, and add shortcuts to the desktop. Wow! Now *that* was a chapter!

Our Windows 95 customization fun is only just beginning, though. In the next chapter, I'll show you how to set up your mouse and keyboard to your liking.

# Chapter 24

# The Made-to-Measure Mouse and Keyboard

## In This Chapter

➤ Making your mouse more reliable

➤ Checking out different mouse pointers

➤ Adjusting the keyboard speed

➤ Another customization compendium that'll help you tame your mouse and make your keyboard fly

In *Star Trek* and other sci-fi stories, the computers of the future are operated by voice commands. You simply say, "Computer!" and a couple of high-tech-sounding beeps tell you the computer is ready to obey your commands. In one of the *Star Trek* movies, the crew of the Enterprise travels back in time to modern-day Earth. There, Scotty (the engineer) has to use a late '80s-vintage PC (a Macintosh, I think). So, of course, he says "Computer!" and is disappointed when nothing happens. Then one of the locals hands the mouse to Scotty who puts it in front of his mouth and yells "Hello Computer!" as though he were speaking into a microphone!

I'm sure few of us have mistaken our mice for microphones (there's an idea for you budding entrepreneurs: micerophones!), but a mouse isn't an obvious tool to wield.

In addition, keyboards pose an interesting challenge for those of us who failed typing in school. Fortunately, Windows 95 has a few customization options that can make both your mouse and your keyboard a little easier to use; we'll check them out in this chapter.

## Messing with Your Mouse's Mind

For many new users, the biggest obstacle to overcome when learning Windows 95 is learning how to use a mouse for the first time. The problems range from controlling it, to getting double-clicks to work properly, to just finding the darn pointer! For the most part, these problems resolve themselves as people get used to the little rodent. However, the Windows 95 programmers were thoughtful enough to include some mouse customization features so each user can set up the mouse just the way he or she likes it.

 To see these options, select the **Start** button, open the **Settings** folder, and select **Control Panel**. In the Control Panel window, select the **Mouse** icon. The Mouse Properties dialog box appears, as shown below. The next few sections take you through using most of the controls in this dialog box. When you're done, select **OK** to put your new mega-mouse settings into effect.

*Use the options in the Mouse Properties dialog box to customize your mouse.*

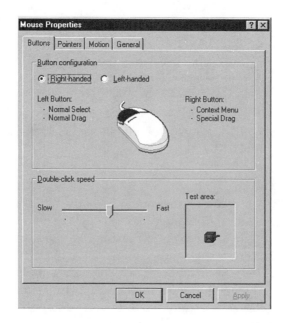

## Setting Up the Mouse for Left-Handers

Most mice and the applications that use them are "handists": they assume the user is right-handed. Southpaws, if you're tired of this politically incorrect discrimination, you can get a small measure of revenge by swapping the left and right buttons on your mouse. All you have to do is select the **Buttons** tab in the Mouse Properties dialog box and activate the **Left-handed** option button. This affects your mouse movements in the following ways:

➤ You now click and double-click with the right mouse button.

➤ To drag something, you press and hold down the right button.

➤ To display a shortcut menu (or a *context menu* as it's called in the Mouse Properties dialog box), left-click on an object.

➤ To perform the "special drag" in Explorer (the one that displays a shortcut menu when you drop a file or folder), you use the left mouse button.

## Controlling the Double-Click Speed

One of the things that a mouse-aware program must do is distinguish between two consecutive single clicks and a double-click. For example, if you click once, wait five seconds, and then click again, that qualifies as two single clicks in most people's books. But what if there's only a second between clicks? Or a half second? This threshold is called the *double-click speed*: anything faster is treated as a double-click; anything slower is treated as two single clicks.

You can adjust this threshold using the **Double-click speed** slider on the Buttons tab of the Mouse Properties dialog box. You have two options:

➤ If you find that Windows 95 doesn't always recognize your double-clicks, set up a slower double-click speed by moving the slider bar to the left.

➤ If you find that Windows 95 is sometimes interpreting two consecutive single clicks as a double-click, set up a faster double-click speed by moving the slider bar to the right.

To test the new speed, double-click on the **Test area**. If Windows 95 recognizes your double-click, a Jack-in-the-box pops up. (Yes, you read that correctly: a Jack-in-the-box. Obviously, some of the Windows 95 designers had *way* too much time on their hands!)

# Trying Different Pointers On for Size

As you trudge through Windows 95, you'll notice that the mouse pointer busies itself by changing into different icons depending on what you're doing. There's the standard arrow for selecting everything from check boxes to files and folders, there's the two-headed arrow for sizing window borders, and, of course, there's the dreaded hourglass icon that appears whenever a program or Windows 95 is too busy to bother with your petty concerns right now.

Surprisingly, the pointers used by Windows 95 in these and other situations aren't set in stone. To see how you can specify different pointers, select the **Pointers** tab in the Mouse Properties dialog box (see the following figure).

*Use the Pointers tab to change the look of the Windows 95 mouse pointers.*

A sample of pointers for the scheme selected

The easiest way to try out different pointers is to choose one of the pointer schemes that come with Windows 95. To do so, select a scheme from the **Scheme** drop-down list, and then take a look at the sample pointers in the box below the list to see what they look like. For example, the following figure shows the pointers you get when you select the Windows Standard (extra large) scheme (which is handy for anyone who has trouble picking out the pointer in a maze of windows).

*Try the extra-large
pointers if you're
having problems
seeing the mouse
pointer on-screen.*

If you're feeling pretty confident, you might want to try your hand at creating a scheme of your own. Here are the steps to plow through:

1. Select the pointer you want to change.

2. Select the **Browse** button, and Windows 95 displays the Browse dialog box.

3. Pick out the pointer you want to use and select **Open**. (Hint: there are lots in Windows 95's Cursors folder.)

4. Repeat steps 1–3 to customize any other pointers.

5. To save your scheme, select the **Save As** button, enter a name in the Save Scheme dialog box, and select **OK**.

# Controlling the Tracking Speed

When you move the mouse on its pad, Windows 95 translates this movement and tracks the mouse pointer on your screen accordingly. How quickly the mouse moves across the screen is called the *tracking speed*. If this speed is out of whack (for example, if you move the mouse furiously but the pointer just creeps along or, on the other extreme, if the slightest hand

**Reinstating the
Normal Pointers**
If you later want to
return your mouse
pointers to their
natural state, select the **Use
Default** button.

tremor causes the pointer to go racing across the screen), your mouse is likely to end up in the nearest garbage can.

The good news is that adjusting the tracking speed is a snap. In the Mouse Properties dialog box, select the **Motion** tab (shown in the following figure) and take a look at the **Pointer speed** slider. You can do two things with this control:

➤ If your mouse pointer is flying around the screen, slow it down by dragging the slider bar to the left.

➤ If the pointer is too slow, drag the slider bar to the right.

If you'd like to test the new setting, select the **Apply** button and try moving the mouse around.

*The Motion tab controls the mouse tracking speed and mouse trails (see the next section).*

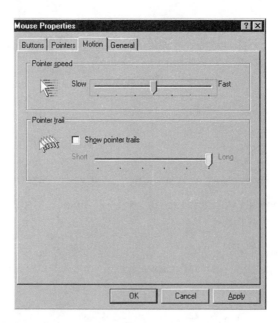

## Happy Mouse Trails to You

Many people who use notebook computers or whose eyesight isn't quite what it used to be have complained they have trouble finding the little mouse pointer on-screen. So Microsoft, ever sensitive, included a "pointer trail" feature in Windows 95. When you activate the Show pointer trails check box in the Motion tab and move your mouse, you see a trail of pointers following the main pointer. Then you can use the slider bar to make the trail longer or shorter. I suppose this does make it easier to see, but I use it all the time just because it's such a way-out, psychedelic effect.

# Customizing the Keyboard

Keyboard connoisseurs can also horn in on the customization carousing. First, though, you need to learn a bit of ever-so-painless keyboard theory:

When you press and hold down a letter on your keyboard, you notice two things. First, there's a slight *delay* between the time you press the key and the time the second letter appears; second, the subsequent letters appear at a constant rate (called the *repeat rate*).

Beginning keyboardists are usually better off with a longer delay and a slower repeat rate. More experienced typists, on the other hand, would probably prefer a short delay combined with a fast repeat rate.

 Fortunately, Windows 95 allows you to change both of these settings. To see how, select the **Start** button, open the **Settings** folder, and select **Control Panel**. When the Control Panel window appears, select the **Keyboard** icon to display the Keyboard Properties dialog box shown in the following figure.

*Use the Keyboard Properties dialog box to adjust your keyboard's delay and repeat rate.*

You control the delay by using the Repeat delay slider. Move the slider bar (by dragging it with your mouse or by using the left and right arrow keys) to the left for a longer delay or to the right for a shorter delay.

As you've no doubt guessed by now, the Repeat rate slider controls the repeat rate. Move the slider bar to the left for a slower rate or to the right for a faster one.

To try out the new settings, head for the **Click here and hold down a key to test repeat rate** text box. Press and hold down any key, and check out the delay and repeat rate. When you're satisfied with these settings, select **OK** to return to the Control Panel.

# The Least You Need to Know

This chapter showed you the ins and outs of customizing your two input devices: the mouse and keyboard. Since Windows 95 was designed with the mouse in mind, you get far more mouse customization options. You can switch between right-handed and left-handed use, alter the double-click speed, select different pointer schemes, adjust the pointer speed, and display cool mouse trails. For the keyboard, you can only adjust the delay and the repeat rate.

For our final look at customizing Windows 95, the next chapter tells you how to use Windows 95 to install programs, how to install Windows 95 components, how to add new hardware, and more.

# Chapter 25

# Adding New Stuff to Windows 95

## In This Chapter

➤ Adding and removing Windows 95 components

➤ Installing new programs in Windows 95

➤ Removing programs you no longer need

➤ Telling Windows 95 about your new hardware

➤ Letting Windows 95 know a piece of hardware has been removed

➤ A treasure trove of techniques for adding on to your Windows 95 house

You know that old saying that "The only difference between a man and a boy is the price of his toys"? Well, they got *that* right! In the transition from little kid to big kid, we go from Hot Wheels to hot cars, from tiny transistor radios to full-blown stereo systems, and of course, from scrawny, pint-sized calculators to brawny, king-sized computers.

For many people (even non-geeks), a computer is the ultimate toy because you can always add new gadgets and doodads to make your machine better, faster, smarter, or just plain more fun. The problem, though, is installing all these hardware and software gizmos. I'm convinced that Murphy must have just finished setting up some kind of computer doohickey when he formulated his famous Law ("If anything can go wrong, it will").

I suppose the makers of Windows 95 must have become fed up dealing with installation irritations, because they built several features into Windows 95 that make setting up both hardware and software practically painless. This chapter checks out these features and shows how they can make your life easier.

# Adding and Removing Windows 95 Components

Like a hostess who refuses to put out the good china for just anybody, Windows 95 doesn't install all of its components automatically when you run the Windows installation program. Don't feel insulted, though, because Windows is just trying to go easy on your hard disk. The problem, you see, is that some of the things that come with Windows 95 are software behemoths that will happily usurp acres of your precious hard disk land. So as a courtesy to you, Windows doesn't install these programs and a few others unless you specifically request them.

"A lot of good this information does me now," you may be grumbling, seeing as how you've already installed Windows 95. But wait! There *is* a way to add any of Windows 95's missing pieces to your system without having to trudge through the entire Windows installation routine. You can just use the handy Windows Setup feature.

To get to Windows Setup, select the **Start** button, open the **Settings** folder, and select **Control Panel**. In the Control Panel window, select the **Add/Remove Programs** icon to display the Add/Remove Programs Properties dialog box, and then select the **Windows Setup** tab. You'll see a dialog box like the one shown here.

*The Windows Setup dialog box lets you add or remove the bits and pieces that come with Windows 95.*

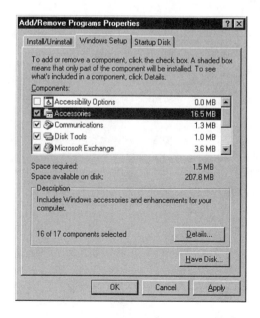

The **Components** box lists the various chunks of Windows 95 that you can add or remove. Note that some of these "components" actually consist of several programs (which I guess we could call "component components"); the Accessories component, for example, includes WordPad, Paint, Calculator, and more. Components with a plain check mark beside them are fully installed. If a check box is filled in with gray, though, it means that some pieces of the component are installed, but others aren't. And finally, if the check box is blank, none of that component is installed.

## How Much Is Installed?

To find out how many of the component's programs are installed, check out the Description box; below the component description, you'll see something like **16 of 17 components selected**. This tells you that the component consists of 17 programs and only 16 of them are installed on your system.

# Adding Windows 95 Components

Okay, it's time to bring out our brass tacks and get down to the nitty-gritty of adding some of these component things. If you're in a devil-may-care, you-only-go-around-once kind of mood, you can install an entire component by activating the check box next to it. To install just one or more pieces of a component, highlight the component and select the **Details** button. A list of the programs in the component appears, as shown in the following figure. Again, select the check box for each program you want to install. When you're done, select **OK** to return to the Windows Setup tab.

*Choose individual pieces of a component you want to install.*

When you finish making your selections, select **OK**. Windows 95 will likely ask you to insert one or more of your original Windows disks (or your Windows CD-ROM). Insert the disk it asks for and select **OK** to continue. Depending on the components you're adding, Windows 95 may ask you to restart your computer. If it does, select **Yes** to let Windows 95 handle this for you. When the restart is complete, the new programs are ready to roll.

## Removing a Windows 95 Component

One of my favorite sketches from the old *Saturday Night Live* shows was called "The Thing That Wouldn't Leave!" It featured John Belushi as a late-staying party guest who wouldn't take any of the hosts' hints about leaving. Instead, he kept hanging around, watching TV, eating their food, downing their drinks, and even making long-distance phone calls!

If you have a Windows component that's worn out its welcome, forget the hints: you can use Windows Setup to give it the old heave-ho. This makes it easy for, say, the artistically challenged to get rid of that Paint program they never use, or for the hopelessly unwired to expunge HyperTerminal from their systems. As an added bonus, removing chunks of Windows from your hard disk also frees up space for programs you *really* need, like Super Mega Video Pinball Deluxe.

Removing Windows 95 components is the opposite of adding them (Duh!). In the Windows Setup tab, deactivate the check boxes for the programs you want to blow away. Again, for multi-program components, select **Details** to see the individual programs, deactivate the check boxes for those you want to nuke, and then select **OK**. Windows 95 removes the components you specified without further delay.

## Great: A New Program! Not So Great: Installing the Darn Thing!

It's a rare computer owner who's satisfied with just the programs that came preloaded on her machine. We all want something bigger, better, faster, *cooler*. Unfortunately, the other definition of "computer user" is "sucker for software marketing hype." So all we have to do is read some breathless package copy ("Most programs offer you everything but the kitchen sink. Well, our new "CodeBloat" suite of applications comes with a brand new kitchen sink, right in the box! Free!") and five minutes later we're walking out of the software store with the latest whiz-bang new program under our arm.

Before Windows 95 came along, you were on your own when it came time to install the program on your system. Now, however, that's all changed. No matter what kind of program you're installing, you can start with Windows 95's Add/Remove Programs

Wizard and take a walk through a series of dialog boxes to get the program's installation show on the road.

### Windows Setup vs. Add/Remove Programs Wizard

Don't get confused by the similarities between Windows Setup and the Add/Remove Programs Wizard. Windows Setup only deals with the accessories and programs that are part of Windows 95 itself; the Add/Remove Programs Wizard handles everything else.

# Installing the Program from the Installation Disks

For starters, crank up the Add/Remove Programs dialog box as described earlier, click on the **Install/Uninstall** tab (if it isn't visible already), and select the **Install** button. The dialog box that appears asks you to insert the first installation disk or the program's CD-ROM. When you've done that, select **Next >**.

The Wizard checks all your floppy and CD-ROM drives, searching desperately for any installation program it can find. When it locates a likely candidate, it displays it in the **Command line for installation program** text box, as you can see in the following figure.

*The Add/Remove Programs Wizard can hunt down your software's installation program automatically.*

If the Wizard correctly identified the setup program, select **Finish** to continue. How do you know the Wizard isn't giving you a bum steer? There are three ways to tell:

➤ The first letter in the text box represents the letter of the disk drive where the Wizard found the program. In the figure shown above, for example, the drive letter is A. This letter should be the same as the letter of the disk drive into which you inserted the disk.

➤ The part after the backslash (\) is the name of the installation program. It should say something like INSTALL.EXE or SETUP.EXE.

➤ Many installation disks tell you the name of the program to run (or it may appear in the manual that comes with the program). This name should match the text box text.

If the Wizard didn't find the program properly, select the **Browse** button, find and highlight the installation program in the Browse dialog box that appears, select **Open** to return to the Wizard, and *then* select **Finish**. In either case, the software's installation program runs automatically.

If you're installing a program that was designed to run with Windows 95, the installation program will probably set up an icon (and maybe even a whole submenu) on the Start menu, from which you can run the program. If you're installing a DOS program or a Windows program that doesn't set itself up on the Start menu, head back to Chapter 23 and read the section titled "Adding Items to the Start Menu."

**3.1** ### Submenu? Program Group?

If the program you're dealing with was written specifically to work with Windows 95, sometime during the installation process you'll be asked which submenu or folder you want the program to appear in. No big whoop there. However, if the program was written for Windows 3.1, it'll ask you which *program group* you want to use. As you know by now, the old Windows 3.1 program groups have been replaced by Start menu folders, so both of these mean the same thing: from what point on the Start menu do you want to be able to start the program?

# Wiping a Program Off Your Computer

People change. The game you were obsessed with last week now bores you; the word processor you swore you couldn't live without seems clunky and awkward compared to the slick new one your neighbor just bought. Hey, don't feel bad for being fickle (or for paying an outrageous price for the program you now hate)—it happens to everyone.

Of course, life's too short—and hard disk real estate is too precious—to have your old programs littering your machine. You need to delete those loser programs to make room for more programs and get on with your life. Fortunately, Windows 95 can remove some software automatically. Therefore, before you start deleting, display the Add/Remove Programs dialog box, activate the **Install/Uninstall** tab, and see if the program you want to delete is on the list of programs Windows can automatically remove. This list contains only programs that meet the following criteria:

➤ The program is written especially for Windows 95.

➤ It was installed using the Add/Remove Programs Wizard.

If you see the program you want to blow away, activate its check box and select the **Add/Remove** button. The program that appears takes you through the necessary steps for obliterating the program.

For software that doesn't meet the above criteria, you'll have to do the pruning by hand. Getting rid of software is a two-part process: you have to delete the files and folders for the program, and then you have to remove references to it from Windows 95.

First, we'll remove the folder (and all its files). In Explorer or My Computer, find the folder that contains the program and delete it. (I covered deleting folders back in Chapter 13, in the "More Recycle Bin Fun: Deleting Folders" section.)

Your next chore is to erase any traces of the program from your Start menu. You learned how to do this back in Chapter 23 (see the section titled "Removing Items from the Start Menu").

# Adding a New Piece of Hardware

One of the best features of Windows 95 is its capability to automatically detect and set up the huge variety of hardware contraptions you can attach to your computer. New CD-ROM? No problem. Different mouse or modem? Piece of cake. Just let Windows 95's Add New Hardware Wizard walk you through it.

It's easiest to just install the new hardware first, and then let Windows 95 figure out what kind of hardware it is. So go ahead and attach the new piece of hardware using the instructions that came with it (hint: bribe a computer-savvy friend to do it). When your hardware is in place, turn the computer and the new device on, and get back to Windows 95.

Then fire up Control Panel by selecting the **Start** button, opening the **Settings** folder, and selecting the **Control Panel** icon. In the Control Panel window, select the **Add New Hardware** icon. In a great cloud of smoke (not!), the Add New Hardware Wizard appears, ready to assist you, as shown in the following figure. The first Wizard dialog box merely displays a couple of not-very-useful sentences; go ahead and select **Next >** to continue.

*The Add New Hardware Wizard walks you through the installation process as painlessly as possible.*

**Don't Panic!**
Don't let the warning in the dialog box intimidate you, and don't worry if it takes the Wizard a long time to detect your hardware. As long as your hard disk is whirring and the indicator bar is moving, you're fine. On the off chance that your computer does stop dead in its tracks during this procedure, calmly shut it off and turn it back on again. When you're back in Windows, you'll need to install the hardware using the instructions in the "Other Ways to Install New Hardware" section that follows.

In the next dialog box, make sure the **Automatically detect installed hardware** option is active and select **Next >**. When Windows 95 tells you it's ready to look for new hardware (and gives you a scary-sounding warning about how this process "could cause your machine to stop responding." Yikes!), select **Next >** again to continue. Your hard disk whirs frantically for a few minutes, and then Windows 95 lets you know what it's found.

If the Wizard doesn't find any new hardware, it tells you so. If that happens, select **Cancel**, shut down your computer (make sure you use the Start menu's **Shut Down** command), check to see if you've attached the new item correctly, and then try again. If it's still a no-go, try installing the hardware using the instructions in the next section.

More likely, however, the Wizard will tell you it's finished detecting and is ready for more. Select the **Details** button to see what the Wizard found, and then select **Finish** to move on.

Next, the Wizard shows you the type of device it thinks you have (see the following figure). If it's right, great. Select **Next >** to continue, and you're done. If it's not right, select the **Change** button, select the real identity of the component, select **Next >** to return to the Wizard, and select **Next >** again.

*The Wizard tries to identify the new hardware, and most of the time it succeeds.*

Select this button if the Wizard guessed incorrectly.

You're done! The new hardware has been successfully set up for Windows' use.

# Other Ways to Install New Hardware

The procedure I just showed you works great—90% of the time. However, there may be situations in which you want to set up Windows to accept the hardware before you install the hardware itself. Or you may run across some hardware that Windows 95 can't or won't recognize. In that case, you'll have to take the manual route.

Instead of telling Windows 95 to automatically detect installed hardware, select the **Install specific hardware** button to pick the hardware type from a list (see the following figure). The Wizard displays an impressive list that includes every kind of hardware you can imagine; and just in case you're more imaginative than the rest of us, there's even an **Unknown hardware** selection you can go with.

*Pick a hardware type from the list, and then pick the particulars from the resulting dialog box.*

Select **Next >** to continue, and the Wizard displays a special dialog box in which you can enter the particulars about the hardware you want to set up (most of which you should find in the manual that came with the device). Just wade on through, supplying the facts as it asks for them and selecting **Next >** ad nauseam, until you reach the end of the interview. (The exact items on the lists vary depending on the hardware type.)

**Check This Out...**

**Have Disk, Will Travel** When you're manually setting up hardware, you'll run across a Have Disk button in some dialog boxes. This button gives you the opportunity to pull setup files from any installation diskette that might have come with the hardware. To use it, just pop the diskette into your disk drive and select the **Have Disk** button.

## Getting Rid of Hardware

As you saw in the previous section, Windows 95 prides itself on being able to tell what hardware you've got. But if you get rid of a piece of hardware, Windows doesn't have any way of knowing it's gone unless you tell it so. For instance, if you get a new printer and disconnect the old one to make room for it, not only does Windows have to be told to look for the new printer (as in the previous section), but it also has to be told that the old printer is no longer available.

To tell Windows you've removed a piece of hardware, select the **Start** button, open the **Settings** folder, and select **Control Panel**. The Control Panel window shows icons for the various types of hardware (printers, modems, keyboards, and so on). Select the icon for the type of hardware you're removing.

For some types of hardware, such as printers, a window opens containing an icon for each of the items of that type that you have installed. Highlight the one you want to remove, and then delete it. When you're finished, close the window.

For other types of hardware, such as modems and keyboards, a dialog box opens with a list of the installed items. To remove one, select it and select the **Remove** button. Select **OK** to close the dialog box.

## The Least You Need to Know

This chapter closed our look at Windows 95 customization by shifting our emphasis from renovating the Windows 95 house to constructing new additions (and, in some cases, tearing them down). You learned how to add and remove Windows 95 components, how to use Windows 95 to install and uninstall software, and how to tell Windows 95 about your new hardware. The next chapter starts our exploration of how to get the most out of a particular piece of hardware: your modem.

# Chapter 26

# Basic Modem Fun

## In This Chapter

➤ What's a modem, and what can you do with one?

➤ Setting up your modem with Windows 95

➤ What online services can do for you

➤ HyperTerminal: the pumped-up communications program

➤ Getting Windows to dial your phone

➤ Your personal on-ramp to that information expressway thing

As you've no doubt figured out by now, computer nerds thrive on jargon and buzzwords. These terms range from the useful (such as *multimedia* and *drag-and-drop*) to the downright silly (*GUI* and *boot* come to mind). Fortunately, most jargon never makes it past the narrow confines of each nerd's subspecialty (which means the rest of us don't have to know about scary-sounding things like *TCP/IP* and *client-server*).

Occasionally, however, the odd buzzword makes it into the mainstream where, tragically, it's quickly trampled to death by media overkill. (I call it the "cachet-to-clichè" syndrome.) The most spectacular example of this was the phrase *user friendly*, which appeared ad nauseam a few years back. The current champ in the overused-phrase category is *Information Superhighway*. Heck, the thing doesn't even exist yet, and we're already sick of hearing about it!

But just as *user friendly* was a good idea before it was knocked silly (after all, who'd want to use something that was *user hostile*?), so too is the Information Superhighway a good idea that's been obscured by hype. In this chapter, we'll ignore the hype, and I'll show you how to use your modem and Windows 95's HyperTerminal accessory to tap into the existing services (such as bulletin board systems and large-scale data marketplaces like CompuServe) that are the precursors of the info autobahn. And, believe it or not, you can even teach your modem to dial your phone when you're making regular phone calls! Stay tuned for the details.

# What's All This About Modems?

Although *modem* sounds like a way to ask for seconds ("Hey, Wilbur, gimme mo' dem black-eyed peas!"), it's actually a little piece of hardware that attaches to your computer. This handy device makes it possible for two or more computers to communicate through yer basic telephone lines. (Which are known as POTS to the online cognoscenti: Plain Old Telephone Service.) Phone lines aren't built to carry computer data, though; they're built to carry sounds. So the modem's job is to convert computer data to sounds that can be sent across the phone lines, and then capture sounds coming in and convert them back to computer data.

**Check This Out...**

**Modem Etymology**
Modem is short for MOdulator/ DEModulator. That's a fancy way of saying that the modem converts computer data to sounds (that's the modulator part) and sounds to computer data (that's the demodulator part).

There are two types of modems: internal and external. An *internal* modem is a circuit board inside the computer, and an *external* modem is a plastic box that connects to one of the computer's ports in the back. Depending on how new the modem is and how much you paid for it, it may have a maximum speed of anywhere from 1,200 bits per second (bps) to 28,800 bps. (A *bit* is the fundamental unit of all computer data; to give you a frame of reference, it takes 8 bits to make up a single character, such as the letter *A* or the number *2*.)

Regardless of the brand, speed, or type, most modems work the same as far as your software is concerned. That's because most modems are *Hayes-compatible*. The Hayes modem commands comprise a standard language used by almost all modems sold today. Don't worry—you don't have to memorize any of the commands; just make sure your modem is Hayes-compatible (it should tell you on the box or in the manual that came with the modem).

## What Can You Do with a Modem?

A modem's purpose in life is to enable you to establish a connection between your computer and another computer: it could be a friend's machine across town, a bulletin board service (BBS for short), your local library, a commercial online service like the Microsoft Network (see "Windows in Cyberspace: The Microsoft Network" at the back of this book), or even the Internet. You can also have a modem dial your telephone for you when you're making a regular phone call, or send and receive faxes (if your modem is a special type called a *fax/modem*). I'll teach you how to get your modem to perform all of these tricks in this chapter and the next couple of chapters. (Need to set up your modem in Windows 95? No problemo. Flip back to Chapter 25 and peruse the section titled "Adding a New Piece of Hardware" to find out all you need to know.)

## A Look at Online Services

An online service is a big, honkin' computer (or a group of big, honkin' computers) you can call with your modem. It contains all kinds of useful and interesting attractions (and, of course, a few useless and dull ones, too), assembled by the company that owns the service. You normally have to pay a monthly fee (and sometimes additional hourly charges) to hook up to an online service.

The offerings vary a bit from service to service, but here are the general categories of amusements you're likely to find:

**Files for downloading** Almost all services have freeware and shareware files available for you to "download" to your computer through the modem connection. You can get full-fledged programs, utilities, graphics, games, or just about anything else under the software sun.

### More Modemspeak

**Download** To transfer a file from someone else's computer to your own. The opposite of this is **upload**, which means to transfer a file from your own computer to someone else's.

**Freeware** Software that costs precisely nothing, nada, zip, nil, zero, the big 0.

**Shareware** A try-before-you-buy system of purchasing software. The creator makes the software available for free to you, and if you end up using it a lot, you're honor-bound to pay a small registration fee.

**Electronic mail (e-mail)**   You can send messages back and forth with almost anyone else who has an e-mail account anywhere in the world: a pen pal in Australia, your grandmother, your ex-wife, or even your high-school guidance counselor (just to let her know how you turned out!).

**Bulletin boards, forums, and newsgroups**   These have different names depending on the service you're using, but essentially, they're all areas where you can post public messages like on a bulletin board, and other people can reply publicly or by private e-mail. People post their classified ads, great (and not-so-great) opinions, and even personal ads for the lovelorn.

**Live chat**   Tired of sending e-mail? With live chat gabfests, you can type a message to someone who's connected at the same time you are, and he or she can type a message right back at you. You can waste entire days having long, involved conversations with total strangers.

**Reference information**   There's a wealth of info out there that's available absolutely free (or for a small fee sometimes). You can read Shakespeare, get the latest stock quotes, look up the population of Butte, Montana, find out the extended weather forecast for Nepal, and much more.

# Which Online Service Should I Join?

There's a staggering number of commercial online services that want your business, so you should shop around before deciding which one to join. Most of the services have try-before-you-buy specials that let you frolic online for a few hours without being charged. Here's a quick look at some of the big players in the online world:

**The Microsoft Network**   As I'll discuss in the section at the back of this book, this Johnny-come-lately online service is brought to you by Microsoft, the makers of Windows 95.

**CompuServe**   This big, business-like online service has been around for many years. It offers all the standard fare: files, forums, e-mail, chatting, reference, and so on.

**America Online**   This fast-growing service is widely known as the place to party online. It's less business-oriented and more tuned in to having fun, and it has plenty of files to download and plenty of friendly people eager to chat with you.

**PRODIGY**   The most family-oriented of the services, PRODIGY has the reputation of having very good offerings for kids. It's easy to use but can be a bit slow and the interface gives ugly a good name.

Most online services require special software, but it's available free for the asking. Services usually cost approximately $10 to $20 a month, with an extra hourly charge of $2 to $10 if you use the service more than your monthly allotment of minutes (usually 120 or 180 minutes is included in your monthly membership fee). Prices vary greatly, so call for details:

| Service | Phone number(s) |
| --- | --- |
| America Online | (800) 827-6364 or (703) 448-8700 |
| CompuServe | (800) 848-8199 or (614) 457-8600 |
| Microsoft Network | (800) 426-9400 or (206) 882-8080 |
| PRODIGY | (800) 776-3449 |

## Other Online Connections You Can Make

You're not limited to using just these big-player online services. You can also connect to local Bulletin Board Services (BBSs) in your town, to smaller services such as GEnie or Delphi, and to the wild and wooly world of the Internet. You can even connect to a friend's computer for private conversation or file-exchanging!

Check This Out...

### Did Someone Say Internet?

The *Internet* is a giant network of computer networks that everyone seems to be talking about these days. Most online services offer Internet access in some form, so unless you're an aspiring computer geek, don't worry about hooking up directly to the Internet. Just join one of the online services and start surfing! One caveat, though: long Internet sessions via most of the major online services will cost you a pretty penny. Check into the costs before you go hog wild on the "Net."

To connect with a service or BBS that doesn't supply its own software, or with a friend's computer, you'll need to use a communications program like Windows 95's HyperTerminal (covered next).

## Getting Wired with HyperTerminal

As I've said, most of the online services come with their own software, which you must have in order to connect to them. However, some services, such as local BBSs, don't have special software. For these, you have to use a generic communications program (or *terminal program*, as modem geeks like to say) to tell your modem what number to dial.

### You Can't Use the Phone Dialer Program to Dial Other Computers

If you've noticed Windows 95's Phone Dialer accessory, you may have been tempted to use it to dial another computer. Alas, however, that's a no-go: Phone Dialer is only for voice calls. (I'll tell you how to use it later on.) You have to use a communications program like HyperTerminal if the computer you're calling doesn't provide special software of its own.

If you've worked with Windows 3.1, you may have suffered with, oops, I mean *used* Terminal, its communications program. You probably didn't like it much, though (most people didn't), because it was pretty awkward and clunky. Fortunately, Windows 95's HyperTerminal is a quantum leap ahead of the old Terminal program. It's almost like a full-featured communications program that you might pay big bucks for in a store!

## Making a Connection with HyperTerminal

To start HyperTerminal, choose the **Start** button, open the **Programs** folder, the **Accessories** folder, and then select **HyperTerminal**. This opens a folder containing just the HyperTerminal icon, as you can see in the following figure. Later, when you create special profiles for certain connections you make, they'll appear in this window, too, so you can access them quickly when you need them.

*HyperTerminal enables you to connect to remote computers with your modem.*

For now, however, let's just start up HyperTerminal by double-clicking on the **Hypertrm** icon. The first thing you'll see is the Connection Description dialog box asking you to enter some information about the connection you want to make. Type the name for the connection you want to make in the **Name** text box, and then, in the **Icon** list, select the icon that best sums up the type of connection you're making. (If you're not sure, just pick an icon that strikes your fancy.) Select **OK** to continue, and the Phone Number dialog box appears, as shown in the following figure.

*The Phone Number dialog box is where you enter (you guessed it) the phone number.*

Use the **Phone number** text box to enter the phone number you'll be calling (the dash is optional). If the call is long distance, enter the area code in the **Area code** text box. If the call is *really* long distance (outside North America), use the **Country code** drop-down list to select the appropriate country code. When you're done, select **OK** to continue.

Now the Connect dialog box appears. If you need to dial a number to get an outside line, if you'd like to dial using a calling card, or if you need to disable Call Waiting, select the **Dialing Properties** button, fill in the appropriate info in the Dialing Properties dialog box, and select **OK**. You're returned to the Connect dialog box, and you're ready for action. Make sure your modem is turned on, and then select **Dial** to dial the number.

### Disable Call Waiting!

As I said earlier, modems work by converting a computer's bits and bytes into tones, and then sending those tones across regular phone lines. If you have call waiting, you probably know that it signals an incoming call by sounding a beep. Because these beeps can wreak havoc on a modem that's transmitting data, you should always disable call waiting before you initiate a HyperTerminal connection. The code to do this is usually *70, but check with your phone company to be sure. Note, as well, that call waiting is turned back on automatically when you complete your call.

# Okay, I'm Connected. Now What?

When you select Dial, the modem dials the number, and your computer connects to the other computer, just like that! If you're calling a BBS, directions appear on-screen telling you how to work with the computer you're calling. Just follow along with whatever it tells you. If you're connecting to a friend's computer, you won't see anything fancy: what you type simply appears on his or her screen, and vice-versa. You can send and receive files to and from each other, too.

# The File Transfer Thing

If you need to receive a file from a BBS or online service (or, more rarely, send one of your own files to the service), you'll generally need to slog through the following steps:

1. Move to the appropriate file transfer area. All services have different sections you can move into and out of. For example, there might be sections for browsing information, getting help, leaving messages, and so on. You usually get a menu of choices; look for a menu item such as Download (if you're receiving), Upload (if you're sending), or Files. If you're transferring files to a friend, skip to step 4.

2. Tell the service you want to receive or send a file (how you do this will depend on the service). You'll be asked to enter the name of the file. If you're receiving a file and you're not sure of its name, you can usually browse through a list of the service's files to find the one you want.

3. You'll also be asked which "transfer protocol" you want to use. This isn't as scary as it sounds because HyperTerminal can only use a few of these protocol things, and there are one or two you'll use almost all the time (I explain everything you need to know a little later).

4. Tell HyperTerminal you want to perform a file transfer (I'll discuss this in detail in a sec).

5. When the transfer is complete, you usually have to press **Enter** or some other key to let the service know you're back.

The next couple of sections take a closer look at steps 3 and 4.

**Transfers Between Friends Are Easier**

If you want to exchange a file with a friend, the two of you first need to decide which protocol you want to use. Then you pull down the **Transfer** menu and select either **Send File** or **Receive File** (as needed), while your friend issues the appropriate "receive" or "send" command in his or her program at the same time. For example, suppose you want to send a file to your friend. You select the Transfer menu's Send File command, and your friend selects the "receive" command in his or her communications program.

# Following Protocol

In diplomacy, *protocol* defines the rules and formalities that smooth communications between nations. Just to get two modems *talking* to each other requires perfect synchronization of various communications settings (most of which, thankfully, HyperTerminal handles for you automatically). If we now want to actually exchange data, that just adds a whole new level of complexity.

The good news is that this complexity is something you and I can safely ignore because the world's modem nerds have worked out various solutions. These solutions are called *protocols,* and, in the same way that diplomatic protocols make cultural exchanges easy, communications protocols are designed to make it easy for two modems to exchange data. The only thing we have to do is make sure both modems are using the same protocol. Otherwise, we'll end up like two diplomats trying to perform different ceremonies at the same time: things just won't mesh properly.

Here's how it works. When you let the BBS know you want to receive or send a file, it eventually displays a list of the protocols it can use and asks you to select the one you want to use during the transfer. Which one should you choose? Well, HyperTerminal supports six different protocols, but two are the most common: Zmodem and Xmodem. Zmodem is better because it's faster, but not all BBSs support it. I've yet to encounter a BBS that doesn't support at least XModem, so that's a good fallback choice. (I'll tell you how to select a protocol in the next section.)

# Receiving and Sending Files

Once you've told the online service the name of the file you want to receive or send and the protocol to use, the service says something like **Ready to send/receive file. Please initiate file transfer.** At this point, pull down the **Transfer** menu and select either the **Receive File** command (if you're receiving a file) or the **Send File** command (if you're sending a file). Note that, in some cases, HyperTerminal selects the appropriate command for you automatically.

If you selected Receive File, the Receive File dialog box appears (see the following figure). In the **Place received file in the following folder** text box, enter the name of the folder in which you want to store the file. If you're not sure of the folder's name, select the **Browse** button, pick out a folder in the Select a Folder dialog box that appears, and select **OK** to return to the Receive File dialog box. To select a protocol, activate the **Use receiving protocol** list and pick out the same protocol you selected in the BBS. When you're done, select the **Receive** button to proceed with the transfer.

*Use the Receive File dialog box to select a folder to store the file and a protocol.*

If you selected Send File, the Send File dialog box appears. In this case, enter the name of the file to send in the **Filename** text box (or use the **Browse** button to select the file), use the **Protocol** drop-down list to choose the same protocol you selected in the BBS, and select **Send** to make it so.

In either case, HyperTerminal displays the progress of the transfer in a dialog box. If, for any reason, you need to abort the transfer in midstream, you can select the **Cancel** button.

When the transfer is complete, HyperTerminal returns control to the service, and you can continue with other service options or log off.

# Closing the Connection

When you've finished using the service, issue the command to disconnect. This command varies depending on what service you're calling, but it's usually something like L for logoff, Q for Quit, or E for Exit. You should log off in whatever manner it expects; don't just hang up! If you're calling a friend, there won't be any special command to issue; you have to manually disconnect by selecting the **Call** menu's **Disconnect** command, or your friend must issue a similar command in his or her communications software.

When you're done using HyperTerminal, exit the program in the usual way (by selecting the **File** menu's **Exit** command). When HyperTerminal asks if you want to save the "session," select **Yes**. Notice that now the HyperTerminal window displays the icon you selected to represent the connection you just set up! To call this same number again, you can just select that icon instead of selecting HyperTerminal itself (see the following figure).

*The icon for the connection you just made is a shortcut you can use to make that same connection again.*

# Automatic Phone Dialing with Windows 95

Have you ever wished you had a telephone with speed dial that would let you program the numbers you call often, so all you would have to do is press a single button and the phone would do the rest? (Those of you who are already blessed with one of these gadgets, bear with me for a minute.) Well, that's the idea behind Windows 95's Phone Dialer.

To take advantage of Phone Dialer, you need both a phone (duh) and a modem. In addition to attaching the modem cable to a serial port in the back of your computer (if you're using an external modem), you also need to rearrange your phone cables:

➤ Run one phone cable from your phone to the "Phone" jack on your modem.

➤ Run a second phone cable from your modem's "Line" jack to the phone jack on your wall.

When all that malarkey is done, you can get into Phone Dialer by selecting the **Start** button, opening the **Programs** folder, opening the **Accessories** folder, and selecting the **Phone Dialer** icon. You'll see a window that looks something like the one shown in the following figure.

*The Phone Dialer works just like one of those fancy telephones.*

Speed dial buttons

Looks just like a telephone keypad, doesn't it? To dial a number, just type it in the **Number to dial** text box (or click on the appropriate numbers with your mouse) and then select the **Dial** button. Through your modem's speaker, you'll hear the phone dialing. When someone picks up at the other end, pick up your receiver and start talking!

If you want to dial the same number again later, activate the **Number to dial** drop-down list and select the number. No retyping is necessary.

## Setting Up Phone Dialer to Work for You

There are lots of handy little extra options you can set for the Phone Dialer. For instance, do you always have to dial a 9 for an outside line? How about a 1 for long-distance? Or maybe you always disable call waiting before you make an important call? Phone Dialer can handle all that for you.

Just pull down Phone Dialer's **Tools** menu and select **Dialing Properties**. You'll see a dialog box like the one shown in the following figure.

In this dialog box, you can specify prefixes for local and long-distance calls, you can set up instructions for using a calling card, and you can even disable call waiting. Just pick the options you want, and then select **OK** to leave.

There are some additional settings you can experiment with to make your own work easier. You'll find them behind the other choices on the Tools menu. I won't go into them all in detail, but here are a couple of tips:

➤ If you're using a calling card, select the **Tools** menu's **Connect Using** command, and select the **Line Properties** button. In the Properties dialog box that appears, select the **Options** tab and, under **Dial control**, specify the amount of time to wait for the credit card tone. The default is 0 seconds.

➤ To adjust the volume of your modem's speaker, pull down the **Tools** menu, select **Connect Using**, and select the **Line Properties** button. Select the **General** tab and adjust the **Speaker volume** as desired.

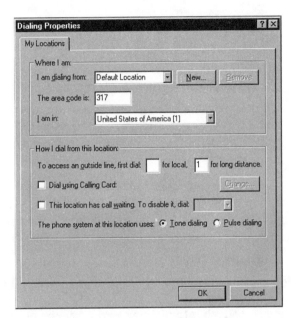

*This is where you set up Phone Dialer for the little extra touches that make life easier.*

### If It's Tuesday, I Must Be in the Office

If you use your computer in different places, such as the office and your home, you might want to set up a different dialing profile for each location. You do this in the Dialing Properties dialog box by selecting the **New** button and filling in the blanks. Then, when you're ready to dial, specify which location you're dialing from by selecting it from the I am dialing from drop-down list.

## Quick Connections with Speed Dial

But you didn't come here to learn how to do simple dialing, did you? You came here to play with the Speed Dial feature. Well, I won't disappoint you.

When you first open Phone Dialer, all eight of the Speed dial buttons are empty. To program one of them, click on the button, and a dialog box appears, as shown in the following figure.

*Use this dialog box to program an empty Speed dial button.*

In the **Name** text box, enter the name you want associated with the number, and then enter the number itself in the **Number to dial** text box. Then select the **Save** button to save the info or **Save and Dial** to save it and go ahead and dial the number right now. (Note that any settings you've defined—such as those for using a calling card—also apply to Speed dial numbers you call.)

If you want to change the name or number associated with one of the Speed dial buttons, you can't just select it like you did when you first entered the info because selecting a button dials the number. Instead, you need to pull down the **Edit** menu and select the **Speed Dial** command. Phone Dialer displays the Edit Speed Dial dialog box.

From here, highlight the button you want to edit, and then modify the data in the **Name** and **Number to dial** text boxes. (You can also assign Speed dial numbers from this dialog box, if you want.) If you want to delete a Speed dial number, select it and then delete the info in both the **Name** and **Number to dial** text boxes. When you're done, select **Save** to return to Phone Dialer.

The next time you want to call any of the numbers on your Speed dial list, just select the button! You may want to keep Phone Dialer running all the time so it's handy.

## The Least You Need to Know

This chapter got our look at communicating with Windows 95 off to a rousing beginning. You learned all kinds of semi-useful info about modems and computer communications, and I showed you how to wield the HyperTerminal and Phone Dialer tools.

For our next communications trick, Chapter 27 takes you on a tour of Microsoft Exchange.

# Exchanging Messages with Microsoft Exchange

## In This Chapter

➤ What's this Exchange thing all about?

➤ Sending and receiving e-mail

➤ Sending and receiving faxes with Microsoft Fax

➤ Setting up Microsoft Exchange to suit yourself

➤ An excellent Exchange excursion that'll help you survive in the have-your-people-e-mail-my-people world

Online aficionados use the term *snail mail* as a snide reference to mail sent through the post office. Why "snail?" Well, regular mail has the nerve to actually take *days* to reach its destination, and that just won't cut it in our fast-paced, I-need-it-yesterday lives. No, in this wired world, communication times are measured in minutes thanks to e-mail systems and fax machines. So how's a body to keep up?

Well, if you have Windows 95, you can put the pedal to your communications metal by using Microsoft Exchange. Exchange is a sort of electronic post office box that you can use to both send and receive e-mail and faxes. It's a one-stop communications shop that lets you read and compose all your digital correspondence from the comfort of Windows 95. This chapter explains Exchange and takes you on a tour of its basic features.

# Installing Microsoft Exchange

The best way to tell whether Microsoft Exchange is installed is to look for the Inbox icon on your desktop, or to select the **Start** button, open the **Programs** folder, and then look for the Microsoft Exchange icon. If you see either one, great: it means Microsoft Exchange is installed.

There are no worries, though, if Exchange is nowhere in sight. You can install Exchange using the Add/Remove Programs utility in the Control Panel. The section titled "Adding and Removing Windows 95 Components" in Chapter 25 gives you the full scoop on this.

# Setting Up Microsoft Exchange

Before we start rolling, let's make sure that Microsoft Exchange has all the info it needs to serve you. To do this, we'll check out, and maybe modify, the Microsoft Exchange profile.

It's like this: Microsoft Exchange can work with a variety of services (the Microsoft Network—MSN, faxing, and Microsoft Mail), but you have to tell it which services you want it to communicate with (this is called your *profile*). In this chapter, we'll be using Microsoft Exchange with MSN (Microsoft's contribution to the online world) and Microsoft Fax (the Windows 95 program that lets you send and receive faxes), so make sure those two are set up, if nothing else.

If you're absolutely sure that MSN and Microsoft Fax are both set up in your Microsoft Exchange profile, you can skip these steps. (But, hey, why take chances? Your machine isn't going to kick the proverbial bucket just because you followed a few measly steps.) Here's how it works:

1. Close Microsoft Exchange, if it's open.

 2. Select the **Start** button, open the **Settings** folder, and select the **Control Panel** icon. In the Control Panel window, select the **Mail and Fax** icon. The Microsoft Exchange Settings Properties dialog box appears.

3. In the Services tab, select the **Add** button to see the Add Service to Profile dialog box. It lists the services that you can set up for Exchange.

4. In the **Available information services** list, highlight the service you want to add and select **OK**.

5. Depending on which service you're setting up, you may get a message telling you that you need to provide some information. In this case, select **Yes**, fill out the Properties dialog box that appears, and then select **OK**.

6. To add more services, repeat steps 3–5. When you're done, select **Close** to return to the Control Panel. Th-th-th-that's all folks!

Okay, now that all that malarkey is over with and Exchange is pumped up and ready to roll, you can get right down to the nitty-gritty of reading and writing e-mail and fax messages. Your first chore is to wake Exchange from its hard disk slumbers by either double-clicking on the desktop's **Inbox** icon, or by selecting the **Start** button, opening the **Programs** folder, and then selecting **Microsoft Exchange**. We'll begin in the next section by showing you how to create and ship out an e-mail message.

# Becoming a Composer: Creating a New Message

Before we get started with this message creation business, you should know that you don't have to be signed in to the Microsoft Network (or to your corporate network if you're using Microsoft Mail) to do it. The idea is that you first create all the missives you want to mail, *then* you sign in to the service or to your corporate network and send everything at once.

There are actually two hoops to jump through to create a message. You first have to add the name of your recipient to the electronic address book Exchange provides for you, then you create the message itself. The next couple of sections fill in the details.

## Populating Your Address Book

Exchange stores the addresses of your e-mail recipients in a handy address book. This is convenient because it saves you the drudgery of having to enter the address of a recipient every time you send them a message. To display the address book, use any of the following methods:

➤ Click on the Address Book button.

➤ Pull down the **Tools** menu and select the **Address Book** command.

➤ Press **Ctrl+Shift+B**.

When the Address Book window appears, follow these steps to add an address:

1. Select the **File** menu's **New Entry** command. The New Entry dialog box appears.

2. Use the **Select the entry type** list to choose what kind of entry you're adding, and then select **OK**. For example, if you're adding an entry for a member of the Microsoft Network, select The Microsoft Network Member.

3. In the dialog box that appears, fill in the appropriate info (such as the member ID and name for an MSN member) and then select **OK**. Exchange returns you to the address book.

4. If you want to add more addresses, repeat steps 1–3. Otherwise, select the **File** menu's **Close** command to return to Exchange.

## Composing the Message

Now you're ready to create some havoc (er, messages) of your own. Here are the steps to follow:

1. Open the **Compose** menu in Microsoft Exchange and choose **New Message** (you can also press **Ctrl+N**). A big ol' message composition screen appears.

2. Select the **To** button to display the Address Book, highlight the name of the person you're sending the message to, select **To->**, and then select **OK**.

3. If you want to send copies to one or more other people, select the **Cc** button to display the Address Book and then, for each person, highlight their name and select **Cc->**. When you're done, select **OK**.

4. Use the **Subject** field to enter a short description of your message.

5. Use the vast expanse below the Subject box to enter the text of your message. Feel free to use the commands on the **Format** menu, or the buttons in the Format toolbar, to spruce up your message. The figure below shows a completed message, ready for transport.

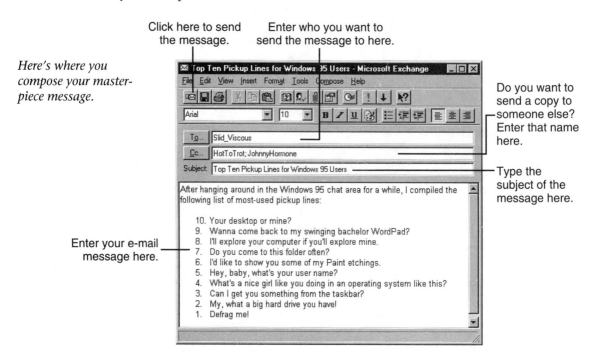

Click here to send the message.

Enter who you want to send the message to here.

*Here's where you compose your master-piece message.*

Do you want to send a copy to someone else? Enter that name here.

Type the subject of the message here.

Enter your e-mail message here.

6. Click on the Send button, or select the **File** menu's **Send** command (pressing **Ctrl+Enter** will also do the job). Note, though, that selecting Send doesn't actually send the message, as you might expect. Instead, Exchange just plops the message in the Outbox folder.

7. Repeat steps 1–6 to compose any other messages you want to send.

8. When you're ready to fire off the messages for real, pull down the **Tools** menu, select **Deliver Now Using**, and then select the service you want to use. For example, to send the messages to MSN, you'd select **The Microsoft Network** (or you can bypass all those menus by pressing **Ctrl+2**).

9. If you're sending the notes to MSN, watch for the Sign In window and then select **Connect**. You're signed in to MSN, your messages are sent on their merry way, and then you're automatically signed off.

# Retrieving and Reading Your Mail

If you've signed up with the Microsoft Network, and if any of your friends or colleagues have sent some e-mail missives your way, the messages will be waiting patiently for you in MSN's central computer. Before you can read these notes, you have to retrieve them to your Microsoft Exchange Inbox.

The easiest way to go about doing this is to sign in to MSN. If there's e-mail for you, a dialog box will show up asking if you want to open your Inbox. Select Yes and you'll see the Inbox window on your screen. (You can also crank up the Inbox by double-clicking the **Inbox** desktop icon, or by selecting the **Start** button, opening the **Programs** folder, and selecting **Microsoft Exchange**.)

As you can see in the following figure, the Inbox window consists of two panels. On the right side of the window is a list of mail you've received. On the left side are the folders into which you can file your mail. (If you don't see the folders, pull down the View menu and activate the Folders command.) As you'll see, some folders, such as the Sent Items folder, get stuff filed in them automatically. You'll learn about filing mail in the section "Moving and Deleting Messages" later in this chapter.

> **Check This Out...**
>
> **Postcards from the Net**
> If you know some people who have e-mail accounts on the Internet, it's easy for them to send messages to your MSN mailbox. All they have to do is address the message to *username*@**msn.com**, where username is your MSN user name. For example, my user name is PMcFedries, so Internet types would send e-mail to me using the address **PMcFedriesd@msn.com**.

This symbol means it's a high-priority message.

*Microsoft Exchange's Inbox window.*

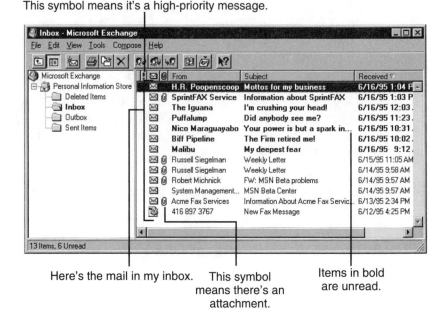

Here's the mail in my inbox.    This symbol means there's an attachment.    Items in bold are unread.

Now that you've got your stack of mail, you can read what your correspondents had to say by using any of the following techniques:

➤ Highlight the message and select the **File** menu's **Open** command (or just press **Enter**).

➤ Double-click on the message.

➤ Right-click on the message and select **Open** from the shortcut menu.

A new window opens to display your message. Note that the message area of the window has a scroll bar so you can view parts of your message that aren't visible at first.

## What Do I Do with a Message After I've Read It?

When you get snail mail at the office, your assistant or somebody from the mailroom probably places it in your "In" basket. You then sort through and read the mail and farm out each message accordingly: some need to be responded to; some need to be forwarded; some get filed; and some get tossed in the garbage. Exchange gives you a similar range of choices after you've perused a message:

➤ You can send a reply to the author of the message.

➤ You can forward the message to someone else.

➤ You can save the message to a different folder.

➤ You can delete the message.

The next few sections give you the details for each task.

# Holding Up Your End of the Conversation: Replying to a Message

One of the few negative consequences about e-mail's ease-of-use is that people aren't shy about asking you to send them info or to respond "ASAP" about one crisis or another. Hey, it was no sweat for them to send the message in the first place, so it should require even less sweat for you to respond, right? Well, luckily for them, that's usually the case, as you'll soon see.

To reply to a message, first use one of the following techniques to tell Exchange what kind of a reply you want to send:

 To send your retort only to the person who sent the message, click on the **Reply to Sender** button, or select the **Compose** menu's **Reply to Sender** command.

 To send the reply to all the recipients of the original message, click on the **Reply to All** button, or select the **Compose** menu's **Reply to All** command.

You'll use the Reply to Sender feature most often because the majority of messages have only one recipient (that's you!). However, the Reply to All option is useful for carrying on group discussions via e-mail. For instance, your boss might send a message to ten people asking for their opinions on the new product line. If you copy your reply to all recipients, you share your opinions not only with your boss, but with everyone else in the group.

## When Is a Private Reply Best?

If you get an official-type message, such as the one welcoming you to MSN, and the recipients include all MSN users or some other mega-group, don't reply to all recipients. You'll flood other people's mailboxes with junk mail and look like an idiot.

Regardless of which option you choose, a reply window appears with the recipient(s) already filled in. Although the subject is also filled in, you can change it if you want.

In the reply window, the original message is automatically repeated for everyone's convenience. You can delete it or leave it as is. Type your response in the allotted space above the repeated message, and then select the **Send** button on the toolbar to jet your reply off to the lucky recipient (who is no doubt waiting anxiously at his or her computer for your reply).

## Psst! Pass it On: Forwarding a Message

Some messages just cry out to be shared with others. It could be a good joke, a brilliant argument, or some howler committed by a clueless correspondent. Whatever the reason, you can pass along a message to someone else by using Exchange's Forward feature.

Forwarding is a lot like replying, except that you have to fill in the To: line because Microsoft Exchange can't read your mind. (Although I hear the Microsoft programmers are working on it.) You'll pick the recipient either from your address book or from the member directory on MSN.

To forward a message for someone else to take a look at, either select the **Forward** button from the toolbar, select the **Compose** menu's **Forward** command, or press **Ctrl+F**. Fill in the To line and then send the message.

# Moving a Message to a Different Folder

Once you've completed all your reading, replying, forwarding, and deleting (see the next section), the messages left in your Inbox will be ones you intend to keep, just in case you need to refer to them later on. But, just as you wouldn't keep all your opened snail mail in your office in basket, it doesn't make sense to have all those read messages cluttering Exchange's Inbox.

The solution is to create new folders to hold related types of messages. For example, if you and your boss exchange frequent e-mail notes, you could set up a folder just to hold his or her correspondence. Similarly, if you subscribe to an Internet mailing list, you could set up a folder to keep the regular mailings you get.

To create a folder in Exchange, select the **File** menu's **New Folder** command, type the name of the folder in the New Folder dialog box that appears, and then select **OK**. The new folder appears on the left side of the Exchange window.

To move a message, you can either drag it from the Inbox and drop it on the folder, or you can pull down the **File** menu, select the **Move** command, choose the folder from the Move dialog box, and then select OK.

# Deleting Messages You Don't Need

Some of the messages you'll receive will be the electronic equivalent of junk mail and you won't want to bother with them again after you've read them. To keep the Inbox tidy, you should delete this detritus by highlighting the message and using one of the following techniques:

➤ Click on the Delete button.

➤ Drag the message from the Inbox and drop it on the Deleted Items folder.

➤ Select the **File** menu's **Delete** command.

➤ Press **Ctrl+D**.

### Whew! Recovering Accidentally Deleted Messages

When you delete a message, Exchange actually moves it to the Deleted Items folder. This is a precaution just in case you change your mind about deleting a message, or if you delete a crucial message by accident. To recover a message, select the Deleted Items folder, highlight the message, and then move it back to its original folder. Keep in mind, however, that Exchange cleans out the Deleted Items folder every time you quit the program. So if you're going to undelete a message, make sure you do it before ending your Exchange session.

# Reading More Messages

While you're reading a message, you can read the next or previous message in the same folder (in this case, your Inbox) just by using the following techniques:

Select the **Previous** button, select the **View** menu's **Previous** command, or press **Ctrl+<**.

Select the **Next** button, select the **View** menu's **Next** command, or press **Ctrl+>**.

# Getting Down to Brass Fax Tacks: Sending and Receiving Faxes

Check This Out...

**Cover Your Fax**
When you create a message and send it as a fax, Exchange tacks on a generic cover page. To choose a different cover page, pull down the **Tools** menu, select **Microsoft Fax Tools**, and then select **Options**. In the Message tab of the Microsoft Fax Properties dialog box that appears, select the cover page you want from the list in the Default cover page section. Select OK to get back to Exchange.

Remember a decade or so ago, when the fax (or the *facsimile* as we called it back then) was the hottest thing around—the new kid on the telecommunications block? How amazing it seemed that we could send a letter or memo or—incredibly!—a *picture* through the phone lines and have it emerge seconds later across town or even across the country. Oh sure, the fax that came slithering out the other end was a little fuzzier, and certainly a lot slimier, but, heck, it sure beat the post office.

Nowadays, though, faxing is just another humdrum part of the workaday world. Any business worth its salt has a fax machine and, thanks to the mass marketing of fax/modems, the lives of many individuals have become fax-enhanced, as well. If you're looking to get into the fax fast lane that lets you send and receive faxes right on your computer, look no further than Microsoft Exchange.

Exchange actually gives you two ways to send a fax. One way is to add the recipient's fax number to your address book, create a new message as if it were an e-mail message (just like you learned to do earlier in this chapter) and then fax it instead of mailing it. (To send a fax that's sitting in your Outbox folder, you can either press **Ctrl+1** or pull down the **Tools** menu, select **Deliver Now Using**, and then select **Microsoft Fax**.) The other way is to use the Fax Wizard (as explained in the next section).

So which do you use? Let's look at the pros and cons. The Wizard is by far the easier of the two ways, but it's less flexible: you can only use a subject and plain paragraphs of text. If you're dashing off a quick message, the Wizard is the right method for you. However, if you want to include attachments, formatting, or any other good message-type stuff, you should go the message route.

## Using the Fax Wizard

To run the Fax Wizard, pull down the **Compose** menu and choose **New Fax**; the Fax Wizard appears. Select Next > to continue.

In the dialog box that appears (see the following figure), enter the recipient's name in the To box, enter his or her fax number in the **Fax #** fields, and, if you're sending the fax overseas, select the appropriate nation from the Country list. Then select the Add to List button to add the person to the Recipient list. Add more recipients if you want to, and when you're finished, select Next > to continue.

On the next screen, you're asked to specify which cover page you want, if any (see the following figure). You can also select the Options button to access a few more options you can change, such as the time of day the fax is sent (if you don't want it sent right away). When you're finished setting options, select OK to return to the Fax Wizard. When you're finished changing the cover page and the options, select Next > to continue.

*Adding recipients is a breeze with the Fax Wizard.*

Next you get a (more or less) blank window where you type your subject and message. Just plunk them in and select Next > to continue.

Next, you'll be asked whether you want to add a file to your fax. If you want to include a file, select the Add File button, pick out the file from the Open a File to Attach dialog box, and select Open to continue. You can add as many files as you want (of course, the more files you add, the longer it'll take to send the fax).

Finally, you arrive at the last dialog box; select Finish to send your fax. The rest of the action happens in the background. Microsoft Fax kicks in and opens WordPad, which displays the fax document and prints it to Microsoft Fax, which sends it. (Don't worry, you won't be tested on that.)

## Faxing from Other Programs

You can fax from almost any program that you can print in, because Windows 95 considers MS Fax to be a printer. You just create your document normally, and then print it using the **File** menu's **Print** command. The trick, though, is to select Microsoft Fax as your printer. (I told you how to select printers back in Chapter 9, in the section titled "Selecting a Different Printer in an Application.") When you select Print, MS Exchange kicks in, along with Microsoft Fax, and guides you through fax creation.

## Receiving a Fax

**Switch back!**
Don't forget to switch your default printer back to your normal printer when you're done faxing.

Receiving faxes with Exchange is no sweat. When Exchange is running, you'll notice that a cute little fax machine appears in the taskbar's information area (in the bottom-right corner beside the time). This means that Exchange is ready to receive any incoming faxes. When a fax call comes in, click on the fax icon to display the Microsoft Fax Status dialog box, and then click on the Answer Now button. Exchange will grab the fax and then stuff it into your Inbox folder. To read the fax, just double-click on it, and Exchange will display it in the Fax Viewer window. For multi-page faxes, use the commands on the **Page** menu to navigate around: **Next**, **Previous**, **First**, and **Last**.

Instead of manually receiving your faxes, you might prefer to have Exchange answer the phone automatically. Easy money. In the Microsoft Fax Status dialog box, pull down the **Options** menu and select the **Modem Properties** command. In the Answer mode section, activate the Answer after option, and then set the number of rings. Select OK and you're done.

## The Least You Need to Know

For folks who like to stay in touch, Microsoft Exchange is a real lifesaver. It helps you manage your mail and faxes in one convenient place.

# Chapter 28

# Common Windows Complaints

## In This Chapter

➤ Handling startup woes

➤ Avoiding General Protection Fault errors

➤ A few Explorer problems

➤ Dealing with unruly applications

One of the biggest problems with computers is that it's so easy to become dependent on them. After having used one for a little while, most people wonder how they ever did without it (I know this may seem hard to believe for some of you, but it really does happen.) So it's all the more traumatic when our once trusty software sidekicks start doing strange and unpredictable things. Suddenly, in true codependent fashion, we find we can no longer function without our programs at our side. Write a letter by hand? How primitive!

So, in an effort to minimize the trauma associated with software problems, this chapter looks at a few of the ways your programs can go bad and offers nontechnical, relatively pain-free solutions.

# Solving Startup Snags

Have you ever had problems starting your car? If so, you know only too well the subsequent emotional roller coaster ride: basic shock is the first to hit ("Oh no!"); then comes denial ("This *can't* be happening."); then anger ("@#$*&!"); and finally frustration ("Why me?"). To make matters worse, this only seems to happen on the coldest mornings when you're late for work (chalk up another one for Murphy's Law).

Windows 95 startup problems can be equally frustrating. When you have a deadline looming or an in-basket full of paper, the last thing you need is for your operating system to refuse to operate. This section lays out several strategies for dealing with Windows 95 startup problems.

## Windows 95 Startup Options

If Windows 95 won't load when you turn on your computer, there are several options you can try to see if you can coax Windows 95 out of the starting blocks. For now, you need to restart your computer using any of the following methods:

➤ Hold down both **Ctrl** and **Alt**, and then tap the **Delete** key.

➤ Press your computer's **Reset** button.

➤ Turn the obstinate beast off, and then turn it back on again.

While your computer gets itself back to its feet, position a finger over the F8 key (but don't press it just yet) and keep a sharp eye out for the following line to appear on-screen:

> **Starting Windows 95...**

As soon as you see this line, slam the **F8** key (you actually have about two seconds to do this). When you do, instead of starting normally, Windows 95 presents you with a menu similar to the following:

> **Microsoft Windows 95 Startup Menu**
> ==================================
> 1. **Normal**
> 2. **Logged (\BOOTLOG.TXT)**
> 3. **Safe mode**
> 4. **Step-by-step confirmation**
> 5. **Command prompt only**
> 6. **Safe mode command prompt only**
> 7. **Previous version of MS-DOS**
>
> Enter a choice: 1

You select an option by pressing the number beside it and then pressing **Enter**. Here's a summary of what each of these options means:

**Normal**   Starts Windows 95 in the usual way.

**Logged (\BOOTLOG.TXT)**   Starts Windows 95 and logs the progress of the startup in a text file called BOOTLOG.TXT in the root directory of your hard drive (C:\>). If Windows 95 fails to start, BOOTLOG.TXT should tell you why. To check it out, restart your computer, press **F8** at the **Starting Windows 95...** message, and choose the **Safe mode command prompt only** option. At the **C:\>** prompt, type **edit bootlog.txt**. Keep your eyes peeled for a couple of lines that look something like this:

> [000A94C1] **Loading Device** = C:\DOS\ATDOSHC.SYS
> [000A94C1] **LoadFailed**     = C:\DOS\ATDOSHC.SYS

This will tell you which file Windows 95 choked on. Other BOOTLOG.TXT keywords to look for are "Error" and "Fail." You'll need to report the error to Microsoft Technical Support.

**Safe mode**   Starts Windows 95 with only a minimal configuration. Specifically, your mouse and keyboard will work, and your video display will be set to VGA. Other goodies, such as your CD-ROM drive and networking, are checked at the door. Always try Safe mode first to see if Windows will start with the minimal configuration. If it does (see the following figure), you can use Windows 95 to try to fix the problem (see "Some Safe Mode Diagnostics," later in this chapter).

**Step-by-step confirmation**   Starts Windows 95 and displays a prompt such as the following at each phase of the startup:

> **Process the system registry {Enter=Y,Esc=N]?**

Press **Enter** to perform the action, and watch your screen for error messages. If you see an error, make a note of where it occurred. You may be able to get Windows 95 to start by rebooting your computer, selecting the **Step-by-step confirmation** option again, and, when you get to the spot where the error happened last time, pressing **Esc** to bypass the process.

*Windows 95 reminds you you're in Safe mode by placing "Safe mode" signs in the four corners of the desktop.*

You're in Safe mode. ——

**Command prompt only**   Displays the command prompt (C:\>) instead of the Windows 95 desktop. Once you're at the command prompt, try to start Windows 95 by typing one of the following commands and pressing **Enter**:

```
win /d:f
win /d:s
win /d:v
win /d:x
```

If one of these commands starts Windows 95 properly, contact Microsoft Technical Support and tell it which command worked. They'll let you know what to do from there.

**Safe mode command prompt only**   Starts Windows 95 in Safe mode and displays the command prompt instead of the desktop. Use this option if Windows 95 fails to start in Safe mode. Try starting Windows 95 using the commands outlined in the previous paragraph.

**Previous version of MS-DOS**   Starts the version of MS-DOS that was previously installed on your computer. You'll only see this option if you installed Windows 95 in a directory separate from the one used by your previous version of Windows. This is the if-all-else-fails option.

If you're running Windows 95 on a network, you'll also see a **Safe mode with network support** option that starts Windows 95 in Safe mode but enables networking.

## Some Safe Mode Diagnostics

As I mentioned earlier, you should always try to start Windows 95 in Safe mode first. If you manage to get it up and running, Windows 95 has a few tools you can use to investigate the problem. Those tools include the Help system Troubleshooters, the Control Panel, the Device Manager, and ScanDisk.

**Help system Troubleshooters.** Windows 95's Help system comes equipped with several "Troubleshooters" that lead you step-by-step through specific problem-solving procedures. (Think of them as the Windows 95 cavalry, riding to your rescue.) To check them out, select the **Start** button and select **Help** on the Start menu. In the Help Topics window that appears, select **Troubleshooting**, and then select one of the topics that appears. For example, hardware conflicts are often a source of startup difficulties, so the topic "If you have a hardware conflict" might be a good place to start. Selecting this topic displays the Hardware Conflict Troubleshooter, shown in the following figure.

The modus operandi of most Troubleshooters is the same: they present some explanatory text and then pose a question. The possible answers are arranged at the bottom of the window. To select an answer, just click on it (or, from the keyboard, press **Tab** until the answer is highlighted and then press **Enter**). If you need to reverse a step, select the **Back** button.

Click on these buttons to answer the Troubleshooter's questions.

*The Help system's Troubleshooters can help you diagnose and solve lots of Windows woes.*

**Control Panel.** To use Control Panel to investigate a problem, select the **Start** button, open the **Settings** folder, and select **Control Panel**. The icons in Control Panel govern the settings for all kinds of devices on your system (such as your video display, your sound card, and your network adapter). Windows 95 may exhibit erratic behavior if these devices aren't set up correctly. Try selecting the icons for your equipment (most of which have been discussed elsewhere in this book) and checking to see if the settings are correct.

**Device Manager.** The third tool available, Control Panel's Device Manager, gives you a forest-instead-of-the-trees look at all the devices installed on your system. A conflict between these devices can cause all kinds of bad things to happen, so the Device Manager examines your system for conflicts and lets you know if there's a problem.

You get to the Device Manager by selecting Control Panel's **System** icon, and then selecting the **Device Manager** tab in the System Properties dialog box. If there's a problem, Windows 95 displays a yellow exclamation mark over the icon of the device that's stepping on another's toes. Use the Help system's Hardware Conflict Trouble-shooter (discussed above) to get things back in sync.

**ScanDisk.** The final investigative tool is ScanDisk. If your hard disk has some files or folders that need fixing, or if some tiny chunk of your hard disk has gone to seed, it could cause all kinds of problems for Windows 95. To make sure your system is fit as a fiddle, run the ScanDisk accessory regularly (as described in Chapter 17, in the section titled "Avoiding Hard Disk Hard Times: ScanDisk").

If Windows 95 won't load even in Safe mode, you can run ScanDisk from the command prompt by following these steps:

1. Reboot your computer. When you see the **Starting Windows 95...** message, press **F8**.

2. Select the **Safe mode command prompt only** option.

3. At the command prompt (the **C:\>** thingy), type **cd\windows\command** and press **Enter**.

4. Type **scandisk** and press **Enter** to start the ScanDisk program. If ScanDisk finds an error, make sure you select **Yes** (or press **Y**) when it asks if you want to fix it.

5. When ScanDisk asks if you want to run a surface scan, select **Yes**.

6. When ScanDisk has completed its labors, select **Exit** (or press **X**) to return to the command prompt.

7. Reboot your computer and see if Windows 95 will start.

# The Last Chance Saloon: The Startup Disk

If Windows 95 won't load in Safe mode, à la mode, or in any other mode, your hard disk likely has a problem that has corrupted the files Windows uses to get itself out of bed in the morning. In this case, your only hope is to boot your computer using your Windows 95 Startup disk. (I told you how to create a Startup disk back in Chapter 13, in the "Creating a Startup Disk" section.)

Place the Startup disk in drive A and reboot your computer. When you get to the A:\> prompt, type **scandisk c:** and press **Enter**. ScanDisk will check the integrity of your hard disk (drive C), let you know what the problem is, and (hopefully) fix it for you. Make sure you run the surface scan when ScanDisk asks.

# Dealing with the Dastardly General Protection Fault

If you used Windows 3.1 regularly, you probably came across more than your share of General Protection Faults. These GPFs (as they were usually called) were particularly nasty errors that could ruin your data and cause your machine to lock up. Why did they occur? Well, applications, like people, have their own "personal space" in your computer's memory. GPFs occur, basically, when one application invades the personal space of another.

Windows 95 improves this situation by making it difficult, if not impossible, for Windows 95 applications to bump into each other. Oh sure, GPFs still exist (Windows 95 now calls them "illegal operations"), but they should appear far less frequently.

## What to Do When a GPF Rears Its Ugly Head

When Windows 95 detects an illegal operation, all sorts of internal bells and alarms go off, and Windows 95 tries to minimize the damage wrought by the wayward program. When Windows has tidied things up as best it can, it displays a dialog box like the one shown in the following figure. Select the **Close** button to terminate the rogue program.

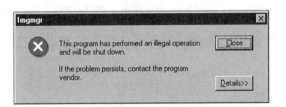

*You'll see a dialog box like this when an application is caught trespassing.*

If things are really ugly, however, the program may just freeze up solid—and nothing you do or say will make it go again. If that happens, press **Ctrl+Alt+Delete** to display the Close Program dialog box. Then highlight the offending application (it should say **Not responding** beside its name) and select the **End Task** button.

Windows 95 does a reasonable job of preventing programs from running amok and locking up your entire machine. So once you've shut down a delinquent application, you can often get right back to work. However, because there's a chance your system may be unstable, it's a good idea to exit the rest of your programs and reboot your computer.

# How to Avoid Those Nasty GPFs

This section looks at a number of ways to prevent illegal operations (or GPFs or whatever you want to call them).

**If you're running an application written for an earlier version of Windows 95, upgrade to a newer version.** As I've said, programs designed specifically for Windows 95 offer the most protection from debilitating crashes. If possible, you should upgrade your existing Windows software to the Windows 95 versions.

**Use ScanDisk to weed out disk errors.** Corrupted or damaged files on your hard disk are another common source of GPFs. To check for (and fix) these problems, use the Windows 95 ScanDisk accessory (as described in Chapter 17's "Avoiding Hard Disk Hard Times: ScanDisk" section).

**Keep an eye on your system resources.** You can bet your bottom dollar that a GPF is just around the corner if your system resources drop below the 20% mark. Keep an eye on them (as described in Chapter 29) if you're working with large applications.

# Explorer Exasperations

Once you get the hang of Explorer (which won't take long if you read the three chapters in Part 3), you'll probably find it's one of the Windows 95 applications you use the most. But, of course, the more you use it, the more likely it is that some operation will go up in flames. The next few sections take you through some common Explorer complaints.

## Explorer Isn't Showing You the Correct Information

Sometimes what Explorer *thinks* is in a folder or on a disk is not what's actually there. (Short attention span, I guess.) You can give Explorer a poke in the ribs by selecting the **View** menu's **Refresh** command, or by pressing **F5**.

## You Have Problems Trying to Copy, Move, Delete, or Rename a File on a Floppy Disk

As explained in Chapter 12, Explorer makes it easy to copy or move files to and from a floppy disk. However, you might run into problems if the following scenarios exist:

## The disk is full.

Explorer, rightly so, won't allow you to copy or move a file to a disk unless there's sufficient space. If the disk is full, delete any unneeded files or use another disk.

## The disk is write-protected.

When a floppy disk is *write-protected*, you can't copy or move files to the disk or delete or rename files on the disk. Here's how to tell whether or not a disk is write-protected:

➤ When a 5¹/₄-inch disk is not write-protected, you'll see a small notch in the side of the disk. If the notch is covered with tape, simply remove the tape to disable the write-protection.

➤ For a 3¹/₂-inch disk, write-protection is controlled by a small, movable tab on the back of the disk. If the tab is toward the edge of the disk, the disk is write-protected. To disable the write-protection, slide the tab away from the edge of the disk.

# You Can't Copy a Disk

As I mentioned back in Chapter 13, Explorer doesn't have a command to copy a floppy disk, so you have to head for the MS-DOS prompt and use the **diskcopy** command, instead. If Windows 95 *still* won't let you copy the disk, try these possible solutions:

**Make sure the disk is inserted properly.** If you're using 3¹/₂-inch disks, make sure they're inserted all the way into the drive. If you're using 5¹/₄-inch disks, make sure the drive's latch is closed.

**Is the destination disk write-protected?** Windows 95 won't copy files to a disk that's write-protected. Check the disk and disable the write-protection as described earlier in this chapter.

**Are the two disks the same type?** The **diskcopy** command is designed to work only with two disks that have the same capacity and are of the same type. (I explained disk capacity and disk types back in Chapter 13, in the section "Types of Floppy Disks"). If you have two different types of disk drives, you can still copy a disk, but you have to use the same drive for both the source and destination.

# You Can't Tell Where the Current Folder Is Located

Once you've drilled down into several layers of subfolders, you may forget the name of the main folder, or even which disk drive you're working with. Although Explorer normally just shows you the name of the current folder, you can change that by pulling down the **View** menu and selecting the **Options** command. In the Options dialog box, activate the **Display the full MS-DOS path in the title bar** check box, and then select **OK**. The title bar and the top of the Contents list show the current drive and the folders leading to the current folder (this is called the current folder's *path*).

# You Can't Tell How Much Free Space Is Left on Your Hard Disk

With applications growing by leaps and bounds, it doesn't take long for a hard disk to run out of room. If you're not sure how much hard disk acreage you've got left, you can find out by using one of the following techniques:

➤ Highlight your hard disk in Explorer's All Folders list, and then select the **File** menu's **Properties** command.

➤ Right-click on the hard disk and select **Properties** from the shortcut menu.

 ➤ Highlight the hard disk, and then click on the **Properties** button in the Explorer toolbar.

In the Properties dialog box that appears, the General tab tells you how much free space is available (see the following figure).

**Check This Out...**

### A Handle for Your Hard Disk

Note that you can use the General tab to rename your hard disk. Why would you want to do this? Well, there's no good reason other than to give your hard disk a more interesting moniker. Just enter a name (11 characters or less) in the **Label** text box.

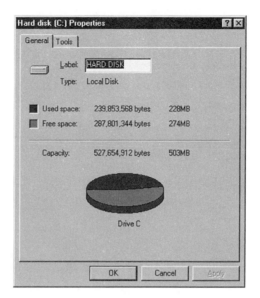

*The General tab tells you how much room remains on your hard disk.*

# The Least You Need to Know

This chapter gave you solutions to some common Windows 95 problems, including difficulties with Windows 95's startup. I told you about the options you can use to start Windows 95, the Help system Troubleshooters, how to handle and (I hope) avoid General Protection faults, and how to solve a few Explorer errors.

The troubleshooting fun continues in the next chapter as we take a look at some problems related to memory, the mouse, the keyboard, and more.

# Chapter 29

# A Smorgasbord of Windows Woes

**In This Chapter**

➤ Tackling low memory problems

➤ Mouse and keyboard conundrums

➤ Patching up printing problems

➤ Dealing with video woes

➤ A veritable cornucopia of computer complaints (and their solutions)

I wish I could tell you that applications were the only thing that could go kaput in Windows 95. Unfortunately, there's a whole host of accidents waiting to happen, and you're bound to be tripped up by at least some of them. This chapter looks at the most common of the problems that fall into this miscellaneous category, including woes related to memory, the mouse and keyboard, printing, and your video display.

## Windows 95 Tells You There Is "Insufficient Memory" to Run an Application

Memory is to Windows 95 what money is to an investor. The more you have, the more things you can do, but if you run out, well, you're out of luck. This section presents a few solutions for those times when money, er, memory is scarce.

## Close down what you don't need.

The most obvious (but the least convenient) solution is to close any running applications that you really don't need. The bigger the application, the more memory you'll save. I've performed careful, scientific experiments to try and determine the optimum Windows configuration. My data tells me unequivocally that the best way to prevent insufficient memory errors is to shut down all your programs and go read a good book.

## Delete the contents of the Clipboard.

When you cut or copy a selection in a Windows 95 application, the program stores the data in an area of your computer's memory called the Clipboard. If you're working with only a few lines of text, this area remains fairly small. However, cutting or copying a graphic image can increase the size of the Clipboard to several hundred kilobytes or more. If you've run out of memory, a chubby Clipboard may be the culprit. To trim the Clipboard and release most of this memory, try one of the following methods:

➤ If you have an application running, highlight a small section of text (a single character or word will do) and select the **Edit** menu's **Copy** command. This replaces the current Clipboard with a much smaller one.

➤ Select the **Start** button, open the **Programs** folder, open the **Accessories** folder, and select the **Clipboard Viewer** icon. When the Clipboard Viewer window appears, select the **Edit** menu's **Delete** command.

## Release some "system resources."

*System resources* are small memory areas that Windows 95 uses to keep track of things like the position and size of open windows, dialog boxes, and your desktop configuration (wallpaper, etc.). You can have megabytes of free memory and still get **Insufficient Memory** errors if you run out of system resources! (Life can be so unfair.) How can you tell if your system resources are getting low? In Explorer, pull down the **Help** menu and select the **About Windows 95** command. As you can see in the following figure, the About Windows dialog box tells you what percentage of the system resource area is still available. You should start to be concerned if this number drops below 30%, and problems may start cropping up when this number dives under the 20% mark.

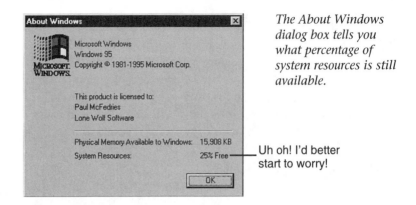

*The About Windows dialog box tells you what percentage of system resources is still available.*

Uh oh! I'd better start to worry!

Although Windows 95 has taken great leaps to improve the way it uses system resources, you may still run into problems with certain applications. (As I write this, the current version of the Microsoft Network is a real resource hog. If you're opening lots of MSN windows, keep a close eye on your system resources.) If you do run into problems, try out these tips for preserving your system resources:

➤ When working with Windows 95 applications, don't leave open any unnecessary document windows.

➤ Turn off program features (such as status bars, rulers, and toolbars) that you don't use.

➤ Run DOS applications full screen instead of in a window.

➤ Turn off the wallpaper on your desktop. The section titled "Wallpapering the Desktop? Why Not!" in Chapter 23, tells you all about Windows wallpaper.

## Load larger applications first.

Because of the way Windows 95 uses memory, you can often start more programs if you load your larger Windows 95 applications before your smaller ones.

## Run the Help system's Memory Troubleshooter.

The Memory Troubleshooter can help out with certain kinds of memory mishaps. Select the **Start** button and select **Help** to display the Help topics window, open **Troubleshooting**, and then select the **Memory troubleshooter** topic.

### Shell out the bucks to buy more memory.

The ultimate way to beat memory problems, of course, is simply to add more memory to your system. (Although, as you've seen, you still need to make sure that your system resources don't get too low.) Unfortunately, memory prices have risen over the past couple of years, so adding any more than a megabyte or two may break your budget. If you do decide to take the plunge, though, contact your computer manufacturer to find out the best kind of memory to add to your system.

# Mouse Mishaps

Using a mouse with Windows 95 is so easy that many people never learn how to work the program with the keyboard. This can present real problems, though, if your mouse decides to go wacko on you. (I once saw an otherwise-composed individual panic badly when his mouse quit on him during a Windows presentation; he didn't have a clue about Windows keyboard techniques.) The next few sections show you how to respond to various mouse problems.

## Your Mouse Pointer Is Doing Weird Things

Some people would say that the mouse pointer *always* does weird things, but some of the weirdness may not be your fault. If you find that your mouse isn't responding or that the pointer is racing all over the screen, you can usually fix it with one of these easy solutions:

**Make sure the mouse is plugged in.**   Yeah, I know, this seems pretty simple-minded, but the Number One Rule when troubleshooting any device is to first ask, "Is it plugged in?" You'd be surprised how often the answer is a sheepish "No."

**Try a mouse pad with a firmer feel.**   A nice firm mouse pad is essential for consistent mouse movements. If the pad is too soft, the roller sinks in too deep, which can cause it to stick.

**Have you cleaned the little guy lately?**   If your mouse is behaving erratically, all you may need to do is clean its insides. A well-used mouse can take in quite a collection of dust, crumbs, and other alien substances that can play havoc on its delicate constitution. Your mouse documentation should tell you the proper cleaning procedure. If your mouse has a roller ball, you can also follow these steps:

1. Remove the cover on the bottom of the mouse.

2. Remove the roller ball.

3. Using a cotton swab dipped lightly in isopropyl alcohol or water, clean the rollers and other contact areas. (I also find a pair of tweezers or needlenose pliers comes in handy for pulling out the mini dust bunnies that accumulate inside the rollers.)

4. Wipe off any excess liquid, and then replace the ball and cover.

## Try a different mouse driver.

Windows 95 supports several kinds of mice, each of which uses its own device driver. If you're using the wrong driver, the pointer may not move at all or it may do some crazy things. To remedy this, you need to change to the correct driver by following these easy steps:

1. Select the **Start** button, open the **Settings** folder, and select the **Control Panel** icon. The Control Panel window appears.

2. Select the **Mouse** icon to display the Mouse Properties dialog box, and then select the **General** tab.

3. Select the **Change** button. Control Panel displays the Select Device dialog box (see the following figure).

*Select your mouse from this list.*

4. Activate the **Show all devices** option button.

5. In the **Manufacturers** list, highlight the name of the company that makes your mouse. Then, in the **Models** list, highlight your mouse.

6. Select **OK** to return to the Mouse Properties dialog box, and then select **Close**. A dialog box appears telling you that you need to restart Windows 95.

7. Select **Yes** to restart Windows 95.

If all else fails, you can often help your mouse regain its sanity by simply exiting and restarting Windows 95.

**Windows 95 Doesn't Always Respond to Your Double-Clicks.**   If Windows 95 ignores some of your double-clicks, you probably need to slow down the *double-click speed*. Refer to Chapter 24 to learn how to do this.

**You Have Trouble Seeing the Mouse Pointer.**   If you use a laptop or if your eyesight isn't what it used to be, you might have trouble keeping track of the little mouse pointer. You may be able to improve things a bit by telling Windows 95 to display "trails" as you move the mouse. You can find complete instructions by turning to Chapter 24 and reading the section "Controlling the Double-Click Speed."

**The Mouse Pointer Moves Too Slowly or Too Quickly.**   The speed at which the pointer moves across the screen is governed by the *mouse tracking speed*. If this just doesn't feel right, you can change this setting to one that's more comfortable. Once again, check out Chapter 24 to get the nitty-gritty.

# Correcting Keyboard Kinks

Although Windows 95's interface is generally easier to use with a mouse, a keyboard is still a necessity. And while the vast majority of keyboard problems are hardware-related, there are a few problems you can take care of yourself.

## Your keyboard is too slow.

Back in Chapter 24, in the "Customizing the Keyboard" section, I showed you how to use the Control Panel to set your keyboard's delay and repeat rate. If your keyboard feels too slow, use the techniques I outlined in that chapter to decrease the delay and increase the repeat rate.

## Your keyboard's F11 and F12 keys don't work.

If Windows 95 is set up with a keyboard driver for an "AT-style" or "XT-style" (83- or 84-key) keyboard, you can poke the F11 and F12 keys until your finger turns blue, but it won't do you any good. (This is especially true if you upgraded your keyboard to a newer model after you installed Windows 95.) To fix this (and save wear-and-tear on your poking finger), follow these steps:

1. Select the **Start** button, open the **Settings** folder, and select the **Control Panel** icon. The Control Panel window appears.

2. Select the **Keyboard** icon to display the Keyboard Properties dialog box, and then select the **General** tab.

3. Select the **Change** button. Control Panel displays the Select Device dialog box (see the following figure).

4. Activate the **Show all devices** option button.

5. In the Models list, highlight your keyboard type. If the specific model is not listed, just highlight the **Standard 101/102-Key or Microsoft Natural Keyboard** option.

6. Select **OK** to return to the Keyboard Properties dialog box, and then select **Close**. A dialog box appears telling you that you need to restart Windows 95.

7. Select **Yes** to restart Windows 95.

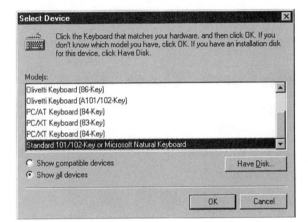

*Select your keyboard type from this list.*

## Your numeric keypad numbers don't work.

Most of the keys on a numeric keypad have two types of characters: a number and a navigation symbol (the arrow keys, Home, End, Page Up, and Page Down). The Num Lock key is used to toggle a numeric keypad between these two types. If you can't get any numbers, simply press **Num Lock** to activate them. Most keyboards also have a NUM LOCK indicator that lights up when Num Lock is turned on.

# Persnickety Printing Perplexities

As I explained back in Chapter 9, Windows 95 makes printing easy because your applications get to pass their printing bucks to Windows 95, which then handles all the dirty work. This, unfortunately, doesn't mean that printing is troublefree. If you're having problems getting your printer to print, the next few sections tell you what to do.

# Windows 95 Reports an Error While Printing

If Windows 95 can't communicate with your printer for some reason, it displays the dialog box shown in the following figure.

*You'll see this dialog box if Windows 95 and your printer aren't on the same wavelength.*

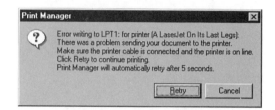

When this happens, try the following solutions:

## Make sure your printer is powered up and online.

Before you start any print jobs, verify that:

➤ Your printer is powered up.

➤ It's online (this means that it's ready to receive output). Most printers have an "Online" button you can select.

➤ The cable connections are secure.

➤ There's paper in the printer.

➤ There's no paper jam.

## Tell Windows 95 to be more patient.

Depending on the print job, some printers take an extra-long time to process the data Windows 95 sends them. If they take *too* long, Windows 95 assumes that the printer is "offline," and you get an error message. To fix this, follow these steps:

1. Select the **Start** button, open the **Settings** folder, and select **Printers**. Windows 95 displays the Printers window.

2. Highlight the printer you're using and select the **File** menu's **Properties** command (or right-click on the printer icon and select **Properties** from the shortcut menu). Windows 95 displays the Properties dialog box for the printer.

3. Select the **Details** tab.

4. Increase the number in the Transmission retry box, select **Apply**, and then print your document again. Start with 120 seconds and, if you still get an error, increase the value in increments of 60 seconds.

5. Select **OK** to return to the Printers window.

## You Can't Select the Print Command from an Application's File Menu

Most Windows 95 applications that can print include a Print command in the File menu. If this command is "dimmed" (that is, it appears in a light gray text and you can't select it), it means you have no printer installed in Windows 95. Skip back to Chapter 9, and read the section titled "Telling Windows 95 About Your Printer," to learn how to install a printer.

# Curing Video Ills

Your video display may be the most important component of your system since you're forced to look at it for hours on end every day. This is especially true for us Windows 95 users because one of Windows' most appealing features is its good-looking graphical interface. But the fanciest interface in the world isn't worth a hill of beans if your display is displaying garbage. If you're having video trouble, read the following sections to learn how to adjust your set.

### Reinstall the video driver.

One of the most common causes of display problems is a corrupt video driver. (The "driver" is the program that translates the otherwise-incomprehensible junk inside your computer into something readable on your screen.) You can usually fix the problem by reinstalling the driver. However, because your display is distorted, there isn't much you can do at the moment to fix the problem. Instead, you need to follow these steps:

1. Press **Alt+F4** and then **Enter** to exit Windows 95 (you may need to do this several times if you have applications running).

2. Once Windows 95 tells you it's safe to turn off your computer, press **Ctrl+Alt+Delete** to reboot.

3. Watch for the **Starting Windows 95...** message and, when you see it, press **F5** to start Windows 95 in Safe mode.

4. Once Windows 95 is back up and running, select the **Start** button, open the **Settings** folder, and then select **Control Panel**.

5. In the Control Panel window, select the **Display** icon and then select the **Settings** tab.

6. Click on the **Change Display Type** button. The Change Display Type dialog box appears.

7. Make a note of what's displayed in the Adaptor Type box (this is the name of your video driver), and then select the **Change** button beside it. Windows 95 displays the Select Device dialog box.

8. If you see your video driver in the **Models** list, highlight it and skip to step 10. Otherwise, activate the **Show all devices** option.

9. Use the **Manufacturers** list and the **Models** list to highlight your display, and then select **OK**.

10. When Windows asks if you want to keep or replace the existing driver, select **Replace existing driver** and then select **OK**. From here, Windows will display instructions for inserting one of your Windows 95 disks. Just follow the bouncing prompts.

If you're having problems with, say, a Super VGA driver, use the previous steps to switch to a VGA driver. If your display is okay with the lower resolution driver, you need to contact the manufacturer for an updated driver for the higher resolution.

Sometimes a display problem is nothing more than a temporary mental lapse on Windows 95's part. Try exiting Windows 95 (press **Alt+F4** and **Enter**) and restarting. If this still doesn't work, exit Windows 95, turn off your machine, and then turn it back on.

# The Least You Need to Know

This chapter took you on a tour of some miscellaneous Windows 95 woes. We examined some simple solutions for memory mishaps, mouse maladies, keyboard kinks, printer problems, and video vexations.

# Windows in Cyberspace: The Microsoft Network

*Cyberspace* is the place you "go to" when you use your modem to connect with an online service, bulletin board service (BBS), or the Internet. It's a purely electronic world, as abstract as angels dancing on the head of a pin, and, like Oakland (to borrow the famous phrase), there's certainly no "there" there. Its populace consists of the usual geek/nerd citizenry, of course, but you'll also find lots of regular folk like you and me. (Well, okay, regular folk like *you*.)

If you'd like to give your modem a whirl and take a day trip or two into cyberspace, but aren't sure how to go about it, then the Microsoft Network (MSN) is for you. It's the easiest online service to use with Windows 95 because it's designed to work directly with Windows 95 itself. If you've been dying to try out the world of online services, now's your chance. Let's check it out!

# Figuring Out If Microsoft Network Is Installed

If MSN is installed, you should have a shortcut for it on your Windows 95 desktop, and there should be a Start menu icon to crank it up (you'll find it inside the Programs folder, as shown in the following figure).

*If Microsoft Network is installed, you should be able to see it on your desktop and on the Start menu.*

Windows 95 puts a Microsoft Network icon on your desktop.

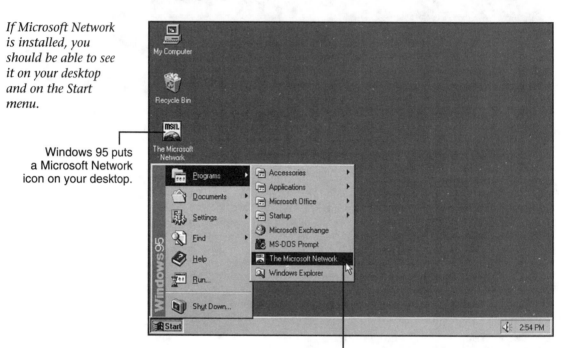

You can also run Microsoft Network from the Start menu.

If you can't find any trace of MSN on the desktop or the Start menu, then it's not installed. Curses! Oh well, there's nothing to do but turn back to Chapter 25 and read the section titled "Adding and Removing Windows 95 Components" to learn how to install any missing pieces of Windows 95.

# Getting Starting with MSN

You can't do the MSN thing without a modem, so your first chore is to make sure your modem is powered up (provided, that is, you're using an external modem; if your modem is lurking inside your computer, you don't have to bother). Now either double-click on the **Microsoft Network** desktop icon, or select the **Start** button, open the **Programs** folder, and select **The Microsoft Network**. The first thing a new user of MSN sees is a welcome screen with a pretty picture at the top and two buttons (OK and Cancel) at the bottom. Select **OK** to continue.

**Not a Microsoft Network Neophyte?** If you've signed on to MSN before, skip to the section "Logging On to the Microsoft Network" later in this chapter. You don't need to wade through all this setup stuff with the rest of us.

Next, Windows 95 asks for your area code and the first three digits of your phone number. Plug those in and select **OK** to continue. The Calling dialog box appears to let you know what's going to happen next. Select the **Connect** button.

Okay, so just what *is* going to happen next? Well, Windows 95 uses your modem to dial a special number that determines the correct local access phone number so you can connect to MSN without making a long-distance call (unless you live in the middle of nowhere, that is). This all happens behind the scenes, so all you have to do is wait for Windows to do its thing (it'll take a minute or two depending on the speed of your modem), and then you'll get to a screen like the one shown below.

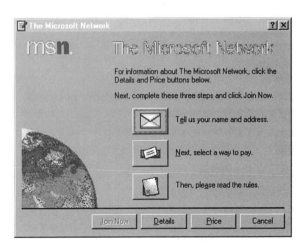

*Three hoops to jump through before you can sign on.*

This dialog box contains three icons that you have to select before you can join the Microsoft Network. Here's a summary:

**Tell us your name and address.** Selecting this button displays a dialog box with a zillion (give or take a few million) text boxes for you to fill out. Using the appropriate fields, enter your name, address, phone number, the names of your pets, and so on, and then select **OK**.

**Next, select a way to pay.** Ah, yes: bucks, shekels, simoleons, moolah, lettuce, the almighty dollar. MSN, as I've said, isn't free, so you'll need to provide a credit card number so MSN can bill you for the charges you accrue. Selecting this button displays a dialog box in which you select the type of credit card you want to use, and then fill in the particulars (card number, expiration date, and so on) in the text boxes provided. When you're done, select **OK**.

**Then, please read the rules.** Selecting this button displays a dialog box with the Microsoft Network Membership Agreement. Read as much of the legalese as you can stomach, and then select the **I Agree** button.

You should now see a check mark beside each of the above options, and the Join Now button is available. If you'd like to know more about just what the heck you're getting yourself into before going further, select the **Details** button or the **Price** button. In each case, read the info that's displayed and select the **Close** button. When you're finally ready to take the plunge, select **Join Now**. The dialog box that appears confirms the phone numbers MSN has selected for you. Select **OK** to move on. In the Calling dialog box that appears, select **Connect** to send your account information to MSN's central computer.

When you select Connect, your modem dials the MSN computer automatically, and you're asked for a member ID and password. The member ID is the name you'll be known by online, so make up one that suits you. Lots of people use their real names and/or initials, such as BSmith, Bob_Smith, or BobSmith. Other people go with something a little more daring, such as RebelYell, FemmeFatale, or ToGeekOrNotToGeek. You can't use spaces, but you can use any number or letter, a dash, or an underscore (_), up to a maximum of 64 characters. MSN will let you know if you choose a name that's already taken or one that contains illegal characters.

For a password, choose any combination of numbers or letters between 8 and 16 characters long. It's a good idea to make up jumbles of numbers and letters that have a meaning you'll remember. For instance, you might use **dog3cats104**, if you have a dog that is 3 years old and two cats that are 10 and 4.

After you've entered your ID and password, select **OK** to complete the signup process. One last dialog box appears to let you know you're now a full-fledged member of MSN. Select **Finish**, and Windows 95 takes you to the Sign In dialog box. This Sign In dialog box is what you'll see from now on when you start MSN. So let's move on and catch up with the rest of the group in the next section.

# Logging On to the Microsoft Network

When you complete the setup procedure, and each subsequent time you crank up MSN, you'll see the Sign In screen shown in the following figure.

*Here's where you log on to the Microsoft Network.*

Type your member ID and password in the appropriate text boxes, if necessary. If you want MSN to remember your member ID and password so you never have to retype them, activate the **Remember my password** check box. When you're ready to continue, select the **Connect** button (yet again!), and your modem dials the Microsoft Network and connects you. Look, ma, I'm online!

### Logging On?

Logging on has nothing to do with felling trees. It just means connecting your computer to another computer through your respective modems and telephone lines. When you tell MSN your ID and password and it accepts you and lets you connect, you're logged on. When you disconnect, it's called logging off.

# What MSN Has to Offer: A Look at Microsoft Network Central

Once you're logged in, MSN takes you to Microsoft Network Central, as shown below. (If, instead, you see the MSN Today window, select the **File** menu's **Exit** command to get to MSN Central; we'll talk about MSN Today in a sec.) Microsoft Network Central is your MSN base of operations. You'll use it to jump giddily between the various services and features offered by MSN.

*Microsoft Network Central is your jumping-off place for the many MSN services available online.*

Each line gives you access to a different area of the Microsoft Network. Here's a rundown of what's available (I'll discuss each one in more detail later on):

**MSN Today**   This item takes you to a daily online newspaper that alerts you to what's going on around MSN.

**E-mail**   This item takes you to your inbox, where you can read, write, file, bend, spindle, fold, and even mutilate e-mail messages. Refer to Chapter 27 for the gory e-mail details.

**Favorite places**   Selecting this item doesn't do much now; it just opens an empty window. But after you've set up your Favorite Places list (as explained later in this chapter), selecting it opens a folder full of your favorite MSN areas for easy access.

**Member assistance**   This option takes you to an online area where you can get answers to questions, help with technical problems, billing information, and other official-type help.

**Categories**   Categories are the heart of MSN. Select this item to begin your journey through a maze of folders that takes you to the category that interests you. (More on this shortly.)

# Getting Around in MSN

The Microsoft Network window changes as you move from place to place, so you'll need to know how to get around. For starters, you select an item in Microsoft Network Central by clicking on it or by holding down **Alt** and pressing the underlined letter in the area's name (for example, press **Alt+O** to select **MSN Today**).

Once you're inside the network, you can usually select an item by double-clicking on it or by highlighting it and pressing **Enter**. To return to the previous window, either select the **File** menu's **Up One Level** command or press **Backspace**. In some cases (such as when you're reading BBS messages), MSN opens a separate window. You can navigate these windows in the usual way (by clicking on them or by using the taskbar as explained back in Chapter 10).

**Checking Your Billing Info**
If you'd like to know what exorbitant charges you've been running up on MSN, pull down the **Tools** menu, select **Billing**, and select **Summary of Charges**. The Online Statement dialog box that appears gives you a summary of the charges you've accumulated in the current billing period. When you've seen enough of the bad news, select the **Close** button.

You can also use the Microsoft Network toolbar to leap around. To display it, pull down the **View** menu and activate the **Toolbar** command. The following table summarizes some of the toolbar's buttons.

## Microsoft Network Toolbar Buttons

| Button | Button Name | Function |
|---|---|---|
| | Up One Level | Returns you to the previous window. |
| | Go to MSN Central | Takes you back to Microsoft Network Central. |
| | Go to Favorite Places | Takes you directly to your Favorite Places list (see below). |
| | Sign Out | Logs you off the Microsoft Network. |

You can also use the drop-down list on the left side of the toolbar to jump back several steps at a time or to select one of the MSN Central areas.

And now, for a whirlwind tour…. The next few sections give you a brief look at three of the Microsoft Network Central areas—MSN Today, Favorite Places, and Categories—and lets you know what they can offer you.

## The Daily News—MSN Today

Select **MSN Today** in the opening window to get your daily dose of MSN news. It changes every day, of course, but the following figure shows what it looked like the day I wrote about it.

*A typical MSN Today newspaper.*

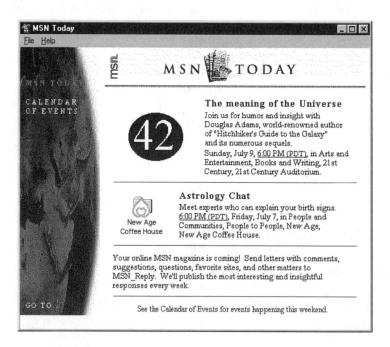

From here, you can also see what's coming up by selecting **Calendar of Events**. Close the MSN Today window when you're finished reading.

## Categories: The Heart of MSN

Most of your MSN life will be spent hanging around in various *categories*. These categories are just subject areas that cover a particular topic, such as sports, entertainment, or computers. Whatever you're into, MSN probably has a category that'll strike your fancy.

To start poking around, click on **Categories** in Microsoft Network Central. You'll soon see a list of category folders similar to the one shown below.

*No matter what your interests are, you'll find them in one of the MSN categories.*

The categories you see are just broad topic areas. To see the subtopics associated with each category, double-click on the category's icon. For example, selecting the Arts and Entertainment folder displays a window with various and sundry subtopics related to the Arts, including a Movies folder and a Comedy and Humor folder. Keep trudging through folders until you find a specific topic that turns your crank. You'll eventually stumble across some of the following goodies:

**BBSs (message boards)**   These are public message areas where you can read notes other people have posted, and even add your own replies to the discussion.

**Classified Ads**   Many areas maintain their own classifieds, where you can buy or sell anything related to the topic.

**File libraries**   Here you can select files (such as games, utilities, and updates of software you own) to download to your PC.

**Chat areas**   The garrulous and the gossipy will love chat areas because you can meet and talk live (that's right: *live!*) with other MSNers who have an interest in the topic at hand.

**Auditoriums**   These are giant chat rooms where you can go to "hear" a lecture from someone famous or important, who might accept typed questions from the "audience."

**Online "books" and help files**   These contain a wide variety of info you can read, and some of them are almost like interactive games you can wander around in!

**357**

**Information kiosks**  If you're not sure what's going on around you (hey, it happens), stop in here to find out where to go and what to do.

 **Suggestion boxes**  Suggestion boxes give you the opportunity to jot a note to the manager of the area to help improve MSN.

Continuing with our tour, let's make a stop at one of the most interesting areas: the BBSs.

# Fun with BBSs

You may have heard the term BBS (bulletin board service) used to refer to locally owned and operated online services in your town. (In fact, Chapter 26 referred to them in precisely this way!) Well, forget that for now.

A BBS in Microsoft Network is a true "bulletin board," in which you can read, reply to, and create public messages on a certain topic. When you enter a BBS area, you see a list of topics. Sometimes the topics are divided into folders that further subdivide them, but eventually you get to a screen that lists many people's public messages (see the following figure).

*If you wade through enough BBS folders, you'll come to the messages.*

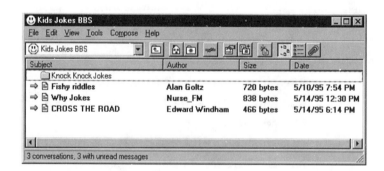

I'll show you how to use BBSs here, and once you know how to do that, you can deal with BBS-like areas such as Classified Ads, Internet newsgroups, and File Areas with no problem because they all work about the same.

## Dealing with Other People's Messages

The basic BBS idea is simple: someone sends a message to the BBS, then the other people on the BBS can read it and, if they feel so inclined, respond to it. This response also appears on the BBS, and people can then respond to the response, and so on. The original message and all its responses are called a *conversation*.

So your first order of business will be to read any messages that sound interesting. To read a message, just double-click on it (or highlight it with the arrow keys and press **Enter**). The following figure shows the "Why Jokes" message.

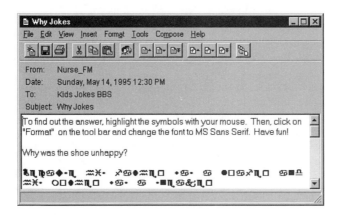

*Select a message title, and the message appears on-screen.*

The gray area below the toolbar tells you four things: the member ID of the person who sent the message (the From line), the date and time that person sent it (Date), the name of the BBS (To), and the subject of the message (Subject). The rest of the window shows the content of the message.

Notice, in the example shown above, that some of the message text appears only as symbols. This is common on MSN, and it's a way of camouflaging the answers to jokes or riddles or the endings of movies and books. To "decode" the symbols, highlight them, select the **Format** menu's **Font** command, and then select a regular font such as MS Sans Serif (which is the one used for most MSN messages) or Arial. When you select **OK**, the symbols transform themselves into regular letters for easy reading. (By the way, the shoe was unhappy because his father was a loafer and his mother was a sneaker.)

When you've finished reading a message, you have a number of options available through the window's menus or toolbar. If an action is not available, the button on the toolbar is grayed out. The following table summarizes your options.

## Commands Available in a BBS

| Command | Toolbar Button | Keyboard Shortcut | Description |
|---|---|---|---|
| Compose→New Message | | Ctrl+N | Compose a new message (see the next section) |
| File→Save | | Ctrl+S | Save the message to disk (you'll be prompted for a name and location) |
| File→Print | | Ctrl+P | Print the message |
| Compose→Reply to BBS | | Ctrl+A | Reply to the message (a window opens in which you type the reply; your response is sent to the BBS) |
| Compose→Reply by E-mail | | Ctrl+R | Reply to the message via e-mail only (the reply goes only to the person who sent the original message) |
| Compose→Forward by E-mail | | Ctrl+F | Forward the message to someone else |
| View→Previous Message | | Shift+F5 | Read the previous message |
| View→Next Message | | F5 | Read the next message |
| View→Next Unread Message | | F6 | Read the next unread message (unread by you, of course) |
| View→Previous Conversation | | Shift+F7 | Read the previous conversation |
| View→Next Conversation | | F7 | Read the next conversation |
| View→Next Unread Conversation | | F8 | Read the next unread conversation |

# Writing Your Own Messages

Anyone can be a follower and answer someone else's messages. But you want more than that—you want to be a bold pioneer and set the pace by writing your own messages. You daredevil, you.

To write your own messages, start in the window for the topic you want to post to. Pull down the **Compose** menu and select **New Message** (or press **Ctrl+N**), and the Compose Message window appears into which you can type your message. Here are the steps to follow:

1. In the **Subject** box, enter a short description of your message. This description is what appears in the BBS window, so make sure it tells people what your message is about.

2. Click inside the large box below the Subject line or press **Tab**.

3. Type your message (see the following figure).

*It's easy to compose your own message.*

4. If you want to format your message, you can use the commands on the Format menu, or you can use the Formatting toolbar. (Most of the formatting options are similar to those found in WordPad, so you should check out Chapter 14 for details.)

5. When you've checked your spelling, dotted all your t's, and crossed all your i's, you can send the message (or *post* it, to use the official term) by selecting the **File** menu's **Post Message** command or by clicking on the **Post** button on the toolbar (you can also press **Ctrl+Enter**).

**My Message Doesn't Appear!** There's a delay (up to a few hours) between the time you post your message and the time it shows up in the folder. Be patient. Don't post a message again if you don't see it right away; eventually all the copies will appear in the folder—and you'll look like a dweeb.

# Downloading a File

Downloading a file is one of the coolest things to do because it's almost like getting something for free. (Well, almost free.) Fortunately, it's also pretty simple to do.

**Almost Free?**
Just what did I mean by that crack? Well, some files are free, but you still have to pay for the online time you spend downloading them. Other files are *shareware*. Shareware is a try-before-you-buy deal, where you download and use the file for free, and if you like it, you send money to the person who created it.

As I mentioned earlier, most files can be found in MSN's file libraries. So, just as you did in the BBS, you'll need to select a category and then wade through the various levels of folders until you find the file you want. The list of files looks a lot like the lists of messages in a BBS. In fact, they *are* messages; they just have files attached, that's all.

Select a message to open it, and you'll see an icon in the message that represents the file to be downloaded (see the following figure). To tell MSN you want to download the file, use any of these methods:

➤ Select the icon, pull down the **Edit** menu, select **File Object**, and select **Download**.

➤ Double-click on the icon, and then select **Download** from the dialog box that appears.

➤ Right-click on the icon, select **File Object** in the shortcut menu, and select **Download**.

*File areas are really just message areas in which each message has a file attached.*

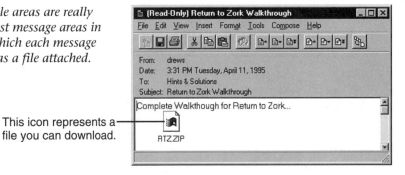

This icon represents a file you can download.

When the file transfer begins, a File Transfer Status window opens so you can watch it go. The file is placed on your computer's hard drive in a folder called Transferred Files, off the Microsoft Network folder on the Start menu. (You can change the destination by selecting the **Tools** menu's **Options** command in the File Transfer Status window.) When the transfer is complete, close the File Transfer Status window.

Some files are compressed with a program called PKZIP, and you have to have the PKZip program to decompress them. Luckily, you can download it from a number of places in MSN. Look in a Utilities folder in almost any area. The file will be called something like PKZ204G.EXE.

# Becoming a Member of the Chattering Classes

I have a friend (a certain manager at Que Corporation, the company that publishes this book) who was born to talk. Even on days when she's frantically busy at work, she still finds time to ask everyone how their weekends were and to update you on her search for the perfect mini-blinds for her dining room. It's people like her who make online chatting so popular.

In online chat, you type your thoughts into the computer, and someone else hundreds or even thousands of miles away, sees them as you type them and responds. It's like having a conversation, except you're typing instead of talking, and you can't see that the "woman" who claims to be a Playboy bunny is really a teenage geek who's yanking your chain.

When you enter a chat area, you'll see a screen divided into three areas. On the left is the conversation that's going on, on the right are the people participating, and at the bottom, well, that's where you type in your two-cents worth. Select **Send** to send your message into the fray.

Here's the conversation.　　　　　　　　　　　　Here's who's involved.

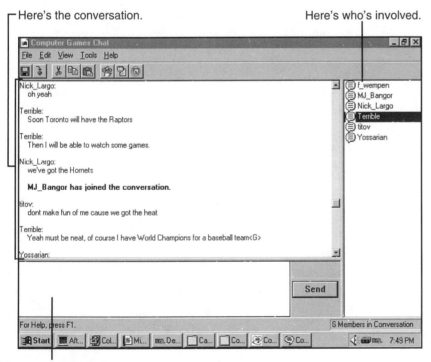

*Your basic chat room. As usual, no one is talking about the specified topic.*

Type your own chat here and select the Send button.

# Favorite Places

Throughout all the categories and most other places you visit, you'll notice a command on the **File** menu called **Add to Favorite Places**. Sometimes there's a button on the toolbar with a heart on it that accomplishes the same thing. (The heart is a nice touch, don't you think? A little cutesy, though.)

When you select Add to Favorite Places, a marker for your current location is added to your Favorite Places list. You can view your favorite places list by selecting **Favorite Places** from Microsoft Network Central; from anywhere else, you can pull down the **Edit** menu, select **Go To**, and select **Favorite Places**. When the Favorite Places list appears on-screen, select any item on the list to go directly to it.

# The Least You Need to Know

Whew! Talk about Europe in a day and a half! There's a lot more to Microsoft Network than I was able to tell you here, but I hope you'll discover that half the fun of working and playing online is finding treasure as you go.

# Speak Like a Geek: The Complete Archive

**386, 486** These are the aficionado's cool short forms for the *80386* and *80486* microprocessors. The microprocessor is the head honcho chip inside your computer that controls the whole shebang. Most people describe it as the "brain" of the computer, so you can think of these numbers as your computer's IQ. In that sense, a 486 machine is "smarter" than a 386 (although the high-end *Pentium* processor would have to be considered the genius of the group). To get the most out of Windows 95, you really should have a 486 or better microprocessor.

**accessory** One of the mini-applications that comes free with Windows 95. Examples include WordPad (see Chapter 14), Paint (Chapter 15), and Microsoft Backup (Chapter 17).

**active window** The window you're currently slaving away in. You can tell a window is active by looking at its title bar: if the bar shows white letters on a dark background, the window is active. (Inactive windows show light gray letters on a dark gray background.)

**application** Software that accomplishes a specific practical task. It's the same thing as a *program*.

**application window** A window that contains a running application, such as Explorer or WordPad.

**ASCII text file** A file that uses only the American Standard Code for Information Interchange character set (techno-lingo for the characters you see on your keyboard).

**background mode** A mode in which a program continues to perform a task "behind the scenes." Typical background tasks include spreadsheet recalculations, document printing, and modem file transfers.

**boot**   Computer geeks won't tell you to start your computer, they'll tell you to *boot* it. However, this doesn't mean you should punt your monitor across the room. The term *booting* comes from the phrase "pulling oneself up by one's own bootstraps," which refers to the fact that your computer can load everything it needs to operate properly without any help from the likes of you and me.

**byte**   Computerese for a single character of information. So, for example, the phrase *This phrase is 28 bytes long* is, yes, 28 bytes long (you count the spaces, too).

**cascade**   A cool way of arranging windows so that they overlap each other but you can still see each window's title bar.

**cascade menu**   A menu that appears when you select certain pull-down menu commands.

**character formatting**   Changing the look of text characters by altering their font, size, style, and more.

**character spacing**   The amount of space a font reserves for each character. In a *monospaced font*, every character gets the same amount of space regardless of its true width. In a *proportional font*, the space allotted to each letter varies according to the width of the letter.

**check box**   A square-shaped switch that toggles a dialog box option on or off. The option is toggled on when a check mark appears in the box.

**click**   To quickly press and release the left mouse button.

**Clipboard**   An area of memory that holds data temporarily during cut and paste operations.

**command button**   A rectangular doohickey (usually found in dialog boxes) that, when chosen, runs whatever command is spelled out on it.

**commands**   The options you see in a pull-down menu. You use these commands to tell the application what you want it to do next.

**Control menu**   A menu common to every Windows 95 window that you use to manipulate various features of the window. You activate the Control menu by clicking on the Control-menu box in the upper-left corner of the window or by pressing Alt+Spacebar (for an application window).

**data files**   The files used by you or your programs. See also *program files*.

**delay**   The amount of time it takes for a second character to appear when you press and hold down a key.

**desktop**   A metaphor for the Windows 95 screen. Starting a Windows 95 application is similar to putting a folder full of papers (the application window) on your desk. To do some work, you pull some papers out of the folder (the document windows) and place them on the desktop.

**device driver**   A small program that controls the way a device (such as a mouse) works with your system.

**dialog boxes**   Ubiquitous windows that pop up on the screen to ask you for information or to seek confirmation of an action you requested (or sometimes just to say "Hi").

**directory**   See *folder*.

**diskette**   See *floppy disk*.

**document window**   A window opened within an application. Document windows hold whatever you're working on in the application.

**double-click**   To quickly press and release the left mouse button *twice* in succession.

**double-click speed**   The maximum amount of time Windows 95 allows between the mouse clicks of a double-click.

**drag**   To press and hold down the left mouse button and then move the mouse.

**drag-and-drop**   Technique you can use to run commands or applications; you simply drag files or icons to strategic screen areas and drop them there.

**drop-down list box**   A list box that normally shows only a single item but, when selected, displays a list of options.

**file**   An organized unit of information inside your computer. If you think of your hard disk as a house, files can be either servants (your applications) or things you use (data used by you or by a program).

**floppy disk**   A portable storage medium that consists of a flexible disk protected by a plastic case. Floppy disks are available in a variety of sizes and capacities.

**focus**   The window that has the attention of the operating system (that is, Windows 95). See also *active window*.

**folder**   A storage location on your hard disk in which you keep related files together. If your hard disk is like a house, a folder is like a room inside the house.

**font**   A character set of a specific typeface, type style, and type size.

**formatting**   The process of setting up a disk so that a drive can read its information and write information to it. Not to be confused with *character formatting*.

**fritterware**   Any software that causes you to fritter away time fiddling with its various bells and whistles.

**hard disk**   The main storage area inside your computer. In the computer house analogy, the hard disk is equivalent to the inside of the house.

**icons**   The little pictures that Windows 95 uses to represent programs and files.

**insertion point cursor**   The blinking vertical bar you see inside a text box or in a word processing application, such as WordPad. It indicates where the next character you type will appear.

**kilobyte**   1,024 bytes. To be cool, always abbreviate this to "K."

**list box**   A small window that displays a list of items such as file names or directories.

**maximize**   To increase the size of a window to its largest extent. A maximized application window fills the entire screen (except for the taskbar). A maximized document window fills the entire application window.

**megabyte**   1,024 kilobytes or 1,048,576 bytes. The cognoscenti write this as "M" or "MB" and pronounce it "meg."

**memory resident program**   A program that stays in memory once it is loaded and works "behind the scenes." The program normally responds only to a specific event (such as the deletion of a file) or key combination. Also called a *terminate-and-stay-resident* (TSR) program.

**menu bar**   The horizontal bar on the second line of an application window. The menu bar contains the application's pull-down menus.

**microprocessor**   See *386, 486*.

**minimize**   To remove a program from the desktop without closing it. A button for the program remains on the taskbar.

**multitasking**   The capability to run several programs at the same time. Figuratively speaking, this simply means that Windows 95, unlike some people you may know, can walk and chew gum at the same time.

**option buttons**   Dialog box options that appear as small circles in groups of two or more. Only one option from a group can be chosen.

**point**   To place the mouse pointer so it rests on a specific screen location.

**port**   The connection into which you plug the cable from a device such as a mouse or printer.

**program files**   The files that run your programs. See also *data files*.

**pull-down menus**   Hidden menus that you open from an application's menu bar to access the commands and features of the application.

**RAM**   Stands for random-access memory. The memory in your computer that Windows 95 uses to run your programs.

**repeat rate**   After the initial delay, the rate at which characters appear when you press and hold down a key.

**scalable font**   A font in which each character exists as an outline that can be scaled to different sizes. Windows 95 includes such scalable fonts as Arial, Courier New, and Times New Roman. To use scalable fonts, you must have a software program called a *type manager* to do the scaling. Windows 95 comes with its own type manager: TrueType.

**scroll bar**   A bar that appears at the bottom or on the right of a window when the window is too small to display all of its contents.

**system resources**   Two memory areas that Windows 95 uses to keep track of things like the position and size of open windows, dialog boxes, and your desktop configuration (wallpaper and so on).

**taskbar**   The horizontal strip across the bottom of the Windows 95 screen. Each running application is given its own taskbar button, and you switch to an application by clicking on its button.

**text box**   A screen area into which you type text information, such as a description or a file name.

**text editor**   A program that lets you edit files that are text only. The Windows 95 text editor is called Notepad.

**title bar**   The area on the top line of a window that displays the window's title.

**tracking speed**   How quickly the mouse pointer moves across the screen when you move the mouse on its pad.

**TrueType**   A *font management program* that comes with Windows 95.

**type size**   A measure of the height of a font. Type size is measured in *points*; there are 72 points in an inch.

**type style**   Character attributes, such as regular, bold, and italic. Other type styles (often called type *effects*) are underlining and strikethru characters.

**typeface**   A distinctive graphic design of letters, numbers, and other symbols.

**window**   A rectangular screen area in which Windows 95 displays applications and documents.

**word wrap**   A word processor feature that automatically starts a new line when your typing reaches the end of the current line.

**write-protection**   Floppy disk safeguard that prevents you from changing any information on the disk. The 5¼-inch disks normally have a small notch on the side of the disk. If the notch is covered with tape, the disk is write-protected. Simply remove the tape to disable the write-protection. For a 3½-inch disk, the write-protection is controlled by a small movable tab on the back of the disk. If the tab is toward the edge of the disk, the disk is write-protected. To disable the write-protection, slide the tab away from the edge of the disk.

# Index

## Symbols

... (ellipsis), 58
3½-inch floppy disks, 144-146
5¼-inch floppy disks, 144-146
386/486 microprocessors, 365

## A

About Windows 95 command (Help menu), 340
accelerator keys, 56
access rights, 259, 262-263
accessories, 14-16, 42, 365
    Briefcase, 205
    Calculator, 203-204
    Calendar, 208
    Cardfile, 211
    Character Map, 248-249
    FreeCell, 214-216
    Minesweeper, 216-217
    Notepad, 202-203
active dialog box controls, 67
active windows, 104-106, 365
Add command (Card menu), 214
Add dialog box, 214
Add Echo command (Effects menu), 238
Add Fonts dialog box, 250

Add New Hardware Wizard, 297-299
Add Printer Wizard dialog box, 97
Add to Favorite Places command (File menu), 364
Add/Remove Programs dialog box, 295-296
Add/Remove Programs Properties dialog box, 150, 292
Add/Remove Programs Wizard, 294-295
Address Book (e-mail), 317-318
Address Book menu (Tools menu), 317
addresses
    inserting, 317
    network addresses, 256-257
Airbrush tool, 172
Alt key, 39
answering, *see* replying
AOL (America Online), 304
application window, 365
applications, 43, 365
    data sharing, 219
    DOS, 221-222
    font selection, 247-248
    switching between, 7
    *see also* programs; software;
appointments, setting, 208-210
Arrange Icons command (View menu), 122

arrowheads, 58
ASCII text files, 365
assigning names
    documents, 84-85
    files, 132-133
    folders, 143
    network PCs, 256-257
audio CDs, 238-240
AutoPlay feature (CD-ROMs), 233

## B

background colors, 167
background mode, 365
Backup, *see* MS Backup
Backup dialog box, 187
Backup Set Label dialog box, 186
backup sets, 180, 186
BBSs, 304
    command options, 359-360
    HyperTerminal program, 305-311
    messages
        composing, 360-361
        reading, 358-360
    Network Central, 358
bits per second (bps), 302
blank cards, *see* cards
books (Help system), 51
booting, 31-35, 149, 328-333, 366
BOOTLOG.TXT files, 329
borders (windows), 107-108
bps (bits per second), 302

# P-Q

Paint
  components, 166-167
  copying/pasting
    drawings, 173-174
  drawing tools, 167-168
    Airbrush, 172
    Curve, 170
    Eraser, 174-175
    Fill With Color,
      171-172
    Line, 168-169
    Magnifier, 175-176
    Pencil/Brush, 171
    Polygon, 170-171
    Rectangle/Ellipse/
      Rounded Rectangle,
      169-170
    Select/Free-Form
      Select, 174
    Text, 172-173
  expanding/hiding
    drawings, 176-177
  starting, 165-166
Paragraph command
  (Format menu), 159
Paragraph dialog box, 72,
  159
paragraphs, formatting,
  159-160
passwords, 25-26, 257, 281
Passwords Properties dialog
  box, 281
Paste command (Edit
  menu), 90, 128, 142
Paste Link command (Edit
  menu), 226
Paste Special command
  (Edit menu), 226
Paste Special dialog box,
  226
pasting
  data to DOS
    applications, 222
  drawings, 174
  linked/embedded
    objects, 226-227
patterns (desktop), 272
Pause Printing command,
  100
pausing print jobs, 100

PCs (personal computers)
  connections, 254-255,
    303
  naming network PCs,
    256-257
  telephone line commu-
    nications, 302
  transferring documents,
    205-208
Pencil tool, 171
Pentium processor, 365
Phone Dialer, 306, 311-314
phone lines, 302-311
Phone Number dialog box,
  307
phone numbers, dialing,
  306-307, 311-314
pixels, 175
Plain Old Telephone
  Service (POTS), 302
play lists (audio CDs), 240
playing
  audio CDs, 238
  FreeCell, 215-216
  Minesweeper, 216-217
  sounds, 235
Plug and Play, 16
pointers (mouse)
  searching, 288
  selecting, 286-287
  troubleshooting,
    342-344
pointing mouse, 37, 369
Polygon tool, 170-171
ports, 97, 369
Post Message command
  (File menu), 361
posting, *see* sending
POTS (Plain Old Telephone
  Service), 302
preventing GPFs (General
  Protection Faults), 334
Previous command (View
  menu), 323
Previous version of
  MS-DOS startups, 330
Print command (File
  menu), 6, 76, 94, 325, 347
Print dialog box, 6, 66,
  76, 94
print jobs, 99-100
Print Preview command
  (File menu), 164

Print Setup command (File
  menu), 99
Print Setup dialog box, 99
Printer menu
  commands, 100
printers
  driver files, 95
  installing, 95-99
    network printers,
      261-262
  selecting, 99
  sharing, 264
  troubleshooting,
    345-347
  *see also* default printers
printing documents, 6,
  93-94
PRODIGY, 304
profiles
  Exchange program,
    316-317
  *see also* user profiles
programs
  closing, 45-46, 340
  deleting, 296-297
  DOS, 14
  files, 118, 182-183, 369
  inserting, 275-277
  installing, 294-296
  running multiple
    programs, 46-49
  selecting printers, 99
  starting, 44-45
    automatic startup,
      277
  switching between,
    49-50
  terminate-and-stay-
    resident (TSR)
    programs, 368
  text editor, 370
  windows, 60
  *see also* applications;
    software
Programs folder (Start
  menu), 44
Properties command (File
  menu), 263, 336
Properties dialog box, 263,
  312, 336
proportional fonts, 245
protocols, 309

**381**

## PLUG YOURSELF INTO...

MACMILLAN INFORMATION SUPERLIBRARY™

que · SAMS PUBLISHING · Hayden Books · que COLLEGE · NRP · alpha books · Brady · ADOBE PRESS

# THE MACMILLAN INFORMATION SUPERLIBRARY™

### Free information and vast computer resources from the world's leading computer book publisher—online!

### *FIND THE BOOKS THAT ARE RIGHT FOR YOU!*

A complete online catalog, plus sample chapters and tables of contents give you an in-depth look at *all* of our books, including hard-to-find titles. It's the best way to find the books you need!

● STAY INFORMED with the latest computer industry news through our online newsletter, press releases, and customized Information SuperLibrary Reports.

● GET FAST ANSWERS to your questions about MCP books and software.

● VISIT our online bookstore for the latest information and editions!

● COMMUNICATE with our expert authors through e-mail and conferences.

● DOWNLOAD SOFTWARE from the immense MCP library:
  - Source code and files from MCP books
  - The best shareware, freeware, and demos

● DISCOVER HOT SPOTS on other parts of the Internet.

● WIN BOOKS in ongoing contests and giveaways!

**TO PLUG INTO MCP:** →

GOPHER: gopher.mcp.com
FTP: ftp.mcp.com

WORLD WIDE WEB: **http://www.mcp.com**

Home Page · What's New · Bookstore · Reference Desk · Software Library · Macmillan Overview · Talk to Us

# Smart People Use Idiot's Guides

*The Complete Idiot's Guide* series provides information in a witty, approachable tone for the intimidated or beginning computer user. Information is delivered in easily digestible bites, with humorous cartoons that empathize with the reader's perspective.

**The Complete Idiot Guide to Word for Windows 95**
0-7897-0378-5
$19.99 USA
Available Sept. 95 (PS

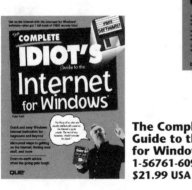

**The Complete Idiot's Guide to Excel for Windows 95**
0-7897-0375-0
$19.99 USA
Available Sept. 95 (PSR)

**The Complete Idiot's Guide to the Internet for Windows**
1-56761-609-7
$21.99 USA

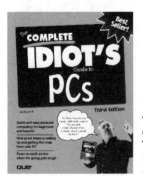

**The Complete Idiot's Guide to PC's, Third Edition**
1-56761-584-8
$16.99 USA

**For more information on these and other Que products, visit your local book retailer or call 1-800-772-0477**

Source code ISBN: 1-56761-495

# Complete and Return this Card for a *FREE* Computer Book Catalog

Thank you for purchasing this book! You have purchased a superior computer book written expressly for your needs. To continue to provide the kind of up-to-date, pertinent coverage you've come to expect from us, we need to hear from you. Please take a minute to complete and return this self-addressed, postage-paid form. In return, we'll send you a free catalog of all our computer books on topics ranging from word processing to programming and the internet.

☐   Mrs. ☐   Ms. ☐   Dr. ☐

 me (first) ⬚⬚⬚⬚⬚⬚⬚⬚⬚⬚ (M.I.) ☐ (last) ⬚⬚⬚⬚⬚⬚⬚⬚⬚⬚⬚⬚

dress ⬚⬚⬚⬚⬚⬚⬚⬚⬚⬚⬚⬚⬚⬚⬚⬚⬚⬚⬚⬚⬚⬚⬚⬚⬚⬚⬚⬚

⬚⬚⬚⬚⬚⬚⬚⬚⬚⬚⬚⬚⬚⬚⬚⬚⬚⬚⬚⬚⬚⬚⬚⬚⬚⬚⬚⬚

y ⬚⬚⬚⬚⬚⬚⬚⬚⬚⬚⬚ State ⬚⬚ Zip ⬚⬚⬚⬚⬚ ⬚⬚⬚⬚

ne ⬚⬚⬚⬚⬚⬚⬚⬚⬚⬚ Fax ⬚⬚⬚ ⬚⬚⬚ ⬚⬚⬚⬚

npany Name ⬚⬚⬚⬚⬚⬚⬚⬚⬚⬚⬚⬚⬚⬚⬚⬚⬚⬚⬚⬚⬚⬚⬚⬚

nail address ⬚⬚⬚⬚⬚⬚⬚⬚⬚⬚⬚⬚⬚⬚⬚⬚⬚⬚⬚⬚⬚⬚⬚⬚

## Please check at least (3) influencing factors for purchasing this book.

nt or back cover information on book ....................... ☐
cial approach to the content ................................. ☐
npleteness of content ......................................... ☐
hor's reputation ............................................... ☐
lisher's reputation ............................................ ☐
k cover design or layout ..................................... ☐
ex or table of contents of book ............................. ☐
e of book ...................................................... ☐
cial effects, graphics, illustrations ....................... ☐
er (Please specify): _____ ☐

## How did you first learn about this book?

in Macmillan Computer Publishing catalog ........... ☐
ommended by store personnel .............................. ☐
the book on bookshelf at store ............................ ☐
ommended by a friend ...................................... ☐
eived advertisement in the mail ........................... ☐
an advertisement in: _____ ☐
d book review in: _____ ☐
er (Please specify): _____ ☐

## How many computer books have you purchased in the last six months?

book only ....... ☐    3 to 5 books ..................... ☐
oks ................. ☐    More than 5 ..................... ☐

## 4. Where did you purchase this book?

Bookstore ........................................................ ☐
Computer Store ................................................. ☐
Consumer Electronics Store .................................. ☐
Department Store ............................................... ☐
Office Club ...................................................... ☐
Warehouse Club ................................................ ☐
Mail Order ...................................................... ☐
Direct from Publisher ......................................... ☐
Internet site .................................................... ☐
Other (Please specify): _____ ☐

## 5. How long have you been using a computer?

☐ Less than 6 months    ☐ 6 months to a year
☐ 1 to 3 years    ☐ More than 3 years

## 6. What is your level of experience with personal computers and with the subject of this book?

| | With PCs | With subject of book |
|---|---|---|
| New | ☐ | ☐ |
| Casual | ☐ | ☐ |
| Accomplished | ☐ | ☐ |
| Expert | ☐ | ☐ |

Source Code ISBN 1-56761-495-7

## 7. Which of the following best describes your job title?

- Administrative Assistant ☐
- Coordinator ☐
- Manager/Supervisor ☐
- Director ☐
- Vice President ☐
- President/CEO/COO ☐
- Lawyer/Doctor/Medical Professional ☐
- Teacher/Educator/Trainer ☐
- Engineer/Technician ☐
- Consultant ☐
- Not employed/Student/Retired ☐
- Other (Please specify): _____ ☐

## 8. Which of the following best describes the area of the company your job title falls under?

- Accounting ☐
- Engineering ☐
- Manufacturing ☐
- Operations ☐
- Marketing ☐
- Sales ☐
- Other (Please specify): _____ ☐

## 9. What is your age?

- Under 20 .............................................
- 21-29 ..................................................
- 30-39 ..................................................
- 40-49 ..................................................
- 50-59 ..................................................
- 60-over ...............................................

## 10. Are you:

- Male .....................................................
- Female .................................................

## 11. Which computer publications do you read regularly? (Please list)

_____
_____
_____
_____
_____
_____
_____
_____
_____

**Comments**: _____

Fold here and scotch-tape to